THE GREAT

EAST ASIAN WAR

AND THE

BIRTH OF THE

KOREAN NATION

COLUMBIA UNIVERSITY PRESS   NEW YORK

THE GREAT EAST ASIAN WAR AND THE BIRTH OF THE KOREAN NATION

JaHyun Kim Haboush

*Edited by
William J. Haboush
and Jisoo M. Kim
with Sixiang Wang,
Hwisang Cho, and
Ksenia Chizhova-Kim*

COLUMBIA UNIVERSITY PRESS
Publishers Since 1893
NEW YORK   CHICHESTER, WEST SUSSEX
cup.columbia.edu
Copyright © 2016 Columbia University Press
Paperback edition, 2021
All rights reserved

Library of Congress Cataloging-in-Publication Data
Haboush, JaHyun Kim.
The great East Asian war and the birth of the Korean nation / JaHyun Kim Haboush ; edited by William Haboush and Jisoo M. Kim with Sixiang Wang, Hwisang Cho, and Ksenia Chizhova-Kim.
pages cm.
Includes bibliographical references and index.
ISBN 978-0-231-17228-8 (cloth)—ISBN 978-0-231-17229-5 (pbk.)—
ISBN 978-0-231-54098-8 (e-book)
1. Korea—History—Japanese Invasions, 1592–1598. 2. Korea—History—Japanese Invasions, 1592–1598—Influence. 3. Korea—History—Manchu Invasions, 1627–1637. 4. Nationalism—Korea—History—16th century. 5. Nationalism—Korea—History—17th century. 6. War and society—Korea—History—16th century. 7. War and society—Korea—History—17th century. 8. East Asia—History, Military—16th century. 9. East Asia—History, Military—17th century. I. Haboush, William Joseph. II. Kim, Jisoo M. III. Title.

DS913. 43.H33 2016
951. 9′02—dc23
2015016431

BOOK & COVER DESIGN: CHANG JAE LEE
COVER IMAGE: BYUN BAK, BATTLE OF TONNAE (TONGNAEBU SUNJEOLDO), 1760, MUSEUM OF THE KOREAN MILITARY ACADEMY

FOREWORD *by William J. Haboush*
vii
MAP OF CHOSŎN KOREA
xiii

Introduction
1

1. The Volunteer Army and the Discourse of Nation
23

2. The Volunteer Army and the Emergence of Imagined Community
53

3. War of Words:
The Changing Nature of Literary Chinese in the Japanese Occupation
73

4. Language Strategy:
The Emergence of a Vernacular National Space
93

5. The Aftermath:
Dream Journeys and the Culture of Commemoration
121

PUBLICATIONS BY JAHYUN KIM HABOUSH
153
NOTES
159
BIBLIOGRAPHY
199
INDEX
213

When JaHyun Kim Haboush, my wife, passed away in January 2011, she had been preoccupied with a research project of many years duration. She died in despair of its fruition, but she did leave a number of files on her personal computer. As her sole heir and literary executor, I have felt a heavy responsibility to at least partially present her program to the historical community that meant so much to her.

As she lay dying she told me where to find her uncompleted writings in her computer. Though she felt them to be much too unfinished to be worthy of publication, she suggested that they be made the subject of a conference or workshop, and she requested that I copyedit them to prepare them for presentation to her colleagues. In consequence I conducted a rather thorough search of her computer and her stored discs and memory sticks. The most complete and usable work was contained in the files she had directed me to.

Since her time as a graduate student, I had read everything that JaHyun wrote. Early in her career it served a real function; I was her first copyeditor. As time passed I did less and less, but the habit of reading her work remained. One of the great pleasures of our relationship was my early access to her work. We often discussed it. As a mathematician, I was in no position to contribute professional historical advice, but as first reader, I could offer a layman's response and sometimes, by responding naively, reveal passages that did not communicate what was intended. In any case I grew familiar with her work habits and use of language. I knew that what she felt to be insignificant or incomplete could actually be quite substantial.

FOREWORD

I had already read many portions of the files she left behind as she wrote, but when I read them together I felt they constituted a coherent whole. After a preliminary copyediting of the files I sent them to three colleagues who had worked with JaHyun: Nancy Abelmann, an anthropologist at the University of Illinois; Martina Deuchler, a professor of Korean history emerita at SOAS; and Dorothy Ko, a historian of China at Barnard College. The three readers were unanimous in their judgment that the files represented important research findings, presented an exciting narrative, merited publication, and would be a meaningful contribution to the study of Korean history. I therefore set about making arrangements to organize them into a manuscript suitable for publication.

I asked these three scholars to prepare and edit the manuscript, and all three were willing and even eager to proceed. The files I had sent to them consisted of an introduction of about thirty-five pages and two very long chapters. The first chapter was devoted to the rise of the volunteer army and the resistance to the Japanese invasion of 1592. Particularly prominent in this chapter were recruitment letters intended to arouse the public and to raise local volunteer forces, guerilla armies really. These letters contain many of the tropes of ethnic nationalism. The second chapter was devoted to the retreat of the government to the northern border and the turn to the vernacular as a means of official communication and the attendant appearance of a vernacular public discursive space. It was also concerned with the emergence of commemoration after the Japanese invasions and its entrenchment in ritual practice after the Manchu invasions of 1627 and 1636–1637. With the vernacular communications of the Imjin War, these rituals of commemoration evolved into occasions for the exchange of some sort of discourse of nation. The chapters were too long, and they required a certain amount of editorial attention. After some experimentation, the three editors decided that it would be best to edit minimally for uniformity of style and to assure that the book would be in JaHyun's voice. The editors decided to divide each of the chapters in two using adaptions of some of the original section headings for the new titles. Splitting the chapters involved a host of editorial and textual decisions. Dorothy Ko noticed that an earlier essay on dead bodies and commemorative literature could logically be used as a fifth chapter, and she modified it to fit the manuscript. Martina Deuchler did an enormous amount of work checking sources and examining references. Gari Ledyard of Columbia contributed a bibliography of JaHyun's work and other supplementary material. I also asked Ronald Toby of the University of Illinois, a historian of Japan whose expertise includes an extensive knowledge of Korean-Japanese relations, to examine references to Japan. In this way the manuscript was assembled and sent out for evaluation.

The reviews of the manuscript were extremely positive, and Columbia University Press decided to publish it. Final preparation required a great deal of technical editorial work. Romanizations were occasionally inconsistent, names appeared without the corresponding Chinese characters, notes were partial or incomplete, and there was no bibliography or glossary. I turned to JaHyun's recent students to rectify these deficits. Jisoo Kim of George Washington University expended enormous efforts to check references in chapters 1 and 2 and did the final editing of the manuscript, and she kindly consented to take a supervisory role, apportioning the work among several colleagues. Sixiang Wang, JaHyun's former undergraduate and doctoral student at Columbia, had organized an electronic archive of JaHyun's papers to accompany their deposition in the rare book room of the Starr Library at Columbia, so he was uniquely positioned to ensure citational consistency across chapters. He also checked *Sillok* citations in all the chapters. Hwisang Cho, JaHyun's student and an assistant professor at Xavier University, supplied the complete notes to chapters 3 and 4. Ksenia Chizhova, another student of JaHyun's and an assistant professor at Princeton University, worked on chapter 5 and the bibliography. In the notes section of the book, those marked [MD] were written by Martina Deuchler; those marked [ED] were supplied by this team of JaHyun's former students.

That is the textual history of this book, but it does not speak to origins or motivation. A major frustration of any historian of East Asian culture or thought, or of any non-Western civilization for that matter, is the distinctness of its evolution relative to the familiar European development. The terminology and conceptual framework of contemporary historical investigation are rooted in the European experience. The logical architecture of the East Asian intellectual edifice requires an entirely different plan of exploration. Things happened in a different sequence, ideas emerged under different circumstances, and terms of discourse were rooted in cultural practice. JaHyun encountered these issues right from the beginning. In the portion of her doctoral dissertation that was published by Columbia University Press as the book *The Confucian Kingship in Korea*, she established that participants in the ritual controversy of the seventeenth century were using notions of ritual propriety and practice to express ideas about royal legitimacy. During the Ming dynasty the Korean king had been perceived as receiving legitimacy through investiture by the Ming emperor. Korean scholar-bureaucrats did not recognize the legitimacy of the Manchu and so it suddenly became difficult to provide a definitive basis for royal legitimacy. Purges occurred when scholarly debate seemed to be undermining royal legitimacy. This view, which finds ready acceptance now, met great resistance among historians of Korea. The accepted view at that time was that the controversy was a power struggle over arcane and irrelevant points of an obscure elitist philosophy. Thus the intellectual output of the Chosŏn bureaucratic scholarly community was not interpreted as meaningful discourse about society or political structure; it was rather assigned to another category of communicative activity.

Even the structure of East Asian studies presented certain problems. China and Japan were studied almost as two entirely separate civilizations. In this context it seemed that the task of a scholar of Korean civilization was to create a third, hermetically isolated corpus of knowledge. What then was one to make of something like Neo-Confucianism? Was one to see it as an alien import or perhaps as a species of intellectual colonization? This very idea was widely expressed in Korean anticolonial discourse in the late nineteenth and early twentieth centuries. JaHyun simply had no use for such parochialisms.

Her educational and intellectual background was broad. She majored in English literature at Ewha Women's University in Seoul and, being a great lover of fiction, was well read in European and American fiction and drama. She often was the only person in the room who had read a work that was mentioned in conversation. After her graduation from Ewha, she spent some time as a film critic and in the film industry in Korea, working as a narrator and a film editor. Soon after her arrival in New York, she took courses in Chinese history and thought and in Chinese language at Columbia. She then completed an M.A. degree in Chinese literature under James Crump at the University of Michigan, writing her master's thesis on the Bao Gong dramas of Yuan dynasty China. Afterward she completed her doctorate in Chosŏn Korean history under Gari Ledyard at Columbia. It is no surprise then that she was particularly aware of cultural exchange and intuitively sought out the cultural matrix, both national and international, in which events were embedded.

As a practicing scholar she of course spent a great deal of time collecting and studying primary sources—official and unofficial histories, diaries and journals, collected works, memorials, memoirs, essays, and letters. She also read a great deal of premodern fiction, which included both shorter pieces in various genres and novel-length narratives, many of which remain relatively unknown. Her range in exploring sources was, in other words, extraordinarily broad and thorough, and she brought it all to bear on her scholarship. In writing *The Confucian Kingship in Korea*, she worked with sources in classical Chinese and the occasional text in Korean, written in *han'gŭl*. The work for which she is best known—the restoration and translation of the memoirs of Lady Hyegyŏng, the wife of Prince Sado and mother of King Chŏngjo—was a vernacular text written by a woman but one that was a reference for royal historians writing in classical Chinese. It left her with an enduring interest in vernacular literature and writing by women as well as a keen awareness of the impossibility of viewing any part of the Korean literary heritage in isolation.

In writing, however, JaHyun frequently found that discussion was constricted by the habit of viewing history as partitioned into distinct regimes with an attendant limitation on the use of ideas and terminology from one regime of history in another context. Events and ideas from Korean history that could quite naturally be discussed using such concepts as "rights" or the "national interest" had to be discussed using other terms.

More recently she was drawn to the study of diglossia in Korea, that is, the simultaneous use of two languages, one sacral and official, the other vernacular. In Korea the languages were classical Chinese, the language of official histories, bureaucratic communication, and much poetry and fiction, and vernacular Korean. She immediately focused on the multilayered structure of the Korean literary heritage. Its reach extended from official writings of the bureaucracy in classical Chinese through more personal communications in classical Chinese and in the vernacular, and vernacular writings by women and others not classed as Yangban aristocrats, to Chinese works, all interacting multidirectionally. She was particularly struck by how the vernacular came to be used for royal edicts. It was this sudden use of the vernacular by a desperate king backed into the northern border of his country that brought her to the study of the great war of 1592. As JaHyun teased out the narrative of the events leading to this incident, she realized that they had induced the emergence of an ethnic and cultural awareness and the construction of a public space of communication in which Koreans of many social strata could participate. It was her excited appreciation of these events that led to this project and this work. She felt that out of this great war at the end of the sixteenth century and the Manchu invasions of 1627 and 1636–1637, Koreans emerged with a discernible sense of themselves as a distinct ethnie united by birth, language, and belief forged by this immense clash of the three great powers of East Asia. She thus argued that Korea arrived at the brink of the seventeenth century a nation. It was her hope that by recounting these events she might initiate a truly regional if not global history of East Asia as an interlocking complex of distinct states joined by ideas and history in a common civilization. She surely would have completed the project had she lived. I can only hope that these assembled fragments will offer a glimpse of her vision. Finally I must offer heartfelt thanks to all those who in sincerest respect and affection toiled to complete this work.

William J. Haboush
Champaign, Illinois

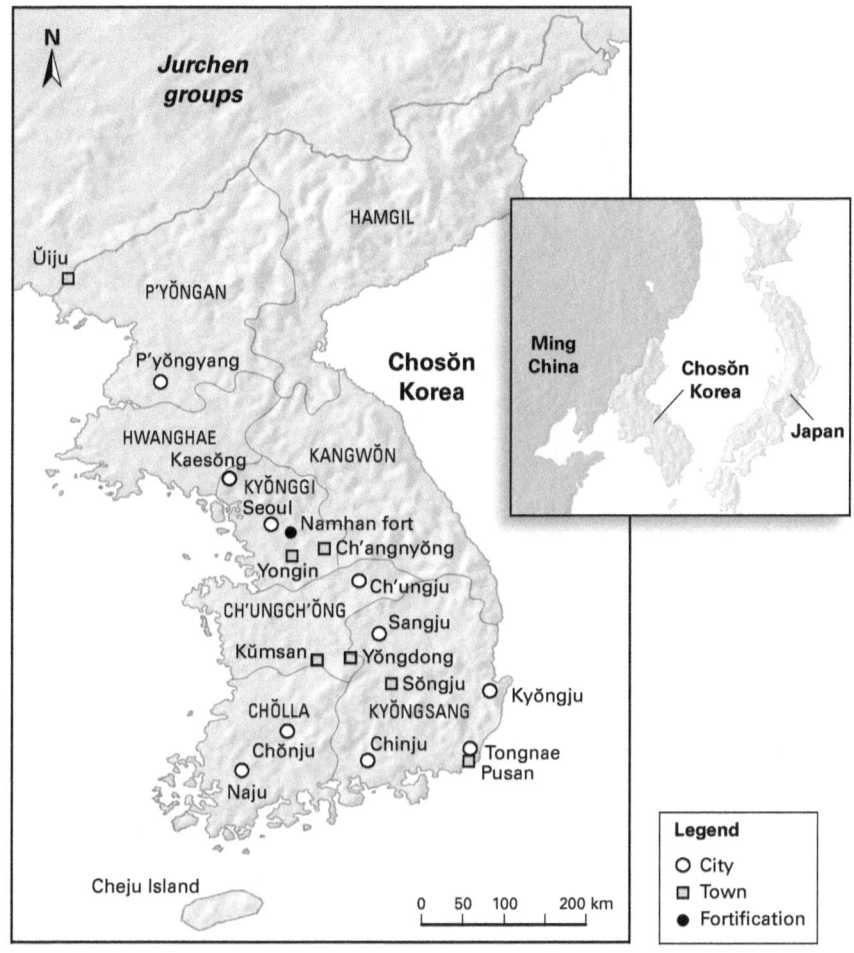

Chosŏn Korea, at the time of the Imjin War (1592–1598). (*Inset*) Chosŏn Korea's geopolitical position between Ming China and Japan.

THE GREAT

EAST ASIAN WAR

AND THE

BIRTH OF THE

KOREAN NATION

In this book I propose that a discourse of nation emerged in late sixteenth-century Chosŏn Korea (1392–1910) and that it continued, in a variety of forms, until the modern era. The discourse emerged when Japan invaded Korea in 1592 at the outbreak of the Imjin War (1592–1598) and was reshaped and intensified after the Manchus attacked the Chosŏn in 1627 and 1636–1637.

The Great Wars in East Asia

The Imjin War and the rise of the Manchus were events of monumental importance in East Asian history. First of all, these were of immense continental scale. Toyotomi Hideyoshi's (1536–1598) invasion of Korea, sometimes referred to as the First Korean War or the Great East Asian War, escalated into a six-year regional war in which the three East Asian countries, Japan, Korea, and China, fought either as allies or as enemies, each state directed by its head, with a commitment of large forces fighting on sea and land using firearms. In fact, this conflict involving more than 500,000 combatants over a course of six years was by far the largest war known to the world in the sixteenth century; in East Asian memory, it remained unequaled in scale until the Second World War. The Manchu incursion into Korea, which Hong Taiji (1592–1643) led with an army of 100,000, ended swiftly when the Korean court surrendered after a forty-nine-day siege of Namhan Fort, to which the Chosŏn court had fled. This was but one in a succession of victories that the Manchus achieved in the course of establishing their empire, which culminated with the conquest of Ming China (1368–1644) in 1644.

INTRODUCTION

Both the Imjin War and the Manchu conquest brought fundamental domestic and regional impacts resulting in regime changes in Japan and China, respectively. Hideyoshi had brought all the domains of the Japanese archipelago under his control after a century and a half of fragmentation and "lawlessness." After his death in 1598, which was in part responsible for the swift withdrawal of the Japanese troops from Korea, his successor was defeated by Tokugawa Ieyasu (1542–1616), who established the Tokugawa Shogunate (1603–1868) that presided over a peaceful and unified Japan until the Meiji Restoration of 1868. In China the Ming dynasty, an ethnic Han dynasty, was replaced by the Manchu Qing dynasty (1644–1911).

The Imjin War and the rise of the Manchu empire implied much more than the rise and fall of ruling houses; they also signaled realignments of power in East Asia and augured a new mapping, both conceptual and territorial, of the region. Hideyoshi invaded Korea as a first step toward constructing a great Asian empire that would include China and beyond.[1] Though the Japanese Army never went beyond Korea, and Japan withdrew from Korea having accomplished none of its stated aims, the invasion announced the emergence of a new force and a new world vision manifest in Hideyoshi's grandiose dream, short-lived though it was. The Manchu conquest of China, on the other hand, can be seen as the culmination of millennia of rivalry between "China" and a "barbarian" other, especially those whom the Chinese categorized as "northern" peoples, against whom the Great Wall had been repeatedly constructed through history. Their relation can be seen as an endless oscillation of aggression, retreat, conquest, and assimilation. That is, Chinese history is punctuated by periods of disunion during which some portion of China proper was occupied by some northern people or peoples, many of whom seem to have been assimilated into the Chinese cultural and ethnic community upon China's reunification. The Mongol occupation of China appears to have diverged from the usual pattern. Yuan China (1271–1368) was one of four khanates with which Mongols ruled over half the world; after their hundred-year occupation ended, many left for their homeland. For the Manchus, the conquest of China was the fulfillment of a long-cherished dream, and by the time the Qing ended in 1911, very few Manchus seem to have reclaimed their ancestral ethnic origins. If the Qing conquest can be seen as the successful establishment of a multiethnic empire, the repercussions of this "barbarian" domination of China, the cultural heartland, reverberated through the region.

Discourse of Nation in Korea

Amazingly, amid this swirl of transformations and realignments in the region, in Korea the Chosŏn dynasty continued, lasting until 1910. Within the structural continuance, however, a movement profound and transformative, historically and historiographically, took place: an idea of nation emerged and circulated. It arose first as a trope among the civilian volunteer army leaders who rose to defend their home and country against the Japanese Army as the Korean Royal Army was struck helpless and Japanese troops swarmed unopposed, razing village and town, terrorizing and massacring their inhabitants, on their triumphant march north. In the call to participate in guerilla warfare, these civilians had to articulate a vision of the land and the people for which the volunteers should fight and risk their lives. Thus began a discourse of nation. This was very quickly joined by other strands of discourse of nation by other groups in different genres and different linguistic spaces. The discourse of nation, initially informed by anti-Japanese sentiment, shifted and intensified after the Manchu invasions.

A number of works have shown that negative encounters with the other often awaken consciousness of nation and lead to the forging of national identity. In Korea, too, each of the encounters, with Japan and the Manchus, respectively, produced a sense of national self, constructed, as it were, in opposition to the other that they faced: in contradistinction to Japan, Korea was predominantly defined by ethnicity and history; against the Manchus, by culture and civilization. While anti-Japanese and anti-Manchu discourses maintained distinct and separate façades, they did not remain separate from each other but were recast in the cauldron of an integrated idea of nation, and they thus acquired additional layers of meaning. In other words, what may seem a monolithic anti-Japanese or anti-Manchu discourse at first glance was in fact a synecdoche for the discourse of nation that was embedded in the mixture of hostilities toward Japan and the Manchus. In fact, the way in which anti-Japanese and anti-Manchu ingredients were positioned and highlighted in various strands of discourse of nation in different eras greatly determined the constitution and shape of that changing discourse.

During the postwar Chosŏn, that is, after both the Imjin War and the Manchu invasions, discourse of nation was carried out in a number of ways, including commemorative activities for the two wars, identity discourse on Korea, and fictional reimagining of the wars. In each of these strands, different themes appeared prominent—in commemoration, patriotism; in identity discourse, Korean culture and history; and in fiction, ethnic continuity—though there were numerous crossovers between these strands. In other aspects, they also exhibited different properties from one another. Commemoration had the widest range of participants, with such diverse agents as the state, localities, families, and individuals competing for possession and appropriation of war memories, and it was performed in both textual and ritual practices.

In reassessing the role of Korea in a changed world order in which "barbarians" dominated China, scholarly elites mainly conducted identity discourse in inscriptional space. Fictional discourse on the individual and collective destinies of Koreans took place outside the inscriptional space, either independent of or opposite to officially sanctioned memory. These multistranded, multidirectional, and multilayered strands of discourse did not move temporally or spatially in a linear or parallel fashion.

All these discourses, however, contemplated Korea's past and sought its future direction. The central concern running through all the different strands was the meaning of the Chosŏn community, in particular, how to imagine the relationship between the individual and the state. Patriotism offered an ideal. In defining patriotism by honoring past actions, various groups of people were in fact creating a set of idealized behaviors for themselves. The Chosŏn state, however, by acknowledging and rewarding what was deemed patriotic service by independently acting individuals, publicly and visibly assumed responsibility for these independent actions and by extension for all its subjects. By confirming the reciprocal ideal of activist loyalty, the people and the state were defining the meaning of both popular sovereignty and the sovereign state. Perhaps it is ironic that the Chosŏn state, whose authority and power were diminished through ineffectual leadership during the Imjin War and the Manchu invasions, survived in Korea while regimes and dynasties changed in Japan and China. It is no exaggeration to say that Chosŏn was sustained and shaped by postwar discourse of nation. The nation, an idea conceived in opposition to Japan and the Manchus, had to be imagined as sovereign.

Historiographical Considerations: Concepts and Vocabulary

In proposing the emergence of a premodern or early modern Asian nation, an idea that has previously not been broached except by E. J. Hobsbawm's terse categorization of Korea, China, Japan, and Iran as "historical nations," I feel that I should attend to several historiographical issues. The nation and the issues related to the nation have been one of the most widely discussed and hotly contested subjects in the academy for many decades. A great deal of scholarly attention has been lavished on the topic, each period favoring its own problematizations and approaches. This is not a place to survey its history, but, as a way of locating my work, I will briefly sample recent trends beginning with the final decade of the twentieth century. In 1990 Hobsbawm said that the period from 1968 to 1988 had been the most productive time on the topic, and he listed eleven books as among the most influential of the period.[2] They are representative modernist works that see the nation as an embodiment of modernity, which developed along with capitalism, industrialization, and political freedom, in which the nation is conceived of and presented through narratives of transformation to modernity. The conceptual frameworks as well as much of the debate and controversy in these works are inextricably entwined with issues specific to Europe. These include the conflict between the continuing practice of patrimony, a practice rooted in feudalism, and the idea of the territorial state, a conflict resolved only by the French Revolution. Ernest Gellner's description of premodern Europe posited the existence of a horizontally stratified class—aristocrats and kings—practicing patrimony but unbound by geography, presiding over a vertically bound class consisting for the most part of those who worked the land and who were hence bound to a specific location.[3] This structural scheme, so specific to postfeudal Europe, became a foundational element in deriving theories of the nation.

In addition, these discussions often involved the conflict between the religious authorities of the ecclesiastical establishment and temporal authorities and their relationship to the vertically bound group or the horizontal group, and more especially the contested loyalties of the vertically bound group to these two authorities. It is interesting to see that Hobsbawm characterizes these works as concentrating on the question of "what is a (or the) nation" and concludes that their attempts to establish "objective criteria" for nationhood have not yielded a satisfactory result. Instead he suggests the concept of the nation as a profitable site for investigation.[4] The desire to define a nation long predated these works, and the search has resulted in incompleteness or ambiguities. The question is raised, for example, in a stirring essay by Ernest Renan, "What Is a Nation?" (1882), which concludes with the impossibility of arriving at a clear definition except as poetic metaphor.[5]

Since Hobsbawm's assessment in 1990, there has been no abatement of interest in the topic, and scholarly inquiry has expanded in new and diverse directions. To name just a few, Linda Colley's *Britons: Forging the Nation 1707–1837* (1992), Liah Greenfeld's *Nationalism: Five Roads to Modernity* (1992), David A. Bell's *The Cult of the Nation in France: Inventing Nationalism, 1680–1800* (2003), and Anthony Marx's *Faith in Nation: Exclusionary Origins of Nationalism* (2003) are interesting examples. These studies pay attention to the different ways in which the ingredients of the nation interacted with historical forces in a given country to give rise to nationalism: the way in which nationalism was continued, shaped, and constructed by the changing dynamics between these elements, and the meaning and impact of the nationalism thus produced within and in relation to outside forces in each country under discussion. By shifting their focus from what a (or the) nation is to how a nation is constructed, the authors highlight the origin and ingredients of nationalism and its trajectory, which are locally embedded and necessarily diverse. These works all view such elements as sentiments, consciousness, perceptions, and memory as important ingredients of the process, and they locate the beginning of the process long before the modern era. They fall into two groups: Greenfeld and Bell subscribe to the central tenet of the modernist camp, while Colley and Marx take revisionist approaches. Bell, for example, maintains that the French developed a stronger attachment to patrie and nation beginning in the late seventeenth century to fill the void left by God's receding presence in human affairs, that this void was replaced by the cult of great French men in the eighteenth century, and that many authors attempted to define "French character," an endeavor that continued after the French Revolution in renewed form to unify diverse ingredients so that it could apply to and homogenize all "citizens."[6]

Colley and Marx contradict the secular basis for nationhood, a long-cherished idea of modernists. They argue that religion served as the driving force for constructing national identity against the other. Colley cites Protestantism as a crucial element in constructing the British identity against the Catholic French in the eighteenth century. Marx argues that European rulers exploited religious conflicts to promote their legitimacy and power in such events as the Spanish expulsion of the Jews in 1492, the Spanish inquisition, the English renunciation of the Catholic Church and adoption of Anglicanism, or the massacre of the Huguenots in the St. Bartholomew's Day Massacre in sixteenth-century France. In locating the origins of English or European nationalism in exclusionary religious passion, Colley and Marx challenge the Enlightenment model of the inclusive or civic nation-state. It appears that scholarly discourse on the nation is no longer bound by the post-Enlightenment model of the nation-state. It also seems that with scholars finding the origins of nationalism several centuries earlier than the modern era, a division between what Anthony Smith calls primordialists and modernists—those who believe that nation has always existed from time immemorial in human society and those who believe that the nation is a product of modernity[7]—is getting blurred. Patrick J. Geary argues for the medieval origins of European peoples.[8]

Concepts of Nation and Modernity in East Asia

The scholarly terrain on the subject of the nation on East Asia presents a rather different landscape. There has been no lack of studies on the Asian nation in Western scholarship, but almost all are on the modern nation. To my knowledge, there has not been a serious study of an East Asian nation that connects or traces it to the premodern or early modern era. This reticence is strange since East Asian states offer interesting examples.

The three countries in the region are referred to as historical states, but they are understood to be differently constituted from those in Europe. These were territorial states from very early on, and in China and later Korea the rulers' legitimacy derived, at least in theory, from the popular affirmation of the people (K. *ch'ŏnmyŏng*, Ch. *tianming*) inhabiting the territory. The bureaucracy was large, consisting of well-educated, literate scholars who, from some point, passed a civil service examination that tested them on the Confucian canon. Bureaucrats wrote in literary Chinese, a common written language in the region, and one of their duties was the writing of histories of previous dynasties that were the major considerations with which the states claimed legitimacy. However, neither rulers, aristocrats, nor bureaucrats formed what Ernest Gellner called "stratified, horizontally segregated layers of military, administrative, clerical and sometimes commercial ruling elite" that sat on top of "laterally insulated communities of agricultural producers."[9] Unlike in Europe, the ruling elites were just as vertically bound as the ruled. While there was no religious authority that challenged the authority of states, China, much bigger in population and territory than the rest, was dominant. Thus smaller states in the region had to contend with the influence of a political state, which had different ramifications from the sacral/secular axis.

Studying a nation in East Asia in the premodern era, however, presents a certain difficulty, which pervades the fields in what is called the non-West: the problem of working under the dominance of a Eurocentric regime of knowledge. Dipesh Chakrabarty says that European thought and its analytical categories served as the framework and standard for the historical inquiry of all societies, including non-European societies, for the entire modern period. He also points out that these concepts have been embedded in our consciousness as fundamental categories of analysis and that the adequacy and legitimacy of this approach to other areas of the world has only begun to be challenged with the advent of colonial and postcolonial studies in recent decades. It is particularly difficult to consider such topics as the nation, which occupies a central place in modern Western historical scholarship. First of all, there are problems of concept and vocabulary—whether and how one can use concepts and vocabulary that took on the meanings grounded in the historical phenomena of one region in discussing phenomena of another. The problems begin with such basic notions as "nation," "sovereignty," "popular sovereignty," and so forth. There have been various attempts on the part of scholars of East Asia to reconcile these usages. The search for equivalence, commensurability, and reciprocity are some of the suggested approaches.

Then there is the issue of temporality. As Chakrabarty points out, the central tenet of Eurocentric historiography is historicism—that modernity and all that embodied it, such as the nation, capitalism, industrialization, and political freedom, were first achieved in the West, and that the rest of the world follows this path in a later time sequence. In locating the modern idea of the nation in sixteenth-century England, for example, Liah Greenfeld says that it was "the first nation in the world (and the only one, with the possible exception of Holland, for about two hundred years)."[10] This may prove to be true, but she has examined only five countries: four European countries and America. In this scheme the history of the world is conceived of and presented as a set of narratives of transformation to modernity in sequential time. For the most part it has been economic historians who have taken up the issue of comparative temporality by discussing East Asia's relative progress toward industrialization. Kenneth Pomeranz discusses how China diverged in its development from that of Europe,[11] while Andre Gunder Frank discusses the inadequacy of the schemes available for comparative study and proposes instead horizontally integrative macrohistory.[12]

Overtly comparative approaches may sometimes produce undesirable results. To begin with, vocabulary has acquired multiple meanings in Western usage, defying simple definitions, and, more noticeably, a constant evaluation and measurement of equivalence or commensurability between one's usage and Western definitions may shift the focus from the subject of study to whether it is similar or different from the European cases. This does not, however, rescue one from the predicament of being caught between a sense of futility and a sense of the necessity of having to work with concepts and vocabulary from the European regime of historical knowledge. Alternatives would include either coining new vocabulary or using terms in the original language, for instance, *kukka*, to refer to state/nation in Korean. If our aim is to expand our knowledge globally, neither of these options seems satisfactory.

Rather I would suggest mutual accommodation between the new user and old usage: the new user searches for and employs words of best approximation from the Western regime; conversely, the new usage should be assimilated into the old word, and the new usage becomes another possible meaning of this word. This had already happened within the Western European context, and it can and should expand in considering other areas. This would also diversify and decenter the European regime of knowledge and rescue the non-West from its monochromatic field of view. In this work I will draw on vocabulary derived from the European regime of knowledge and will, when possible and desirable, identify the sources of my insights. However, my concepts are embedded in local material and local context.

Concepts of the Nation in Historical Scholarship in Korea

If the idea of a premodern East Asian nation is novel in historical scholarship conducted in the West, the idea of a sixteenth-century

Korean nation is also unfamiliar in Korea. Scholarly discourse in Korea on the Korean nation is deeply contentious. By and large it is bifurcated between primordialists and modernists. A majority of scholars of premodern Korea in the Korean academy seem explicitly or implicitly to subscribe to the primordialist view. In this regime of knowledge, the antiquity and homogeneity of the Korean race is assumed. Many of the components that mark an ethnic group, such as a collective name, a common ancestor, a shared history, a distinct culture, a specific territory, a sense of solidarity—the components that Anthony Smith calls *ethnie*—are discussed in the context of the a priori existence of a "Korean" nation, which is thought to have maintained its cohesive identity through historical changes. National sentiment is taken for granted as the natural expression of an omnipresent sensibility inherent to the inhabitants of Korea. There are a great number of studies on the Imjin War, for example, and many refer to Korean nationalism during the war, but it is presented as a preexisting condition, though "strengthened" and "heightened" by the experience. Scholars of the modernist camp, consisting mostly of historians and social scientists working on periods from the late nineteenth century on, subscribe to the historicism of Western historiography. They present the nationhood of Korea as a narrative of transformation, locating its arrival in the modern period, sometime in late nineteenth or early twentieth century, under the auspices of new ideologies and visions from the West.

The matter is further complicated by a division between primordialist and modernist camps, which is enmeshed with another divide between nationalist and antinationalist historiography. This phenomenon is too complex to discuss in full detail. Suffice it to say that it is ideologized, and politicized, as much of the postcolonial discussion of history in former colonial societies tends to be. Nationalist history began in Korea in the late nineteenth century as a defensive strategy against an outside menace, and it was informed by a desire to sanctify and empower Korean history and culture as a source of inspiration for the preservation and revitalization of Korea. Depending on the needs of the time and individual scholar's inclinations, different periods and different segments of the Korean population were chosen to embody the glory of Korean history. Sin Ch'aeho (1880–1936), revered as the first great historian of the nationalist school, singled out the ancient period, promoting it as a time during which "Korea" reigned over a vast territory, including Manchuria, and was a major force in the East Asian region. Chosŏn, the regime that was annexed by Japan, was bitterly criticized: it lost strength and uniqueness because its elite, having adopted an alien Confucian culture from China, became effeminate and corrupt, and the people, the mass, in which the true vitality of the Korean people inhered, was suppressed. That Sin, a socialist writing during the Japanese colonial period, chastised the elite of a regime that had lost its sovereignty to Japan with a class-driven denunciation and rendered its ruling ideology as foreign seems logical. This vision of an enervated and morally bankrupt Confucian civil ruling elite and an "imported" Confucianism as the culprits in Korea's decline and ruin was not confined to Sin; in fact, it dominated Korea's vision of its past for the greater part of the twentieth century. It is worthy of note that Sin's class-driven view of Korean society was resurrected and used as a rallying point to empower the people in the mass movement for democracy of the 1970s and 1980s.

After the liberation from Japan in 1945, scholars in both North and South Korea stressed the antiquity of the Korean race and its culture, and different agencies including government authorities in both states exploited it. Tangun, who was the mythical progenitor of the Korean race and the first founder of the Korean state but who first appears in the thirteenth-century text *Remaining Stories from the Three Kingdoms* (*Samguk yusa*), was hailed as a national symbol of the ancient, unified, and divine origin of the Korean race. At the same time, the question of modernization emerged as a prominent issue for historical inquiry in South Korea, and the period immediately preceding the modern era, the late Chosŏn of the seventeenth and eighteenth centuries, came into focus. Countering the view that the Korean path to modernity was guided and engineered solely by foreign regimes, especially the colonial regime of Japan, and imported technology and ideas, scholars of nationalist history proposed the so-called theory of internal seeds for industrialization and capitalism, pointing at commercial activities and the writings of scholars of the practical learning (*sirhak*) school in the late Chosŏn as proof of the domestic origins of modernity. Many scholars who subscribed to the primordialist view of the nation seem to have joined the nationalist camp on this issue. The thesis of domestic origins of Korean modernization elicited a strong reaction from certain quarters, especially from historians of Korea working in the United States, who viewed this line of inquiry as lacking in objectivity and a spirit of scientific inquiry. For about two decades the disagreements between the nationalist and the antinationalist camps were sharp, though some interesting works were produced in this contention.

Regimes of Korean history both inside and outside Korea became increasingly diverse beginning in the 1990s. Many scholars in Korea moved beyond the internal seeds thesis, while some younger scholars working in the West criticized American scholars of the antinationalist school as orientalists, not so much in their own scholarship as in their view of Korean scholarship. Diversity also brought calmer scholarly waters, and the nationalist and antinationalist camps are no longer occupied with incipiency of Korean modernization or the lack of objectivity of Korean scholarship. Despite these changes, an argument for the emergence of a nation in late sixteenth-century Korea may not be a comfortable affair. Nationalists or primordialists will think this a nonissue, an anomaly, and regard the timing as late or puzzling, while modernists and antinationalists might suspect it of emerging from nationalist leanings.

My proposal of the emergence of a nation in sixteenth-century Korea is based on my finding that a discourse of nation appeared when the Japanese invaded Korea, that it continued, shifting and acquiring an extra dimension after the Manchu invasions, through the entire Chosŏn period, and that this process was a visible, traceable, and documentable phenomenon. I decided to put forth the thesis of the emergence of a nation because I feel that the term "nation" is the most suitable frame for a historical phenomenon of such intensity and passion extending through the totality of Korean society and persisting through several centuries, not because I wish to determine whether the Korea of the premodern era was a nation by the criteria of bifurcated paradigms. In fact, I do not subscribe to either school.

By locating the beginning of the Korean nation in a sixteenth-century war, I do not mean that national sentiment or national consciousness had not existed or manifested itself prior to that. The Imjin War was not the first foreign invasion that Korea had suffered. The Mongol attacks on Koryŏ during the thirteenth century, for example, were extensive, prolonged, and fiercely resisted, even though the Koryŏ state eventually succumbed and lived under Mongol domination for a century. Michael Rogers persuasively argues that the appearance of the Tangun myth in the Mongol-dominated Koryŏ displayed Koreans' consciousness of their distinct ethnicity and a yearning for a unified identity for the entire Korean community.[13] There are numerous other symbols and images that appeared sporadically at different points in history, which can be interpreted as expressions of national sentiment or national consciousness. These earlier manifestations, however, were brief, isolated, and disconnected and did not cohere to become a connected, contextualized discourse.

Neither do I subscribe to the modernist school of thought concerning the nation. This work may be described as a narrative of transformation into a nation but not to modernity. Discourse of nation spread eventually to involve almost all groups, through the means and materials of Chosŏn society, both textual and ritual, and it was carried out with the technology of the premodern and early modern era. This is a study of a premodern and early modern nation in a specific time and place. I do not present the Korean case as representative of other East Asian states, not to mention a wider Asia. While Korea, China, and Japan, three states of the four that Hobsbawm called historical nations, shared a number of political and cultural attributes, each is distinctly situated in relation to the nation or, for that matter, to modernity.

Historical Considerations: Trauma and Discourse

What indeed were the historical contingencies that gave rise to the discourse of nation in Korea at this time? What led to such a momentous movement? True, I chose wars as the main sites that led to the emergence of discourse of nation, but not every war elicits discourse of nation. These issues will be discussed in depth in succeeding chapters, but I will mention several here. The first is the sheer depth and acuteness of the trauma caused by the wars. With the Imjin War, it was not only the immensity of the catastrophe but also the extreme shock and surprise of Koreans, unprepared as they were for an invasion from Japan. This was partly due to the nature of the diplomatic relations between Korea and Japan, and partly to Koreans' conception of the world order. Considering their proximity, Korea and Japan had remained remarkably, though not entirely, free of negative encounters. There were two hostile confrontations that did not quite escalate into warfare, one in the seventh century and the other in the thirteenth.[14] They left no imprint on Korean historical memory. The vituperative rhetoric of a demonic Japan that historically minded Koreans developed in the post–Imjin War period made no mention of prior collisions. True, Japan was one of Korea's national security concerns, though a far less serious one than the northern borders. When Japan fragmented into civil strife between the Japanese pirates known as *wakō* (K. *waegu*) that frequently marauded the southern coastal regions of China and Korea and the huge number of trade missions, some fraudulent, sent to the Korean court by the shogun and feudal lords in the decentralized polity, "Japan" became a troublesome and confusing place. The Chosŏn entered into the Kakitsu Treaty in 1443 with the Sō feudal house of Tsushima, and Korea's use of Tsushima as a mediator with Japan to control piracy placed Japan at an even further remove from Koreans.

Korea was preoccupied with constructing a society of civil culture and securing its place in what may be termed the Sinocentric world order.[15] In 1592, entering the third century of the Chosŏn dynasty, Korea had experienced two centuries of stability as a centralized state. It had enjoyed an uninterrupted peace of two hundred years. The successful diplomatic relations that Chosŏn Korea had forged with Ming China as a tributary state solved many of the security problems along the northern border. The continuing peace and security permitted the Korean political and intellectual elite to focus on constructing Korea as a Small Brilliant Center (*Sojunghwa*),[16] a term coined in both emulation of and competition with China, the original Brilliant Center (*Chunghwa*). In the geo-cultural imaginings of sixteenth-century Koreans, Japan was hardly present. Thus when Hideyoshi's invitation to join the Japanese campaign against China, accompanied by a threat of invasion if Korea were to be unwilling to cooperate, arrived at the Korean court in 1591,[17] it was greeted with incomprehension, rage, and misunderstanding.[18]

The Japanese Army did come, in May 1592, and announced its arrival with the massacres of thousands if not tens of thousands of residents of Pusan and Tongnae. These mass killings set the stage for "one of the most cruel and unprovoked wars that the world has ever witnessed," in the words of the Japan-centered scholar Yoshi Kuno, writing in 1937 during the Japanese colonial rule of Korea.[19] The Japanese Army, 158,700 strong, well-trained, and well-armed, swiftly marched north with little resistance from the Korean Royal Army, pillaging villages, looting towns, and capturing and killing inhabitants. As Korean civilians were subjected to widespread carnage of a nature they had never imagined they would witness in their lives, initial wide-eyed disbelief grew into a realization that their very existence and modes of life were at stake, and that the only way to preserve their lives, their families, their property, culture, and country was to fight and defend themselves against the intruders. A volunteer army movement sprang up and quickly spread nationwide. One volunteer leader after another sent out impassioned exhortations to other civilians, creating a vision of Korea in which all were united in an inseparable and cohesive community, and for which all should fight risking death. The movement was inseparable from tropes of the imagined community of Korea and patriotic duty to it with which they mobilized volunteers. The tropes and the movement were created and defined in mutual interaction. This strand of discourse of nation was almost simultaneously joined by others, initiated by different individuals and groups who also were motivated by their concerns for ethnic and cultural identity under the threat of extinction.

The trauma that the Manchu invasions brought to Koreans was of a different kind: a profound and gnawing sense of humiliation that they had surrendered to "barbarians" and thus were besmirched with "barbarism." The ceremony in which King Injo performed a ritual act of surrender to Hong Taiji in February 1637, the only one that a Korean king performed to a foreign ruler in recorded history, imprinted an indelible sense of shame on the entire Korean political body. The Manchu conquest of China in 1644 led Koreans to believe that civilization was lost to China, and that they had to find a way to preserve it in Korea. This gave them a sense of mission with which they recovered a cultural sense of self, even a cultural identity, and rededicated themselves to the Korean Brilliant Center. Nevertheless the nightmarish vision of the ceremony of surrender seems to have continued to haunt the full spectrum of the Korean elite. Living under ritualistic and diplomatic subservience to the Qing, the Korean civil elite, in shame and impotent rage, turned to the Imjin War and transformed it from a war of error and tragedy into one of victory and unity. Unlike the Manchu invasions that resulted in a shameful defeat, the Imjin War ended with Japan's unconditional retreat. Even in Japan it is referred to as the Dragon-Head and Snake-Tail Campaign (*Ryo-to ja-bi*) because Hideyoshi undertook it in pursuit of a grand vision of Asian empire but ended it having accomplished none of his professed aims.[20] The Imjin War offered sites under which Koreans could bury their shame and on which they could project visions of uncompromised heroism and patriotism. Discourse of nation, which was rendered even more imperative and urgent after the Manchus undercut their cultural identity, grew into a layered complex of ethnic and cultural components, hidden and visible, encompassing shame and pride, remorse and determination.

The second contingency was the existence of a certain type of local elite nurtured by the two centuries of Chosŏn Confucian civil rule. Commonly held scholarly views attribute the ineffectual management and consequent disasters of the two wars to the Chosŏn's excessive attention to civil culture at the expense of military prowess. This is undeniable. The Chosŏn pursued national security policy primarily by means of diplomatic negotiations supplemented by military solutions only when it was absolutely necessary. I argue, however, that this same civil culture also produced the local elites who considered themselves the guardians of the Korean state and culture and who, when it came under attack, rose to fight for it, risking their lives. It is not surprising that as privileged products of Chosŏn society, they were vested in the system. What is remarkable is that when the government could not fulfill its role as defender of Korea, they stepped in. The civilian elites were private individuals with no obligation to fight, and they had neither experience nor training in warfare, but they voluntarily rose in arms against a well-armed Japanese army. They fought calling themselves the "Righteous Army" (*Ŭibyŏng*), which, except as an entity with an abstract meaning as a punitive force of justice, had no historical precedent. These voluntary militias sprang up quickly in all eight provinces.

The most immediate question is what caused the local elites to lead this unprecedented and extraordinary patriotic movement. What in the identity of the local elites led them to meet this national challenge as they did? In terms of Chosŏn political culture, their mobilization can be described as activist loyalty, that is, the concept of loyalty translated into action. One may attribute their source of inspiration to the Confucian notion of moral autonomy, but the movement has to be grounded in their particular and local sense of identity as men of Chosŏn. Insofar as it was a voluntary and participatory action on behalf of the state taken by a huge number of civilians, it is akin to an assertion of popular sovereignty. This movement transformed the political culture of the Chosŏn, and the local elites were correspondingly transformed by the experience. Catapulted into prominence during the Imjin War, the local civil elites continued to exhibit a sense of participatory ownership of the Chosŏn. They remained, after the cataclysmic Manchu invasions and through several centuries of postwar commemoration of war dead, a commanding force in shaping and defining the Korean state and culture. One may attribute the state's tireless participation in the commemorative activities to its desire to win them over, but it also felt a need to take a role as ultimate guardian and custodian of memories of the wars.

The third factor was the existence of a diglossic linguistic space of classical Chinese and vernacular Korean, or, more properly, of parallel linguistic spaces in the two scriptural media. The discourse of nation spread through two linguistic spaces in constant interaction with oral narratives, facilitating its appearance in many different strands and genres, some interconnected and intertextual and some separate. These dual linguistic spaces enabled the movement to become more participatory, open, and far-reaching. The discourse of nation that began in the diglossic space remained diglossic through the long years of postwar discourse. This phenomenon differs from the common view that places the classical and vernacular languages in dichotomy both in spaces of action and in era, the classical being seen as religious, regional, and premodern, and the vernacular seen as secular, national, and modern. Benedict Anderson terms classical languages sacral and includes classical Chinese among them.[21] However, the dichotomy worked somewhat differently with classical Chinese, as the Confucian canon, the most representative texts in it, comprised not religious but political and moral texts. Moreover in Korea there was another dichotomy of function between classical Chinese and vernacular Korean—classical Chinese was seen as regional, public, and male while vernacular Korean was local, private, and female. The discourse of nation, however, broke the division and transcended the boundary between the two linguistic spaces, providing accessibility and acquiring diversity. In this again, discourse of nation and diglossic linguistic spaces were mutually reinforced and shaped by each other.

The fourth factor was the ready availability of commemorative channels in postwar Chosŏn and the eager participation by a wide range of agents in these activities. The Chosŏn was a Confucian society with remembrance as a core organizing principle of life, and so it possessed a built-in infrastructure for commemoration in its ritual and everyday life. Paul Connerton maintains that ceremonies that involve bodily practices more than textual transmission constitute social memory.[22] Commemorative rituals of war dead during the Chosŏn encompassed a great variety of forms—textual, ceremonial, and combinations of both—and they were performed in different units and localities, from domestic family rites through semiofficial ceremonies at local institutions to public rites by the state. Availing themselves of these opportunities for ritual commemoration in all its forms, these agencies actively engaged in constructing, propagating, and transmitting memories of the wars that were deemed meaningful and useful.

Postwar memories can largely be divided into two groups by the way they were constructed and perpetuated. One was disparate, produced and circulated by individuals and groups in different localities. Memories in this group were multiple, fragmentary, and marked by the premodern and preindustrial state of communication technology. Another group was unified and systematized by the state. Acutely aware of the symbolic value for the politics of legitimation, the Chosŏn state embarked on a project to nationalize memories of war, appropriating the role of curator and custodian. It collected all categories of memories; it performed commemorative rituals to those who died during the wars, including those who died anonymously; it enshrined and immortalized heroes; it conferred posthumous honors on those deemed to have rendered meaningful service to the country and rewarded their descendants. The process of nationalization of memories was interactive, multidirectional, and multilayered. In selecting from and transforming disparate and personal memories into the collective and public memory, the state solicited the views and listened to the suggestions of local authorities and individuals in near and remote areas. The main theme of the politics of memory was patriotism, by whose criteria merit was measured and rewards were requested and conferred. The state seems to have been an obvious arbiter. What is apparent is that the Chosŏn state made itself into the undisputed custodian of national memory.

This is not to say that all individual and local memories were transferred into the state's storehouse or that all claims of meritorious services were honored. Nor did it mean that the state's versions of memory or its vision of meritorious service necessarily coincided with that held by individuals in distant localities. Different agencies continuously competed for the possession and appropriation of memories of wars. What mattered was that the state left channels open for popular participation in commemoration and for recommending persons and acts for public commemoration, and that the people felt a sense of agency and participation in the politics of memory, transforming personal memory into public commemoration.

Approaches and Organization

The basic scheme of this book consists of adopting two different temporal perspectives: discourses that appeared during and immediately after the war, and postwar commemorative discourses. Though history is inherently retrospective, I will attempt a forward gaze, moving with those experiencing war and, later, those contemplating postwar issues (although some of these narratives were compiled later), and a backward gaze inherent in commemorative writings and activities.

I will begin by discussing compelling images of the war created by narratives that were written during or immediately after the wars. These images remained the emotional core on which postwar memories were constructed and structured. In addition to those from Imjin War, there were those from the Manchu invasions. Some were new and some revived the use of old channels and spaces of communication, but these nearly simultaneous though disparate strands appeared, interconnected above all by the theme of the imagined community of Chosŏn.

The Imjin War was an epochal event in which hundreds of thousands participated directly. Three states fought, each closely directed by its respective head, assisted by ministers, staff, and advisors for the course of war. There were thus three armies and three navies deployed, commanded by generals and admirals, some of whom acquired immortal fame. In Korea, where the battles were waged, there were also thousands of volunteer army members, moving amid a population of millions suffering the ravages of war, not to mention the hundreds of thousands killed or taken prisoner. The Imjin War was to be writ large in tales of heroes and victims. The three states entwined in battle each had its own unique perspectives, with separate legends and corresponding hagiographies and canons of heroes and victims. As befits a war that occupies a central place in their defining imaginings, Koreans canonized and deployed a huge number of heroes in the aftermath of the Imjin War, the most honored among them arguably being Admiral Yi Sunsin (1545–1598) and a number of volunteer army leaders. Non'gae, a courtesan who threw herself into a river, bringing a Japanese general with her, also earned legendary status.[1] I will argue that the Imjin War became the war that defined or redefined "Korea" as an imagined community in Korean historical discourse, so that these heroes became the patriotic faces of Korea.

Yi Sunsin was a state military officer. His famous admiralship qualities—a superb strategist who never lost a battle, an inventor of the famous battleships known as turtle ships (*kŏbuksŏn*), and a fearless soldier who, when felled in the final battle as the Japanese retreated from Korea, ordered

1

THE VOLUNTEER ARMY AND THE DISCOURSE OF NATION

that his death be kept secret until the fighting was over—achieved near mythic status, and he became *the* hero of popular Korean history and the exemplar of patriotic virtue in contemporary South Korean elementary textbooks. But Yi's special place in Korean history does not rest only on his being a superior admiral. More important still to his heroism and his status as a "sage-hero" (*sŏng'ung*) (as the popular 2004–2005 television drama, *Pulmyŏl ŭi Yi Sunsin*,[2] refers to him) was his unwavering loyalty to the very throne that rejected and humiliated him. Indeed, the Chosŏn state had not always appreciated or valued him. Despite the early victories he earned for Korea, Yi Sunsin was recalled in the midst of the war and demoted to the lowest soldier rank (*paegŭi chonggun*). It was only after his successor, the infamous Wŏn Kyun (?–1597), suffered a drastic defeat in which the entire fleet was destroyed and he himself was killed that Yi was reappointed as commander of the navy. Though his disgrace and fall lent humanity to this seemingly perfect man, Yi Sunsin's story is after all that of a soldier.

What of the volunteer army? Known as the Righteous Army (*Ŭibyŏng*), it consisted of countryside civilians who formed volunteer army units and waged guerilla warfare against the Japanese Army of 158,000 after it landed and swept across Korea.[3] Benedict Anderson has argued that "the idea of the ultimate sacrifice comes only with an idea of purity, through fatality." He elaborates that "dying for one's country, which usually one does not choose, assumes a moral grandeur" because of "an aura of purity and disinterestedness."[4] In this vein, the leaders of the volunteer army, despite their civilian status and the absence of any obligation to fight, felt compelled to rise for their country. Although none of the members of this army have achieved the instant name recognition of Admiral Yi Sunsin in the popular media, arguably they achieved an even greater moral grandeur precisely because of their "aura of purity and disinterestedness." Collectively they occupy a place of honor in the Korean historical imagination that is no less revered than that of the great naval hero.

Not surprisingly, the volunteer army movement has received a great deal of attention from historians in contemporary Korea. There are innumerable studies on different aspects of the army. Some consider the movement on a local or national scale and evaluate its effectiveness as an army; others discuss its relations with the state, focusing on the social and political constraints under which the volunteer army operated; and some examine its effects on the socioeconomic positions of the local elites before and after the war. By far the greatest number of studies detail the deeds of individual leaders, most often in a timeless heroic narrative mode well-suited to biographies of national heroes highlighting selfless acts of courageous devotion to the country in the face of impossible odds.[5]

Despite the enormous attention devoted to the volunteer army, I believe that the army's political and historical significations have yet to be properly examined. Issues such as the texture of the political culture from which the movement emerged and the changes wrought have not been adequately addressed. For example, while the missives of exhortation the leaders of the volunteer army sent out are casually quoted in the secondary literature, they have not been properly appreciated as an integral component of the movement. I believe these missives to be foundational communiqués from which discourse of nation emerged. Still unexamined are the process and political meaning of the immortalization of volunteer army leaders as patriotic symbols in postwar Chosŏn.

Thus missing in modern scholarship is proper recognition of the exceptional nature of the volunteer army. We can perhaps attribute this oversight to a primordialist vision of the nation as timeless, so that patriotic uprisings in the face of foreign invasion can be seen as natural. In this view, the rise of the volunteer army was an admirable venture worthy of endless encomium but not a remarkable historical phenomenon deserving to be studied for its origin, impact, and meaning. It is also possible that centuries of adulation may have turned these figures into familiar images, depriving them of the aura of wonderment with which they were viewed by their contemporaries and by postwar Chosŏn society.

This primordialist view, however, flies in the face of history. Just as the Japanese invasion was unanticipated, so too the volunteer army was unimagined. The Chosŏn was a state that fit Max Weber's definition of a state: it possessed a monopoly on legitimate violence. Private armies and private possession of arms had been outlawed since 1400.

Local elites, who were a majority of the leaders of the volunteer army, were scholars not warriors. Thus when the civilian-volunteer army first appeared it was greeted with bewilderment and awe. The volunteer army had to get state permission to organize and bear arms and, at some point, to be made a part of the royal army. Although it is disputed whether government encouragement or the appearance of the volunteer army came first, and it is known that the relationship between the government and the volunteer army often was complex and even tense, nonetheless the government encouraged and supported the movement. Awe and wonderment at the appearance of the volunteer army lasted for centuries, and these "structures of feeling," to borrow Raymond Williams's phrase, lay at the heart of their becoming national heroes.[6] This was true during the war and remained so through centuries afterward, as various agencies competed to appropriate and honor volunteer army fighters and leaders. Eventually, it is hardly an exaggeration to say, nearly every family scrambled to claim an ancestor who had been active in the volunteer army. Posthumous honors were showered on them, shrines were built in their name, and their resistance activities were researched, revealed, narrated, and even published—an industry that continues to this day in Korea.

The volunteer army is hard to characterize. On the one hand locally based, on the other hand it grew into a nationwide force as well as a national movement. Then again it was a military movement, but its growth was inextricably intertwined with the emergence and expansion of the communicative space that connected Koreans to one another, and in which they exchanged discourse on an imagined community of Chosŏn. It was at this moment of crisis—when the Chosŏn community seemed to be irrevocably torn asunder—that Koreans fashioned an alternative communicative space through which a nation emerged. In this and the subsequent chapter, I am foremost interested in the local and national components of the army and in the way its activities were subsumed into a national movement. I will argue that a vision of national community emerged between the space of action and the space of communication. I will concentrate on what I call the horizontal space of communication that was created by volunteer army leaders, and on the way in which the discourse on the Chosŏn community evolved from one limited by social status and region to one that extended to all inhabitants of Korea.

Prelude

I have already mentioned that on the eve of the Imjin War, the identity and aspirations of Japan and Korea were nearly opposite: Korea, having enjoyed two hundred years of uninterrupted peace, aspired to be a society of civil culture, while Japan, having just been unified under Hideyoshi after many years of civil strife, was intent on building a huge Asian empire through invasion, with Korea as its first target. The irregular and inadequate communication that existed between Korea and Japan for decades prior to the war also contributed to their mutual incomprehension. The ambassadorial mission of investigation that Korea sent to Japan in 1590 amply displays this. The Korean court dispatched the embassy to investigate whether Hideyoshi genuinely intended to invade Korea as he had threatened in his missives. The embassy, headed by Hwang Yun'gil (1536–?) and Kim Sŏng'il (1538–1593) as ambassador and deputy ambassador, respectively, the first since 1443, left in April 1590 and returned a year later. This ill-fated mission would become notorious in the narration of Korean history. In their audience with the king upon return, the two were queried for their views as to whether Hideyoshi was planning an attack. Hwang replied affirmatively; Kim negatively. Later historians often attributed their conflicting views to their differing factional affiliations and cite the incident to refer to the sorry factionalism of the Chosŏn bureaucracy.[7]

Perhaps the greater misfortune of the embassy was that it inadvertently conveyed the wrong message to Hideyoshi. When the Korean investigative embassy arrived, the official mediator between the two countries, the Sō feudal house of Tsushima, led Hideyoshi to believe that the Korean envoys had come as tributaries and that Korea accepted his demand for cooperation in the invasion of China.[8] Thus he ordered his own envoys, Keitetsu Genso and Sō Yoshitoshi, to accompany the Korean embassy on its return to Seoul to present his letter to the Korean king. This letter invited Koreans to join in his planned campaign against China. After describing his pacification and unification of Japan, he announced his dream of building a greater Asian empire:

> A man born on this earth, though he might live to a ripe old age, will not, as a rule, reach a hundred years. Why then should I rest grumbling in frustration where I am? Disregarding the distance across the sea and across the mountain reaches that lie between us, I shall in one fell swoop invade Great Ming. I have it in mind to introduce Japanese customs and values to the four hundred and more provinces of that country and to bestow upon it the benefits of imperial rule and the culture of the coming hundred million years.

He then gave an ultimatum:

> Your esteemed country has done well to make haste in attending our court. To the farsighted, grief does not approach. Those who lag [in offering homage], however, will not be granted pardon, even if this is a distant land of little islands lying in the sea. When the day of my invasion of Great Ming arrives and I lead my troops to the staging area, that will be the time to make our neighborly relations flourish all the more. I have no other desire but to spread my fame throughout the three countries, this and no more.[9]

This letter left no doubt as to Hideyoshi's intention to invade.[10] From this point on, the Korean government made some attempt to devise defense plans: it chose and placed talented men in charge of crucial military posts, fortified the fortresses of walled towns, and streamlined weapons.[11] These measures were half-hearted and were rebuffed and resented by local residents.[12] The Chinese scholar Li Guangtao justifiably characterized the confused manner in which Koreans approached the Japanese this way: "Korea adopted a policy of trying to hide its mistakes by going to sleep and ignoring the threat as if hoping the Japanese would be gone when they woke up."[13] No one seems to have believed or wanted to believe in the likelihood of an imminent invasion. This would perhaps have required too large a leap of both imagination and disposition.

Even taking into consideration Chosŏn incredulity and unpreparedness for the war, Korea fared miserably, especially in the early phase of the war. Though the navy continued to function, the Chosŏn Royal Army could offer no resistance to the invaders. Narrative after narrative, private or official, portrays this period as one of unmitigated doom. The Japanese vanguard army landed in Pusan on May 23, 1592, and the first battles fought in Pusan and Tongnae set the stage for what was to come. On May 24 a Japanese army of 18,700 led by Sō Yoshitoshi and Konishi Yukinaga encircled the port town of Pusan, despite Korean resistance led by Chŏng Pal, the commander of the navy of Pusan, and entered the town.[14] On May 25 the Japanese Army attacked Tongnae and overcame fierce resistance led by the magistrate, Song Sanghyŏn, within a day. Both Chŏng Pal and Song Sanghyŏn were killed, and Song, because of the dignified manner in which he met his death, became one of the heroes of the war. Other government officials in charge, including Kim Su, governor of Kyŏngsang Province, either ran away or were unwilling to come to the site of battle. The number of people killed in battle or after the Japanese occupation began seems to have been quite high.[15] One Japanese source put the number killed in Pusan at 30,000, although it is likely that the real number was considerably lower.[16] Another Japanese document describes the massacre at Tongnae: "We beheaded about 3,000 people and took 500 as prisoners of war."[17]

It must have been profoundly shocking and terrifying for Koreans to see a huge number of Japanese on their land. Most of them had never seen foreigners, not to mention a foreign army, and certainly not a foreign army attacking with sword and arquebus, a kind of musket. As news of the power and mercilessness of the Japanese army spread, very few towns mounted even token resistance, and residents fled to mountains and other hiding places.[18] The Japanese Army, which reached its full planned force of 158,800 in Korea after a very short period of time, marched north to the capital in three groups taking three different paths,[19] burning towns and killing residents on the way. The Korean Royal Army made several attempts at resisting the invaders, but the fighting always ended disastrously for them; they were decimated at battles fought at Sangju on June 4 and Ch'ungju on June 6.[20] The Korean government invested all its hopes of defending the capital in successfully stopping the invaders at Ch'ungju and devoted all its remaining resources to this battle. Thus the miserable defeat there, for which commander Sin Ip earned infamy, represented the destruction of the final Korean defenses.[21] In a hastily called meeting, the terrified Sŏnjo insisted on leaving the capital for the North. Despite strong opposition voiced by a majority of officials, it was decided that the capital would be temporarily moved (p'ach'ŏn) to P'yŏngyang.

It hardly needs to be mentioned that the power of the monarchy was vested in the symbolism of "court-and-capital" as "a microcosm of supernatural order" and "the material embodiment of political order."[22] The removal of the royal court, thus separating the court from the capital, would destabilize the very basis of the power of the state and was thus a frightening prospect. Chosŏn took several desperate measures: it sent envoys to the Ming requesting military assistance; it appointed Prince Kwanghae as heir apparent; and it dispatched Princes Imhae and Sunhwa to Hamgyŏng and Kangwŏn Provinces, respectively, to recruit additional soldiers.[23]

The tale of the Sŏnjo court's flight to the North rings both pathetic and perilous.[24] Worse still, the powerlessness and irresponsibility of the government symbolized by this flight were communicated time and time again as it repeatedly took flight. Indeed, a pattern emerged in which the royal entourage would depart from the capital as news arrived of the approaching Japanese. In this instance the king in a public announcement of June 7 assured fearful residents of safety and protection,[25] only to renege by departing surreptitiously two days later, leaving behind vulnerable residents totally exposed. The government appointed Kim Myŏngwŏn commander-in-chief of the Korean Army, directing him to encamp with the remaining soldiers of Kyŏnggi Province along the Han River and to guard the city wall.[26] In a short time the army crumbled as soldiers took flight. Enraged mobs attacked the palace, setting fire to several buildings.[27] The *Miscellaneous Record of the*

War describes Seoul on the eve of Japanese occupation: "The people of the city have all fled. The knaves of the town have formed themselves into groups and whenever they see beautiful women or valuable goods, they take them by force, paying no attention to the status of the people they are violating. In this disorder, father and son, husband and wife are separated from each other, and take flight."[28]

The Japanese troops, which had taken different routes, converged on the capital and, on June 11, entered the evacuated capital completely unopposed. In Kaesŏng and P'yŏngyang the same set of events was repeated: the king's promise of protection and security to the residents followed by furtive departure of the royal entourage, causing the cities to fall into chaos and lawlessness and eliciting in turn a burst of rage from the residents. Descriptions abound of the state of disorder into which cities fell even before the arrival of the Japanese armies.[29]

Had there been any hope that government troops could recoup and muster some sort of offensive, it was dashed in the debacle of the battle of Yongin in Kyŏnggi Province near the capital. On July 14 the governors of the three southern provinces, who also were serving concurrently as commanders-in-chief of the army, leading a newly recruited army of 60,000, suffered a massive defeat in an ill-advised, poorly strategized battle. While scores of brave souls died in the fighting, all three governors fled.

What appears to have been a dysfunctional Korean military may require some explanation. Although a detailed discussion of the Chosŏn's military system is beyond the scope of this work, I will briefly explain its basic ingredients. The royal army consisted of two components: the palace guard, which was the military body that protected the king and his family, and the general army. The latter consisted of five commands (*owi*), each of which was responsible for protecting specific areas in the capital and certain provinces. In other words, the military was organized as a centripetal system with the provincial offices attached to one of the five commands, whose headquarters were in the capital.

Despite an appearance of cohesiveness, it was a system that evolved over time, and each part was only loosely connected to the others.

Several factors seem to have been at work. Each command had been established at a different time for a specific purpose, and each had a distinct organization and composition. The Chosŏn state maintained the principle of universal military service for men between the ages of sixteen and sixty on rotation but in reality allowed very flexible arrangements depending on status, residence, and inclination. Moreover there was a great deal of difference in the operation of the army in the capital and the provinces. In the capital the five commands were staffed continually at a more or less fixed number, whereas in the provinces, although the number of leadership posts was specified, they were filled only when a crisis demanded and soldiers were conscripted. Thus the military does not seem to have maintained a fixed independent bureaucracy. On these occasions civilian officials took on additional duties as military commanders. There were exceptions—specific commanders were appointed in the navy and sometimes stationed in the troublesome border regions to the north.[30]

As peace continued, provinces had few active military men. There is little evidence that the regulations specifying that men between the ages of sixteen and sixty be in reserve and in training during the slack farming season were put into practice. This negligence of military affairs caused anxiety for some people. The most renowned instance was the proposal of 1582 by the famous scholar-official Yi I (1536–1584) that argued for a stronger and more systematic arrangement.[31] Any military reform, especially involving an increase in the army, required fiscal arrangements, a tremendously difficult proposition in an agrarian economy. It does not appear that the Chosŏn elite felt the need for it.

When the Imjin War broke out, the governor of each province served as the military commander of his province, as was required by his position. Even during the war, when most Korean territory was under Japanese occupation, the Chosŏn bureaucracy did not disappear but went underground. Though vested with leading the Royal Army on the battlefield, these governors were civilian officials, unschooled in the arts of war. They were not known for valor; indeed many are known to have fled the battlefield when, or even before, the situation proved to be unfavorable. The defeat at Yongin amply testifies to this view.

After the Imjin River defense fell, there was no further plan for obstructing the Japanese advance. Unimpeded, the Japanese Army pursued the royal entourage. By the end of the seventh month, Sŏnjo's court was hiding in the border town of Ŭiju. To make things worse, early in October Princes Imhae and Sunhwa were captured by Katō Kiyomasa, reputedly the most ferocious Japanese general.[32] To add insult to injury, it was discovered that this event had been accomplished with the help of a Korean, Kuk Kyŏng'in, who captured the two princes and their entourage and handed them over to the Japanese.[33] The incident seems to have been considered the ultimate humiliation to the Korean monarchy and grist for the expression of popular disenchantment.[34] It was as though almost the entire territory was given over to the pillaging Japanese, and the people's faith in government plummeted to its lowest level. O Hŭimun's (1539–1613) *The Records of Trivial and Insignificant Matters* records a verse from a widely circulated song that satirized the government: "Though we may build a high wall around the city, who would defend us against the enemy. The wall is no wall; the people are the wall."[35]

The Rise of the Righteous Army

It was against this background of demoralization, panic, and loss of faith in government that the volunteer army emerged. From its inception it was both local and national. All volunteer army units were locally based and remained so to a great extent; they were initiated by local elite who mobilized residents with the immediate objective of defending homes, families, and localities. However, the army also projected a national aspiration and vision, in that local interests were tied to national destiny. What transformed the volunteer army into a national movement from what could have remained disparate local activities was the creation of a horizontal space of communication by volunteer army leaders. To recruit volunteers, local leaders sent a succession of open letters of exhortation (*kyŏksŏ*) and circulars (*t'ongmun*) to an ever wider circle of people, creating an imagined Chosŏn community that came to include every Korean, transcending social status and region. In this way military action and a discourse of nation moved forward hand in hand.

There was another, though related, force at work that influenced the course of the volunteer army movement: the ambivalent, tense, and shifting relationship between the volunteer army and the state. As mentioned above, Chosŏn was a centralized state committed to Confucian civil rule, and it enforced strict regulations against armament and the formation of armies by private individuals.[36] A violation of this prohibition was deemed an act of sedition and was punished as such. Thus the volunteer army was a contradiction in terms, arising as it did under a colossal and imminent sense of crisis, a sense that also seems to have guided the state's response to this unprecedented predicament. On its flight north, the central court had already resorted to desperate measures, militarizing civilians and relinquishing its monopoly over the military. This was announced in mid-June in the royal edict of self-castigation in which the monarch blamed himself (*choegisŏ*) for the tragic situation into which the country had been plunged and asked the people to take up arms against the invaders to preserve the country.[37]

Urging the people to take up arms not under the control of the state was a radical move, unprecedented and not to be repeated during the Chosŏn dynasty. The volunteer army rose with pledges of loyalty to the state, and the state responded with promises of support and recompense. The government publicized specific rewards for killing Japanese. Chŏng T'ak's *The Diary of the Dragon and Snake War* contains a memo that he, serving under the Crown Prince, sent to Sŏnjo to propose and report on a systematic way to reward those who brought in the severed heads of Japanese. These rewards included promises to raise the social status and grant additional privileges to those who could provide evidence of their military accomplishments.[38] This reflects an implicit assumption that many Koreans were seeking to improve their status.[39] While the volunteer army regarded the state as its raison d'être, the state saw the volunteer army as a means of survival, at least for the duration of 1592, until the Chinese Army arrived toward the end of 1592. Nevertheless, if the volunteer army was reassuring, its very existence signified to the state its own failure and inadequacy. Moreover, the question of state authority over the army emerged as an issue: should the volunteer army be given total autonomy and if not, how and to what extent should it be made subject to state sovereignty? Should there be a uniform policy or case-by-case control?

These elements—local versus national, and volunteer army versus the state—played out somewhat differently in various regions. The volunteer armies of Kyŏngsang and Chŏlla Provinces, which are viewed as having been two of the most active, represent opposite poles in their appearance, structure, vision, and relation to the state. The first volunteer army to proclaim itself the "Righteous Army" was in Kyŏngsang, the province the Japanese landed in and quickly occupied. Narratives abound describing the confusion and desperation surrounding the emergence of the volunteer army. The Chosŏn officials in charge, from Governor Kim Su down to the heads of towns, fled, leaving the region to fall into complete disarray.[40] From this chaos appeared Kwak Chaeu (1552–1617), who is believed to be the first volunteer army leader. Kwak's story is instructive. He was a private scholar with neither a position nor a relationship to officialdom, but he began to mobilize civilians into a volunteer army, which he named the Righteous Army. It is said that Kwak sought and found brave people proficient in archery and began guerilla warfare with a unit of fifty people in his hometown of Ŭiryŏng on either June 1 or June 3, eight or ten days after the Japanese landing at Pusan.[41] He financed the army with his own funds but still needed help and appropriated grain from the state granary to feed his soldiers.[42] In the context of the long-standing Chosŏn prohibition against private armies, Kwak's act was greeted with incredulity and suspicion. The *Miscellaneous Record* describes the initial reaction: "People thought he was stark mad. Some thought he was engaged in stealing. The magistrate of Hapch'ŏn reported to the governor that Kwak was a thief, and this scared volunteers away."[43] Kwak's mobilization of the volunteer army could have been interpreted as an insurgency against the state, and indeed, when he later came into conflict with Governor Kim Su, Kim would bring this very charge against him.

The problem of illegality was resolved by the state's lifting of the ban on private armies through the edict of Sŏnjo, mentioned above. The court also instructed officials on site to encourage the mobilization of civilians. For occupied areas, new posts such as recruiter were created and granted substantial authority. Kim Sŏng'il, who was on the way to the capital to be interrogated for his inaccurate report on Japan, was exonerated and instead appointed to the newly created post of chief recruiter of the army for Kyŏngsang.[44] Kim moved quickly to legally sanction the volunteer army. The *Miscellaneous Record* reports that after Kim interviewed Kwak and encouraged him to find more recruits, volunteers returned. Sometime in mid-June Kim sent out a letter of exhortation to the residents of Kyŏngsang Province encouraging them to rise and join the volunteer army.[45] With this official imprimatur, Kwak's army grew and its guerilla warfare became much more effective.[46]

One notices a swift and profound transformation in the way in which the volunteer army was perceived. In their glowing accounts of Kwak, both private records and official histories display the change. The *Revised Veritable Records of Sŏnjo*, in an entry within two months of his first appearance, lauds Kwak's loyalty, integrity, and bravery, "which earned soldiers' trust and led many volunteers to join him in the battle."[47] It recounts that he started out with a few tens of men, but that his followers soon numbered more than a thousand. It also describes him "as a principled scholar who mobilized the Righteous Army with empty hands and inspired soldiers with righteous spirit."[48] Other accounts refer to Kwak's fearlessness, his imaginative tactics that elicited awe from the enemy (including his self-styled title of "Red-Robed General Descended from Heaven" (*ch'ŏn'gang hong'ŭi changgun*), his extraordinary speed of movement that enabled him to evade enemy bullets, his sudden and unpredictable methods of attack, and his care for the livelihoods of the local residents.[49] In these encomiums, Kwak was transformed into an iconic figure symbolizing courage and an uncompromising commitment to principle. In the telling he was even endowed with superhuman powers. Kwak's tale vividly illustrates the near mythical ascent of the Righteous Army even at this very early stage.

While Kwak quickly earned fame and trust, the sphere of his guerilla activity was confined to his province and even to an area near his home village. This was also true of other volunteer army units that appeared in Kyŏngsang Province in the early stages. News of the royal court's flight from the capital and the capture of Seoul by the Japanese galvanized the local elites. More than anything else, it symbolized the terrible disarray and peril into which the state had fallen. With legal obstacles cleared, and possessed of a sense of urgency, the volunteer army gained momentum in the provinces. There also seems to have been a groundswell of support from residents, many of whom had witnessed the atrocities inflicted by the invaders. One witness account reports that residents who had been hiding in mountains and valleys began to form groups that attacked and killed many Japanese.[50]

In June and July many other civilian leaders appeared with newly recruited armies of varying size. Chŏng Inhong of Hapch'ŏn, for example, a former official of the Censorate, formed an army consisting mostly of his students, and Kim Myŏn of Koryŏng, another former official, became prominent leading a small army. Chŏng Inhong and Kim Myŏn coordinated forces and fought effectively.[51] After one such battle, they received a letter from Sŏnjo praising them: "Why does the royal army always get defeated so easily and why does the Righteous Army invariably win? This is because the former is bound by punishment by which the law cannot be upheld whereas the latter is galvanized by just principle which does not allow them to contemplate retreat."[52]

The volunteer army in Chŏlla Province proceeded on a different trajectory. The Japanese march north in 1592 did not pass through this western province, and for more than half a year Chŏlla was the only region that was not occupied by the Japanese Army. Thus the country looked on Chŏlla, situated in a fertile area rich in resources, as the hope for the restoration. The mobilization of a volunteer army in this province thus had special meaning, quite different from other regions. However, the bureaucratic structure in Chŏlla remained intact, and hence the need for civilian armies was questionable. True, in view of the new state policy of militarization of civilians, a plethora of official messages, from the throne and the governor down to town magistrates, encouraged the raising of volunteer armies.[53] Nonetheless, Governor Yi Kwang, even though he did not enjoy a sterling reputation, actively recruited new enlistees for the royal army.[54] An even more crucial question was that of an objective. Unlike other regions, Chŏlla Province was neither being destroyed nor immediately threatened by this prospect. What should the mission of a Chŏlla volunteer army be?

Kim Ch'ŏnil (1537–1593) and Ko Kyŏngmyŏng (1533–1592), the first two leaders of the volunteer army of Chŏlla, reformulated the army's objectives, setting their military goals and articulating an idea of a unified Chosŏn community. Kim and Ko, older scholars, were hesitant to compete with the governor but were disillusioned by his evasive and ineffectual military campaigns. A decisive moment for Kim was the discovery that the royal army of sixty thousand, heading north under the command of Yi Kwang, had turned back at Kongju and returned to Chŏnju upon hearing that the court had left Seoul.[55] Kim quickly summoned residents of his town, Naju, to a meeting and, in a passionate appeal for "determined action transcending life or death," was able to secure three hundred men, horses, and expenses for them. After declaring the formation of his army on June 25, he began a march to the capital on July 11.[56]

Ko Kyŏngmyŏng seems to have entertained a grander vision. He announced the formation of an army on July 8 at Tamyang and, as an attempt to expand it, immediately began to send out open letters not only to the residents of Chŏlla but also to other provinces as far away as Cheju Island, exhorting them to take up arms and pleading for assistance in procuring arms and provisions.[57] Ko too was affected by the incompetence of the royal army. The disastrous defeat of the royal armies of the three provinces at Yongin on July 14 seems to have convinced him that he had no choice but to take steps to publicly challenge the enemy. On July 19 he led his army, in an impressive formation with colorful flags, on a march north toward the capital. These volunteer armies were no longer merely local guerilla forces defending local territories but a force that sought to retake the capital, return the court to it, and reestablish the order of the Chosŏn state.

Summoning a People:
Letters of Exhortation and the
Emergence of a Discourse of Nation

I have already mentioned that the expansion of the volunteer army proceeded in tandem with the emergence of a communicative space of discourse, and that open letters of exhortation greatly shaped the nature of this space.[58] Letters of exhortation and other genres of open letters at this time were written specifically to mobilize the volunteer army and seek donations to finance it. The writers were aware of the affective power of language and the importance of appeals to emotion.[59] In constructing a vision of a community for whose protection they were asking their audience to sacrifice their lives, they drew on metaphors and imagery from the Korean landscape, common ancestry, and a shared history. These metaphors resemble the elements of discourse that Anthony Smith describes as signifying the transformation from ethnie to nation.[60] The goal and the content of national imaginings for Koreans at this time, however, were immediate and urgent, and the vision they presented was also impregnated with danger, anxiety, and determination.[61] The writers constructed a vision of Korea as the sacred and inviolable land of Koreans and Korean culture—a land that was being trampled, its people killed and defiled, and its culture soon to be annihilated by barbarous Japanese. As their choice of name—the Righteous Army—revealed, they argued that it was the moral duty of all Koreans to rescue, defend, and restore Korea. These components were intimately interwoven in the rhetoric, but the letters were a call to arms, employing every possible mode of persuasion to propel readers to action. Ultimately it was a contemplation on personal and collective identity—on the meaning of living and dying as moral human beings, and of remaining a Korean and not being transformed into a "bestial" other. Constructed in defense against the cruelties inflicted on Koreans, the rhetoric is searing and inflammatory.

The discursive space was interpenetrating and dynamic; each writer tailored his rhetoric to the time of his writing, the occasion, and the audience, and different writers interacted with and were influenced by the responses. As this space was constantly reconstituted with hundreds of letters coming from and going to different directions, it is impossible to fully reconstruct the evolving process and the content of this discursive space. Here I will discuss the letters of Kim Sŏng'il and Ko Kyŏngmyŏng, which set the process in motion. I will return to other letters later.

The letters by Kim and Ko parallel the distinct characters of the volunteer armies of Kyŏngsang and Chŏlla Provinces. Kim's letter, addressed to "magistrates, generals in outlying areas, children of officials, gentlemen of leisure, soldiers and the people" and sent out in mid-June, is the first letter known to have specifically asked people to join the volunteer army.[62] Since Chosŏn was a Weberian state maintaining its monopoly of legitimate violence as the only agency that could legitimately send out a letter exhorting the people to take up arms, it is not surprising that the first letter was sent by a royal messenger. The letter is considered a masterful piece of writing, and its format seems to have been a paradigm for others.[63] Its metaphors, imagery, and logic of persuasion are frequently repeated in other letters. Nevertheless, it differs in tone from most letters by civilians in that, as an official, Kim had to defend the government, and his tone is more commanding than persuading. After lamenting the terrible state into which the country has fallen and the miserable and irresponsible way in which officials and generals of the province behaved, it shifts its gaze downward: "The easy crumbling of Yŏngnam [Kyŏngsang Province] to the enemy should not be attributed solely to irresponsible magistrates, generals, and officers; soldiers and the people cannot escape their share of responsibility." It stresses the justness of the cause and calls for retribution against the cruel invaders: "When those black-toothed [Japanese] barbarians landed on our soil, they were intent on occupation; they took our women as concubines; they exterminated our men to the last one, attacked villages burning them to the ground; looted the treasure of the government and private households. A poisoned air pervaded all; blood flowed through ten thousand *li*.[64] Who dares to speak the sufferings of our remaining people!"

Kim's letter is also revelatory in its equating of the local and the national. It speaks of the ethical imperative to remain a human being and a person of the Chosŏn: "Can you sully that body of yours trained to honor propriety and music? Can you accept the [barbarian] custom of shaving your hair and tattooing your body? Can you bear to turn over to Japanese thugs the dynastic mantle that we have guarded for two hundred years? Can you let the thousands of *li* of our mountains and rivers turn into the caves and dens of Japanese thugs?" It then constructs a unified national vision by conjuring up the images for ethnic Koreans: "the great principle that binds lord and subject is the law of Heaven, the way of Earth. Therein resides the inalienable way of morality (*tori*) for all. We are the people who acquired blood and spirit from this land, who are nurtured by its crop. Can we just watch, unconcerned and unaroused, as our ruler's carriage flies north, our dynasty is overturned, our people are set out to rot like heaps of fish?" Later the national vision is embodied in locality, in this case, in the special quality of Kyŏngsang Province. The letter points out the crucial role the province played in the brilliant and long history of Korea: "Our Yŏngnam has been called the treasure-house of the talented. It is known to all that during the thousand years of the Silla dynasty, the five hundred years of Koryŏ, and the two hundred years of this dynasty, the fame and the exemplary virtue of its loyal subjects and filial sons and the indefatigable thirst for justice of its people have shone in history. All scholars and all the people acknowledge that its beautiful customs shrouded in integrity and honor are first in the East."

Then the letter moves to the present:

> In our time, T'oegye [Yi Hwang; 1501–1570] and Nammyŏng [Cho Sik; 1501–1572],[65] working in one generation, have promoted the Way and made the hearts and minds of the people clear. They took as their own responsibility discipline and order and trained and taught many young students. Scholars and students were deeply inspired by their teaching; many emulated them even without benefit of studying with them in person. How countless the scholars who pored over the books of the

sage and the wise who emerged proud and self-confident in their learning and their ethical way of life?

Finally it strikes to elicit ethnic rage: "These grass-clothed, wormlike island barbarians are impossibly disgusting. They pillage and occupy our land, kill and abuse our people! How can you not seek ways to drive them out, to annihilate them?" Speaking in an authoritative official voice, perhaps it is natural that Kim foregrounds and closes the letter with national vision while highlighting local specificities.

Ko Kyŏngmyŏng's letters of exhortation are completely new, not only in their content but also because of the space of communication they forged. Ko was renowned for his fine prose,[66] and, as might be expected of a fine stylist, he composed a number of exhortations addressed to various groups, which, taken together, are viewed as a definitive declaration of the rationale for the voluntary army. Two of them—one addressed to all Koreans and one to residents in four provinces—are particularly noteworthy. In fact, they were the first ones with which a private person legitimately addressed all Koreans and half of the Korean population, respectively, and they created a new nationwide horizontal space of communication. Previously only the throne had the privilege of addressing all Koreans in royal missives from the ruler to the ruled, in what can be thought of as a vertical space of communication.

The letter in which Ko addressed all Koreans, sometimes known as "the letter written on horseback" (*masang kyŏngmun*) because he purportedly wrote it in haste while riding, is praised for its emotional power.[67] While it is addressed to the widest possible audience, it is written in a confessional mode. Though Ko uses some of the same metaphors, images, and logic as Kim Sŏng'il does, he does so from the perspective of a private person. Fully aware of the fatal nature of his decision to accept the patriotic duty to bear arms, Ko gives reasons for doing so. Indeed, the letter resembles a brief spiritual autobiography that chronicles an awakening to the inevitability of choosing this path: "I am an aging scholar with a loyal heart. I took this role with an undivided heart with nothing more than devotion to my lord.... This was in complete disregard for the meagerness of my power." The letter is constructed very much in the Habermasian mode of communicative rationality:

> Who among the living with blood and spirit is not angry and who would wish to die without vengeance for the atrocities visited upon us? . . . Men so brave as to capture bears and wrestle tigers arrived like wind and thunder; a multitude on chariots passed through the gates, gathering like clouds and rain. . . . No one was forced; none hesitated. All followed the dictates of their loyal, devoted hearts. At this critical moment when the country is at stake, we do not spare our bodies. We are the Righteous Army; we are not bound by duty. The strength of our army is the justness of our cause; comparison to the enemy's strength is no concern of ours.[68]

In speaking of how, in time of trial, personal morality would inevitably be transformed into patriotic action, Ko extends this personal vision to everyone in his audience: "Big or small, there is no difference; we unite under one goal. Far and near, all rise on these tidings." He argues that all Koreans are moral, that all would share his sense of justice, and that all would decide on loyalty despite the extraordinary risk:

> Magistrates, all! Scholars and commoners (*samin*), all on roads and byways! Can your loyal hearts forget your sovereign? Rightful duty calls upon us to die for our country (*sun'guk*). Each within the limits of your ability, whether with weapons or food, whether mounting on horseback, charging into battle, or rising from your rice paddy, casting aside your plow to join in battle, each do your utmost to reclaim your righteous heart. If anyone has strategies to cease this chaos, let us act with him.

In a letter sent to the people of four provinces—two middle ones, Ch'ungch'ŏng and Kyŏnggi, and two northern ones, Hwanghae and P'yŏngan—seeking food provisions to assist the army, Ko emphasizes the interconnectedness of all the provinces and the importance of working together. He states that though the three southern provinces are the heart of Chosŏn, since Ch'ungch'ŏng and Kyŏngsang are occupied by the invaders, Honam (Chŏlla) Province would have to bear most of the burden: "We know that both the government and the people rely solely upon Honam. Thus, with the resolve to die ten thousand times, we appealed to people, and with their hearts filled with devotion to the country, multitudes gathered like clouds." Appealing to their moral sense, he seeks their help: "We are planning to go north to exterminate evil. However, it would be too difficult for us to carry food provisions such a distance. You are committed to righteousness; we urge you to combine your strength and help us. How can a great deed be accomplished by one singly?" He then focuses on the interdependence of all regions: "There is no place within our borders that is not the land of Chosŏn. We feel that if we are assisted by the volunteer armies of Ch'ungch'ŏng and Chŏlla, we will be able to restore our land to us. We sincerely hope that with renewed determination to die for the country, you will help us with food for the army."[69]

Perhaps the most powerful and enduring tropes summoned by Ko's letters were a romanticized vision of volunteers choosing to fight for the justness of the cause entirely of their own free will yet responding to destiny and the equally romantic idea of dying for one's country. Here we encounter the aforementioned vision evoked by Anderson: "The idea of the ultimate sacrifice comes only with an idea of purity, through fatality." As the famous phrase of the letter has it, "no one was forced; none hesitated," the volunteers' choosing the path of fatality is based solely and completely on a moral imperative. In the letter, they assume a "moral grandeur" and an "aura of purity."[70] In presenting the choice of dying for the country as a morally autonomous yet inescapable path for Koreans, Ko redefined the concept of loyalty as an activist ideal, akin to "popular sovereignty." This vision seems to have deeply touched an emotional chord in readers of the time.

Dying for the Country: In the Mind and on the Battlefield

It was, however, the volunteers' actual dying en masse for the country that galvanized the population. Ko Kyŏngmyŏng's impressive army of six thousand suffered a total defeat at the battle of Kŭmsan in the month of its formation. The army, joined by a contingent of the royal army, attacked a Japanese battalion garrisoned at Kŭmsan, a Japanese headquarters on the edge of Chŏlla, on August 3. After two days of intense fighting, first the royal army and then Ko's army were destroyed. Ko, his second son Ko Inhu, and many of his colleagues died in this battle.[71] Ko had solicited and received pledges from other volunteer army units, including that of Cho Hŏn (1544–1592) from Ch'ungch'ŏng Province. Cho Hŏn arrived after Ko's death, and on October 23, together with Yŏnggyu, a Buddhist monk who had mobilized an army of monks, he waged another battle at Kŭmsan. Cho and his army of seven hundred as well as Yŏnggyu and his monks all died in battle.[72]

The defeat of Ko's army, the first test of a large volunteer army unit, which had been watched with anxious hope tempered by skepticism, must have been a terrible blow for the movement. Alarmed by the potentially negative impact, many sent out letters of exhortation. Different themes were introduced. One was that not only was the act of dying for the country supremely noble, but this noble act was extended to all as a moral requirement. This idea reached a new heights of urgency and poignancy, represented by a letter from Song Chemin (1549–1602), who came to the scene after the battle. The letter displays a palpable sense of desperation: "From the appearance of the Righteous Army proclaiming firm determination, the hearts of the people (*insim*) have regained some self-possession; their antipathy for the invaders has soared. But the Righteous Army suffered defeat; the morale of the populace has plummeted to a nadir." The emotional center is the nobility of Ko's dying: "He gave his life for the country (*sun'guk*) to repay his indebtedness to the sovereign. Following his father, his son died too. These acts of loyalty and filiality were the product of a single family. In dying, they left behind glory that burns brilliantly for eternity. A person has only one death. Chebong [Ko Kyŏngmyŏng] fulfilled his mission and died in the right place. We need not weep for him."[73]

Eager to pass the torch, Song cast his net more widely. He radically expanded the circle of those required to offer patriotic action. The people he called to arms are not only those who have maintained their Heaven-sent humanity but also those who have lost it and their virtue as well: "Ah! Humanity and right principle (*inŭi*) are the qualities everyone receives from Heaven; no one is different from anyone else in this. Despite equal endowment, there are those who, blinded by greed for selfish gain, lose their true hearts. There may be those who, despite human appearances, took on the hearts of beasts. We cannot always expect loyalty or filiality. The extermination of the invaders is not something desired only by loyal subjects or principled scholars, but something that even the disloyal and unfilial wish for." Clearly Song felt that he could not afford to exclude anyone, and in his argument he employs the Mencian theory of human nature, according to which people are originally and naturally good. By this logic, no one is beyond redemption. Since the Mencian notion of the goodness of human nature was the basis of the Neo-Confucian worldview, Song's logic must have been familiar. What is interesting is that he inverts this familiar trope: he does not reason that because a person has innate goodness, he will fight for family and country; rather, he argues that no rational person could but feel compelled to fight for his own survival, that of his family, and that of the people of his province, and that in the process his true nature, which he might have lost, will reemerge. By this logic, by embracing his Koreanness, he regains his humanity.

While Song expanded inclusivity by relativizing one's exhibited virtue, Yi Chun (1560–1635) specifically focuses on the insignificance of social status. In his exhortation written in the winter of 1592, Yi stresses the fundamental equality of all Koreans as loyal subjects and moral human beings: "When it comes to loyalty and the sense of justice, from the descendants of scholars to slaves in mangers, there is no difference; all are equal."[74] The idea of equality implicit in many letters is made explicit here.

Another theme that appeared after the battles at Kŭmsan was the idea of revenge—that Koreans could not let the martyrs' deaths go to waste unavenged. A letter by Ko Chonghu (1554–1593), Kyŏngmyŏng's first son, written five months after the death of his father and his brother Inhu, exhibits the theme. After his father's death, he mobilized an army and took the title general of the Righteous Army of Vengeance (*Poksu ŭibyŏngjang*). In a letter titled "Oath of Revenge Sent to All the Towns of the Province [of Chŏlla]," Ko uses a familiar trope, the duty to avenge the death of a loved one, but he also links family to nation: "Because I could not turn away from fighting the Japanese thugs, I dared to unexpectedly don the golden belt [of a general], but if brave men do not gather, with whom shall I be able to avenge the enemy of my family and my country (*kaguk*)?" He recalls the inseparable bond of the people of the province: "Is it not true that all in our province, whoever they might be, are brothers and sisters sharing the same womb (*tongp'o chi min*)? Did we not mount the platform together and, in blood, pledge ourselves to my deceased father? We patted our shoulders and shook one another's sleeves. We may have even gazed upon one another! Even though we may not have seen one another face-to-face, we live in a close, mutually connected community. Even in a hundred generations, we would feel for one another; how much more true is this for us born in the same age!" He then expands the sphere of the community, transforming personal revenge into a national project: "Towns should look across their boundaries, and counties should see beyond their borders; please do not view this matter as the affair of others. All within the four seas are brothers. A single peck of crops will do. Even in the last room [of Hell], one finds loyalty and faithfulness. Can we ignore affairs of such urgency as those of the present?"[75]

Tropes of Ethnie and the Discourse of Nation

Discourse of the imagined Chosŏn community spread rapidly nationwide. Although I have concentrated on the horizontal space of communication created by exhortations by the volunteer army leaders, this space was a part of interpenetrating multidirectional and multilayered space, closely connected to vertical space as well. We have already observed the consistent themes across many exhortations. Indeed, within a short span of time, by the autumn of 1592, tropes and images of imagined community had become the common currency of communication binding different groups across different spaces. These lines of communication work as conduits through which we can envision the ways in which sixteenth-century Koreans imagined themselves and their country. Although there were many variations on the themes, they can be grouped into several larger categories. Befitting the emergence of a discourse of nation in the face of invaders, the most common theme was the atrocities inflicted by the invaders. Such phrases as "our parents were killed, our wives and children were taken prisoner of war, our houses were burned to the ground, and our livelihood that has sustained us for generation upon generation has evaporated overnight"[76] or "the black-toothed [barbarians]" "charging like wild boar," "like black bees," "raped our women, ransacked our properties" abound.[77]

A second central image is that of Korean land—its sacralization, laments over its violation by the enemy, Korean embeddedness in it, its inseparability from ethnicity, and its interconnectedness. The land was sacralized for being "ours": "This is the land in which the souls of our ancestors reside, in which our parents received beneficent nurture and our brothers and children were born, in which we formed families and enjoyed closeness with friends and neighbors. How unspeakably degrading would it be if suddenly one morning a calamity made us servants and concubines to these barbarians and compelled us to work as slaves to a brutish enemy?"[78] Thus its defilement by the enemy was even more unbearable: "The mountains and rivers of Yŏngnam have become caves and dens of tigers and leopards while the plants and grasses of Hosŏ are contaminated with the stenches of dogs and sheep";[79] "Our mountains and rivers are bathed in shame. How can anyone with spirit not feel deeply aggrieved?"[80] Koreanness was in turn inseparable from the land: "We have been nourished by food produced from this land. We are all subjects of the ruler, not only those on official salaries";[81] "Anyone who lives in this land surrounded by the sea, no matter who he/she is, is the child of the Yi royal house?",[82] "The entire land of our country is [inhabited by] one people who share the same womb";[83] "There is no place in our land which does not belong to our dynasty. The army from the two Ho[84] is sufficient to restore our country";⁸⁵ "Tamna (Cheju) is indeed a part of our territory."⁸⁶

A third constellation of tropes evoked "Korean culture," its glorious history and civilized customs, pride in the local history and culture of various regions, and chagrin over its destruction. Exhortations claim such ideas as "the people's hearts are loyal," "The sagacious twelve kings of our dynasty with their virtue have benefited the people. We know vividly that our civilized Small Brilliant Center (*Sojunghwa*)⁸⁷ will not turn barbarous overnight!"⁸⁸ "The beautiful virtue of our country,"⁸⁹ and "during the long years of peace, the people have been accustomed to royal grace and benevolent governance."⁹⁰ Pride in local history and culture was also explicit: "Honam [Chŏlla] is called the region of decorum. It is the place where talented people are congregated, and it is the place where the people are like unmovable grass that resists strong and fast wind. All will become loyal subjects during this terrible national crisis";⁹¹ "In our province (Kyŏngsang), propriety is observed, and customs among people are generous vividly displaying that the traditions of one thousand years of Silla still remain";⁹² "The scholars and the common people of three Han [southern part of Korea] have lived under the benevolent rule of the sagacious dynasty, and received great moral instruction."⁹³

Some exhortations lament the very destruction of Korean culture: "Within three months of the war, the provinces of Yŏngnam, Hosŏ, Kyŏnggi have become the sweet home of the enemy. The place of civilization and propriety in which exquisite material culture and refined customs have been flourishing for two hundred years was desecrated one morning by cruel bloody ransacking, our people and their ways mercilessly cut down like weeds, their [refinement] reduced to the state of birds and monkeys."⁹⁴

A fourth trope was an individual's moral duty and commitment, a moral being here defined by the logic of the Confucian worldview. As a civilized being, a Korean could not entertain the possibility of becoming a barbarian: "If you betray your country and submit to the enemy, how can you find peace, and how can you bear to shave your head and blacken your teeth?"⁹⁵ "Our sense of knowing shame has been deeply ingrained in our civilization of two hundred years, and thus we pledge that we cannot possibly live with the Japanese enemy."[96] "The officials and the people of this country cannot become barbarians. Nor can the costumes of our court be exchanged for those of barbarians."[97] This impossibility is due to Koreans' inborn humanity: "All of you are born with the talents and physique to render useful deeds to our sovereign. We have been born into a time that values the civilization. How can we not show our devotion to the country?"[98] "If we possess one ounce of human heart we cannot eat or sleep in peace. We wail and weep."[99]

A fifth trope appears with the question of who should rise up to give their life for the country. The issue discussed was who should be willing to sacrifice themselves out of loyalty to the dynastic state. Some pointed at scholars as the group that had received more favors and privileges: "How can the elite of each town, who have received so much more grace from our state, bear to sit still?"[100] "The state nurtured scholars for two hundred years. . . . This is the time to sacrifice our bodies to save our country."[101] Much more common was rhetoric that appealed to all Koreans: "We would be most happy if anyone, regardless of high or low status, who is brave, capable of handling bow and arrow and talented, were to come";[102] "I sincerely hope that when this letter arrives, all will take up arms, that all will arise in passionate devotion and accomplish great deeds";[103] "Whether the sun and moon will shine again in this land depends entirely on our common people";[104] "All who are loyal to our sovereign, and who love our country, whether they have a civil or a military post, are of high or low status, young or old, whether a slave, or are among the nine categories of lowborn, or whether they belong to any of the miscellaneous categories, all come to the station of *Samnye* on the 27th."[105]

The sixth trope equated defeat with an unbearable loss of civilization. This logic was embedded in calls to die for the country: The assertion that keeps appearing is that surrender to a barbaric other is tantamount to a fundamental loss of civilization and hence humanity: "When we remember our indebtedness to our king, unless we are willing to become beasts, we cannot live under the same Heaven with the enemy. We have no choice but to rise in determination ready to give our lives for our country";[106] "It is much more honorable to die.

How much more is this true when your own flesh and bones and your relatives are all being slaughtered by this enemy? If you are to die, is it not better to die fighting them? If you avoid fighting to seek life but do not find a way, we shall face another disaster like the one we face today. If we are determined to fight, and if we are not afraid of dying, then there is no reason that we must die. We may thus avoid death and receive endless blessing";[107] "Although we hate to die, there is no way for us to escape since the net is spread everywhere, and even if we seek to live, it would be as unbearable as living among dogs and pigs. Since it result in death no matter what we do, it is better to die with principle. Give your life for principle."[108]

The final trope was the dream of restoration and peace: "If the volunteer army can make the people see the vast, clear sky again, and since you many not even die, wouldn't it be lovely to celebrate the joy of restoration (*chunghŭng*)?"[109]

These tropes were the leitmotifs of ethnic nationalism. Taken together, they fashioned a vision in which all Koreans, as members of one community, shared the responsibility of defending Korea, and all localities were integrated into a unified Korea that all needed to defend. No longer were civilians passive subjects who looked toward the state for protection; they had become active agents responsible for driving out the invaders, preserving the country, and restoring its way of life. After all, their community had to be defended from barbaric domination to preserve its special moral and civilized way of life.[110]

2

THE VOLUNTEER ARMY AND THE EMERGENCE OF IMAGINED COMMUNITY

By continuing to explore the issue of volunteer army, this chapter deals with how and to what extent the missives reached their intended audience, and whether the tropes and images discussed in the previous chapter became meaningful symbols to a wider populace.[1] The volunteer movement became a national movement in part because of the successful creation of an affective image of an imagined community of Chosŏn. Evidence shows that the writers of exhortations made great efforts to see that their messages reached and affected their intended receivers, including those who were not lettered.[2] If we assume that at least to a limited degree there was a correspondence between conceptual and actual audience, what was the mechanism through which this was achieved? The letters were disseminated through the utilization of the public and private technology of communication available at the time, and in a combination of written and oral forms. Once a letter was completed, it was copied in tens or hundreds of duplicates, each of which was sent to places where a person of responsibility would receive it,[3] read it aloud to congregations, and instruct those who could to repeat the process. Evidence indicates that copies were made either by woodblock print, usually at county schools that had printing facilities,[4] or by hand copying. What is notable about this endeavor is that it was the collaborative labor of a community. It required the cooperation of those in charge at schools and, in the case of hand-copied manuscripts, the services of the educated. Evidence indicates that a great many rendered service.

In time of peace the country was connected through postal stations, which were responsible for the circulation of government missives, chief among them the daily court gazette (*chobo*), and which provided lodging and transportation, often horses, to officials in transit. Although these stations did not function in occupied areas during the war, some of the routes were used to disseminate official letters as well as letters by volunteer army leaders and soldiers. The landed elite had long since developed a private system of postal exchange relying mainly on their own slaves and servants as couriers. During the Imjin War, a more elaborate private postal network seems to have been established. Apparently utilizing and in some cases privatizing some fragments of official facilities and routes of communication between the central government and provincial and local offices, and using private couriers, they were able to disseminate information so that they could maintain and even expand the space of communication.

Modes of Dissemination and the Reception of Exhortations

It is difficult to determine the speed and efficiency of this mode of communication during the Imjin War. We have only a few records of dates of receipt of dated missives. Communication in the occupied areas, especially during the first days of the war, seems to have been quite slow. Cho Chŏng (1555–1636) reports in his *Diary of the Imjin War* (*Imjin ilgi*) that the exhortation that Kim Sŏng'il, the chief recruiter of Kyŏngsang, sent out on June 14, 1592, arrived in Sangju of the same province on August 13. He reports two days later, on August 15, that Chŏng Inhong, Kim Myŏn, and others were mobilizing the army, and that they had gathered more than six thousand people.[5] Chŏng Inhong appeared on the scene with his army on July 5, and so the news seems to have acquired speed as time went on. It could well be that it took time to devise the routes in the early phase of the war, and that the network functioned better once the system was in place. Missives in Chŏlla Province fared much better since it was not occupied. O Hŭimun, staying at Changch'ŏn, northern Chŏlla, records in *The Trivial Matters* that a letter of exhortation dated August 3 by Kwŏn Yul (1537–1599), the magistrate of Kwangju, administrative center of southern Chŏlla, arrived on August 6, three days later;[6] and that a circular letter dated June 22 from Yŏngdong, the northwestern point of Chŏlla that borders on Kyŏngsang and Ch'ungch'ŏng Provinces, also arrived three days later, on June 25.[7] A circular letter of July 26 from volunteer army leaders of Anŭp in Kyŏngsang crossed the provincial border and arrived at Changch'ŏn on the following day.[8]

Royal edicts were disseminated with greater care, lest they be intercepted by the enemy. *The Trivial Matters* reports that Sim Tae (1546–1592), bearing a copy of the royal edict of June 4, arrived in Chŏnju, the provincial capital of Chŏlla, on June 20, that copies of the royal edict that he brought were sent to various towns, and that a copy arrived in Changch'ŏn, in northern Chŏlla, through Chinan.[9] It appears that once it arrived at Chŏnju, copies were made and disseminated, at least in unoccupied Chŏlla Province, through the usual routs of communication. The *Miscellaneous Record* also says that a copy of an edict, on a torn piece of very poor quality paper, sent through the governor arrived in the Namwŏn area on June 23.[10] While it is unclear whether this was the same edict as the one mentioned in *The Trivial Matters*,[11] it shows that copies of edicts circulated to the far reaches of Chŏlla Province.

These narratives also note the performative scenes in which these letters reached their audiences. In an appointed location with a congregation, a letter was ritualistically handed over to a person of influence in the locality who, after receiving it respectfully, solemnly read it aloud to an audience, which is described as having responded with deep emotion. This mode of dissemination—relying on oral delivery—was to a large extent necessitated by the low literacy rate. Though the literacy rate of premodern Korea has yet to be determined, the rate for literary Chinese in which letters of exhortation were written was far lower than that for vernacular Korean. Exhortations and circular letters were almost always written in literary Chinese, and this meant that the person who read the letter to a congregation had to make an impromptu translation into Korean and deliver it in language accessible to ordinary people. Some letters included specific authorial instructions on the importance of addressing and affecting the illiterate: "We should also let those not versed in letters get this news. Make certain that they hear the gist of this letter in words that are accessible to them so that they will be moved."[12]

This form of delivery was a common mode of communication between agencies that insisted on using literary Chinese and the majority of Chosŏn Koreans. An important reason for staging communal readings seems to have been performative—to maximize effectiveness. It has been noted that religious meetings in Europe adopted the strategy of reading a text aloud to a congregation for emotional impact, that this had nothing to do with whether people read the same text silently in private, and that those who were moved by hearing it also propagated the messages to those who were not present.[13] Given that the production and dissemination of letters of exhortation were politically charged, those involved in the process must have looked for the most "socially anchored" forum[14] and gravitated toward communal readings. One gets the impression that even in occupied areas surveillance was sporadic, and that communal readings were staged, if furtively. This is not to say that there were no other modes of dissemination—copies were made by individuals to be read silently and to preserve and record the missives—but communal readings are the mode of dissemination most frequently referred to in narratives.

The setting and the oral delivery were important, but the centerpiece of these readings was the letter. Given the voluntary nature of the Righteous Army, the writers were acutely conscious of the requirement that their language be powerful enough to move readers or listeners to offer that which was most precious to them, their lives and property. They operated in a literary culture that believed that only when words were spoken with passion and sincerity, not merely with artfulness of phrase, could they acquire the power to elicit the same from the reader or listener.[15] Thus, while they calibrated letters to the audience to which they were addressed,[16] they did so with a conviction that purity of emotion was connective tissue. It is also interesting to note that evaluations of the letters are focused almost exclusively on their effects on the reader. A preface to the collection of exhortations by Ko Kyŏngmyŏng and his associates praises Ko's famous letter of exhortation to the people of all provinces as "so passionate and heartfelt that when anyone read it, their hair stood on end and tears began to roll down their cheeks."¹⁷ A chronological biography (*yŏnbo*) of Ko Kyŏngmyŏng, admittedly hagiographical, says that wherever his famous exhortation letter arrived, "all those refugees hiding in the deepest recesses in mountains or valleys, competed to read and copy it, and some even shed tears."¹⁸

The knowledge that letters were being transported and made available in reasonably authentic form enabled readings to be held widely, and so they were disseminated to great distances and to audiences of great variety. With growing scholarship on print culture in recent years, we are aware of the cultural impact of imprints. As I mentioned in the introduction, what is interesting about Korean book and print culture was that "prints" in various materials—movable type, woodblock prints, and handwritten manuscripts—coexisted and circulated simultaneously. A recent study of the book culture of China shows that, while the flourishing of commercial publishing led the imprint to become the dominant form in the sixteenth century, it neither replaced nor eliminated manuscripts from circulation, and that manuscripts continued to exert influence on the style of imprints.¹⁹ It is Korea's pride and joy that movable-type printing was invented in Korea much earlier than in the West. However, printing in movable metal type remained largely under government monopoly.²⁰ Moreover, Korea had a much smaller commercial market than China, and the use of woodblock prints and manuscript copies was more prevalent and persisted longer.²¹ Commercial printing did not become common until the nineteenth century.²² Woodblock prints and hand-copied letters during the Imjin War were reproducible, transferable, and transportable with relative speed. The letters often had instructions on how and to whom they were to be disseminated.²³ What seems clear is that when writers addressed their letters to all residents of their province or the people of Korea, they envisioned that their letters would be read or heard by the people and that this was the case to a qualified extent.

What was new was not just that the letters were addressed inclusively but that private individuals created a conceptual horizontal national space of communication with these letters. Also new was that the technology and facilities of the communicative national space, both vertical and horizontal, were opened to use by private individuals. Previously the person in charge of a certain administrative unit could communicate with the people under his jurisdiction. Private individuals had their own networks, which included family and relatives, friends, and professional colleagues. Rarely did a private person address fellow residents of a geographical unit, not to mention larger regions. It appears that in spite, or perhaps because, of the urgent and adverse condition under which channels of communication had to be opened, a wider and more inclusive space of communication was constructed and maintained. This actual emergence of a national space of communication paralleled the creation of a conceptual space—the national community.

MILITARY ACTIVITIES OF THE VOLUNTEER ARMY UNITS

The military activities of the volunteer army grew, and they grew in tandem with the expanding space of discourse of nation. The deaths of Ko, Cho, other leaders and volunteer soldiers at the battles of Kŭmsan inspired participation in the movement rather than discouraging it. From sometime around August 1592, new Righteous Army units of varying size in different locations announced their formation almost daily with open letters of exhortation. By late summer there does not seem to have been a province without several Righteous Army units.[24] The *Miscellaneous Record* reports in November that there were twenty-eight large units of the Righteous Army in Chŏlla, that all eight provinces had a similar number, and that there were innumerable smaller formations of the army.[25] Apparently they came in all sizes, shapes, and compositions, and they changed over time. Perhaps the most renowned were units consisting of Buddhist monks.[26] The eminent monk Hyujŏng of P'yŏngan Province, for example, with his equally famous disciple Yujŏng, formed an army of a thousand monks.[27] There were groups ranging from ten or a dozen people, consisting mostly family members servants and slaves, such as the one led by Sŏng Ch'ŏnhŭi of Ch'angnyŏng, to huge groups such as the one of six to seven thousand led by Ko Kyŏngmyŏng.[28]

The Righteous Army was vested with much hope, especially during the first year of the war. Sometimes it was spoken of as if it were invincible, and this view was shared by the court.[29] True, it does appear that from the Korean perspective the voluntary army was the only game on land until the Chinese Army arrived. To what extent was the view of voluntary army's prowess grounded on its military exploits? There are a tremendous number of studies devoted to this topic in Korea; I will be able to present neither a comprehensive picture of the volunteer army as a military force nor a discussion of studies on it. However, the most celebrated tropes of commemoration in postwar Chosŏn were the volunteer army's displays of indefatigable loyalty on the battlefield against great odds, both individually and collectively. For this reason I will briefly assess the voluntary army's military activities.

Despite exhaustive studies on the volunteer army, there does not seem to be any agreement on a precise number for the Righteous Army or, for that matter, of the royal army. The numbers obviously fluctuated. The report on its military force that the Chosŏn government submitted to the Ming on February 11, 1593, puts the combined number of the royal army and the Righteous Army at 172,400.[30] The accuracy of this number has been called into question, and because of the way the report is written, it is difficult to sort out the Righteous Army from the royal army. Ch'oe Yŏnghŭi believes the number to be an exaggeration, but he suggests that the ratio between the two armies was about four to one.[31] This puts the Righteous Army at about 43,000. What is conveyed in this report is that the state regarded the Righteous Army as a legitimate component of its military force paralleling the royal army, and that it constituted a significant portion of the force. The relationship between the volunteer army and the royal army was complex and fluid, and it spanned a wide variety of arrangements, from official recruiters mobilizing volunteer army units[32] to groups of Righteous Army attaching themselves to the royal army,[33] and a number of royal army units joining the Righteous Army.[34] Most studies, however, maintain that despite blurring and overlapping between the volunteer army and the royal army, the distinction did not disappear. They cite the distinguishing features of the Righteous Army: civilian leadership, the voluntary nature of its membership, its relative autonomy in its field of operation, and private financing.³⁵

It is widely known that one of the main reasons that the Korean Royal Army could not compete with the Japanese in the early phase of the war was that firearms gave the invaders a huge advantage. Then how did the Righteous Army fight, and what arms were they able to procure? We read quite often of how poorly equipped the civilian volunteers were.³⁶ A recent study by a military historian brings another perspective. Kenneth Swope maintains that the muskets the Japanese used were effective only at a certain range, that missile weapons were almost as important as firearms, and that in this respect the Korean bow and arrow, strong, speedy, flexible in usage, and wide of range, was very effective.³⁷ Although narratives are generally reticent about the weapons that the Righteous Army used, from the time Kwak Chaeu mobilized the Righteous Army, we hear of archers. One of the circular letters mobilizing the volunteer army describes the qualification as "irrespective of high or low, those who have brave hearts, and those who know how to handle bow and arrow."³⁸ A description of the second battle of Chinju makes it clear that bows and arrows and the lance were the main weapons of the Korean Army.³⁹ The practice of archery and the production of bows and arrows were commonplace in Korea,⁴⁰ and it is most likely that this was the main weapon on which the Righteous Army relied.

With these tactics the volunteer army was quite successful in guerilla warfare.⁴¹ In Kyŏngsang Province guerilla activities produced visible results. In August Chŏng Inhong, with 2,800 soldiers, took over the town of Anŏn.⁴² Kwak Chaeu was famous for his guerilla tactics, and his army succeeded in securing towns such as Chŏng'amjin, Hyŏnp'ung, Ch'angnyŏng, and Yŏngsan in the eastern part of Kyŏngsang Province.⁴³ This made it possible for the Righteous Army to attack continuously to recover towns in western Kyŏngsang Province. The recovery of Sŏngju and Kaeryŏng in western Kyŏngsang was accomplished by the combined efforts of Chŏng Inhong and Kim Myŏn of Kyŏngsang, with the help of the Righteous Army led by Yim Kyeyŏng and Ch'oe Kyŏnghŭi of Chŏlla over a period of four months starting in mid-November 1592 and finally succeeding in

March 1593.⁴⁴ When, in February, in the middle of this attack, the state ordered that Yim's and Ch'oe's armies stationed in Kyŏngsang march north to join forces with the Chinese Army in the allied army's planned attack on the capital, the scholars of Kyŏngsang and Chŏlla Provinces memorialized the throne protesting the order. The memorial stated that the safety of seven towns in Kyŏngsang was entirely dependent on the Righteous Army of Chŏlla. In fact, the mere possibility that the volunteer army units of Chŏlla might be evacuated from the region caused such fear that some residents fled the area, creating further confusion. The state rescinded the order.⁴⁵ The prominent role played by the Righteous Army of Chŏlla in securing towns of neighboring provinces was common knowledge. Moreover, securing the region made it possible to keep the routes between Kyŏngsang, Chŏlla, and Ch'ungch'ŏng open for Koreans, and, with Admiral Yi Sunsin's naval victories, it cut the invaders' supply lines. This is regarded as the major factor that destabilized the Japanese.⁴⁶

Larger formations of the volunteer army, however, had mixed results. First of all, large formations often consisted of combined units from different regions, combined with contingents of the royal army. Perhaps the best-known battles in which combined forces of the volunteer army and the royal army fought together were the first and second battles of Chinju. Chinju was regarded as a strategically crucial post for the preservation of western Kyŏngsang, the supply of provisions to the navy on the southern coast, and the safeguarding of Chŏlla from the enemy. Thus both invader and defender made great efforts to occupy this city. A number of battalions of Japanese, numbering around 30,000, besieged Chinju walled town on November 9, 1592. Korean forces consisted of 3,800 people led by Magistrate Kim Simin inside the walled town, 2,000 led by Ch'oe Kyŏnghŭi, and a number of units of several hundred each sent by Kwak Chaeu, Chŏng Inhong, and other voluntary army leaders. Some were stationed at strategically selected locations outside the walled town before the battle began, and some, such as a unit of Buddhist monk-soldiers led by Sin Yŏl, arrived during the fighting. The description of the battle, which lasted three days, from November 10 to 13, is colorful. The Japanese army relied mainly on muskets, while the weapons used by the Korean Army ranged from cannons, to bows and arrows, to burning arrows and stones thrown by the old and the young, to boiling water poured by women. Against all odds, the battle ended with victory of the Korean force. The main credit was consensually attributed to Kim Simin. He is portrayed as a consummate Confucian leader who led by example and by his concern for those below him. He is reputed to have shared his food with them, and even when bullets flew, he stood calmly, pleading with them that "the entire country has fallen, and there are only a few places that have been preserved. The preservation of this walled town will directly influence the fate of this country. If this walled town crumbles, then it will be the end of our country. Moreover, if we are defeated, the thousands of souls taking refuge within will be made ghosts cut down by enemy swords. Please remember that only when we fight bravely without fearing for our lives can we survive!" Soldiers are said to have responded and to have fought bravely.[47]

The second battle of Chinju, fought from July 18 to 27, 1593, was far more ferocious and tragic. The order to attack Chinju was issued again by Hideyoshi himself, who is reported to have been chagrined by the earlier defeat.[48] As this took place after the Japanese retreated from P'yŏngyang and Seoul, the Japanese force was huge—93,000, led by key generals, including Konishi Yukinaga and Katō Kiyomasa, all gathered at Chinju. Realizing the terrible odds against them, the leaders of the Righteous Army conferred and disagreed on the wisdom of fighting. Kwak Chaeu insisted that it would be suicidal and hence was to be avoided; Kim Ch'ŏnil asserted that it would be unconscionable to abandon Chinju.[49] The exact size of the Korean force is not clear, but it is estimated that to have been between 8,000 and 15,000 men.[50] Despite fierce resistance that lasted for nearly ten days, the Japanese took the walled town. Many leaders died, including Ko Chonghu, Ch'oe Kyŏnghŭi, and Kim Ch'ŏnil. Obeying Hideyoshi's orders, the Japanese massacred whomever was found inside the walled town, 60,000 people in all.[51] This battle also produced a female hero, the courtesan Non'gae, who is alleged to have enticed a Japanese general and, embracing him by the waist, threw herself into the Nam River, taking him with her.[52] While the battle was a tragic defeat, scholars believe that because Japanese also suffered tremendous losses in this battle, they did not push on to Chŏlla, and in this way it contributed to the preservation of the province free from Japanese occupation.⁵³ This battle was indelibly imprinted on Koreans' collective memory, making Chinju a main site for commemorative activities for the Imjin War dead.⁵⁴

Popular Sovereignty and the Local Elite

The extraordinariness of the volunteer army as a movement was recognized very early after its appearance, and ever since it has received inordinate attention. Its military effectiveness has received mixed reviews. What has received most attention and been uniformly valorized is its symbolic role as the embodiment and motivator of popular will, referred to as the hearts of the people. Narrative after narrative, even including the official historiography, highlights this. The *Veritable Records of Sŏnjo*, for instance, in an entry of December 19, 1592, quotes a memorial that the Office of the Censor-General (Saganwŏn) sent to the throne: "After the invasion, the hearts of the people [toward the government] fell to the ground. Once men of principle rose, calling forth justice (*ŭi*), soldiers and the people (*kunmin*) responded to them and joined their army. That the state (*kukka*) survives until today is owed completely to the efforts of the Righteous Army (*ŭibyŏng chi yŏk*)."⁵⁵ An earlier entry of July 9, 1592, of the *Revised Veritable Records of Sŏnjo* is even more direct: "Although [leaders of the Righteous Army] did not accomplish much, they gained the hearts of the people and thus, through them, the state sustained itself."⁵⁶

These narratives represent the volunteer army in two different modes: as a metaphor for popular will to resist the invaders, and as a metonym for the state's loss of the people's hearts, which were restored through its intervention. Chosŏn based its legitimacy on the Confucian concept of the Mandate of Heaven, which was confirmed, theoretically, by gaining the people's hearts, a kind of popular sovereignty. Hence, by the terms of Chosŏn political ideology, gaining and losing the people's hearts directly bore on the legitimacy of the regime. How can we interpret the idea that the volunteer army gained the people's hearts after the state had lost them? It does not appear, however, that the volunteer army or any of its leaders were viewed as an alternative or challenge to the current dynastic mandate. True, the state displayed a certain anxiety over this possibility, and the war was a genuine crisis, but popular anger represented disappointment in the government rather than doubt in the legitimacy of the Chosŏn state. As the official historiography repeatedly affirmed, the volunteer army was valorized for its role as the inspirer and bearer of the people's hearts on behalf of the state. How did it bring this about? The leaders of the volunteer army were local elites, who were mainstays of the Confucian civil culture that had prevailed in Korea for two centuries of peace. How were they able to transform their identity in a wartime emergency? What kind of ideological tools were available to them, and how were they able to assemble them into a wartime activist ideology of patriotism? How were they able to mobilize the population?

I contend that they were able to turn the people's hearts by reconceptualizing popular sovereignty, which enabled them to redefine and reassign the roles of constituents of the Chosŏn state. Before I proceed, a note regarding the way I use the term "popular sovereignty" might be in order. My usage is embedded in Korean political tradition and hence differs from the way in which it is used in the Western context. Popular sovereignty has been one of the key ideas in modern Western political thought, and there is a voluminous literature on it as a political concept and on the way in which it was interpreted, implemented, and utilized. It would be foolhardy even to attempt any systematic comparison between the two traditions. Without going into specifics, however, we may observe very broadly a few conspicuous differences in usage between the Western and Confucian contexts. At its basic level, in the West popular sovereignty was the Enlightenment ideal that came to be associated with the republican and democratic polity.[57] In Confucian political thought, popular sovereignty was an ancient political ideology associated with dynastic legitimacy by the concept of the Mandate of Heaven. That is, the possession and the loss of the Mandate of a ruling house depended on gaining and losing popular support.[58] It was conceived of more as metaphor and was used by the ruling house that prevailed as an ex post facto justification. It was not associated with political process that translated popular support into a political regime. Another fundamental difference was that whereas Rousseau's popular sovereignty justified the transition of human society from isolated, free, prepolitical existence into an existence within polities, in Confucian imagining in which the past began with a polity, popular sovereignty was the concept that explained the conditions and changes of power.

Popular sovereignty was a central trope in the rhetorical and conceptual makeup of the Chosŏn state. The Chosŏn dynasty, founded with the Confucian vision of an ideal state as model, based its legitimacy on the receipt of the Mandate of Heaven. This Confucian concept of popular sovereignty was explicitly evoked at the founder's coronation edict of 1392: "I was told that the people's wishes are such that Heaven's will is clearly manifested in them and that no one should refuse the wishes of the people, for to do so is to act contrary to the will of Heaven. Because the people insisted so steadfastly, I yielded finally to their will and ascended the throne. Now that we are at the threshold of a new beginning, I must show abundant grace, and I hereby announce the following policies for the benefit of the people."[59] In the subsequent two centuries, as the political culture of Chosŏn became increasingly Neo-Confucian, the rhetoric of popular sovereignty became a site on which the monarchy and the bureaucracy competed for power and authority with each other: bureaucrats pointed at the possible loss of popular sovereignty as a way to advance their counsel, whereas the king flaunted his possession of it to counter bureaucratic arguments. In the pre-Imjin Chosŏn state, however, the notion of popular sovereignty was used with the understanding that the state as a ruling body held a monopoly of responsibility to maintain the people's welfare and to safeguard the country. In this vision of good rule, the people were projected as passive objects to be protected. When the Imjin War broke out, this formula changed. Permitting private individuals to mobilize civilian armies, and thus implicitly relinquishing the state monopoly on the military, was the first step in the development of a more expansive popular sovereignty.[60]

It was the provincial elites who radically changed the concept of popular sovereignty and reassigned the roles of various constituents of the Chosŏn social structure. The relationship between the state and the people was always thought to be reciprocal: the king (and his government) owed benevolent rule, whereas the people owed loyalty to the king. In their exhortations the volunteer army leaders went beyond reciprocity and stressed interdependence. As we have seen in their exhortations, they repeatedly pointed out that during two hundred years of peace, the government had nurtured the people. At this time of crisis when the king was in flight and the state was in peril, it was their turn to rescue the king and restore the state. Not only did they belong to the king; the king also belonged to them. The loyalty each owed to the king needed to be translated into sacrificial action: willingness to die for the country. By redirecting responsibility to flow from the people to the state, they rendered moot the issue of the state's failure and invigorated the people's spirit to fight to preserve their state. What made local elites credible and inspiring was that they were at the forefront of this movement, taking up arms and dying for the country.

Who were these local elites, and what in their sense of identity compelled them to act as they did? Civilian leaders of the Righteous Army came from a number of backgrounds, and they ranged widely in age, experience, and relationship to the central government. There were those who had recently migrated from the capital or from some other region to their present places of residence and those who had inhabited one place for a long time. There were those who had previously served in the bureaucracy and those who had always lived as private scholars. As a group they did share certain common attributes in that their primary identity consisted of the yangban—aristocratic—status, and prominent standing in their locality. While the yangban was a bureaucratic class in its origin, it was an ascriptive privilege that certain lineages could claim and transmit to their descendants with no need of confirmation from the government.[61] The social prestige of these lineages, however, depended on a continuous maintenance and renewal of cultural capital, and this was achieved through adherence to the Confucian way of life. The way in which the ingredients of the Confucian mode of life evolved over time displayed an expanding influence of the Neo-Confucian intellectual and scholarly apparatus and its ethos. Such towering figures as Yi Hwang (T'oegye) and Yi I (Yulgok), the founders of the school of principle (*li*)[62] and the school of material force (*ki*)[63] in Korea, respectively, not only took Confucian scholarship to new heights of sophistication but also led the Confucian establishment in a geographical expansion. Private academies were founded in numbers in the provinces, and the centers of learning located in different provinces competed with and supplemented the educational establishment in the capital area.[64] The migration of elite lineages into localities away from the capital continued. All these movements and changes led to the forging of an intricate web of relationships between the intellectual establishment and the power elite both in the capital and in the provinces.

By the sixteenth century there was a certain homogenization in what constituted the essential elements of the Confucian mode of life. In addition to such standard features as the observation of Confucian ritual and the acquisition of Confucian classical learning, providing moral leadership to the local population emerged as an important ingredient. The elite displayed great concern to disseminate Confucian mores among the local population beyond the confines of the educated. Scholars in nonmetropolitan areas seem to have taken activist roles in "civilizing" the local population quite seriously. Spearheaded by such scholars as Yi Hwang and Yi I, the movement to adopt community compacts and localize the practice to suit each locality seems to have spread throughout Korea.[65]

This project of Confucianizing local society had a dual impact. It strengthened and solidified the privileges of the local elite. The central government also valued their role as mediators and implementers of its long-standing program of the Confucianization of Korean society. At the same time the civilizing project subscribed to the transformability of the local population and the possibility of moral suasion, which was in turn based on the Mencian vision of the original and natural goodness of human nature. This emphasis on the common attributes of human beings highlighted an alternative system of evaluating individuals on the basis of moral qualities and merit. The coexistence of two distinct systems of organizing society was not new. Like most societies, Korea exhibited the tension between an inherited class structure and alternative systems of evaluation. The ascendancy of Neo-Confucianism neither diminished nor offered a better resolution to the conflict between these two systems, but it did accelerate the fusion between the two systems of evaluation.[66] That is, social status was encoded with signifiers of virtue. The elite were expected to display more virtue. Qualities of individual moral character such as humanity and righteousness came into the play more visibly. The moral leadership that was expected of the local elite in promoting a local Confucian society by example and the active promotion of Confucian precepts were closely intertwined with this fusion.

The Confucian vision impelled the elite to construct their identities as Confucians dually along axes of civilization and nation. Confucian identity was civilizational in that all Confucians accepted the supremacy of Confucianism and the Confucian way of life as the means of sustaining civilization and humanity. Confucians, however, also defined their identities "nationally" in that, as members of the ruling elite, they viewed themselves as coextensive with the state and were committed to maintaining it by providing moral leadership since, in their understanding of the concept of loyalty (*ch'ung*), their duty to the state was seen as one of the cardinal virtues of Confucianism. These two modes of defining one's identity as a Confucian were not thought to be linked or mutually reinforcing, but the way in which they interacted and found expression in individual and collective consciousness differed widely depending on the time, place, circumstances, and individual perspective. The same can be said of the way in which the concept of loyalty was interpreted, ranging from an unswerving loyalty to one's lord to patriotic duty to one's country or an evaluative moral duty to principle. When peace reigned, in accordance with the prevailing Neo-Confucian ethos that stressed the individual cultivation of morality, they regarded loyalty as an individual moral duty to principle. Many scholars, for example, took for granted as their prerogative to choose not to serve in government if they wished, even when the king strongly asked for their service. They saw their primary duty as pursuing their own moral cultivation and helping to enact a moral vision in the society in which they lived.

When the war broke out all this had to change, and they had to make new sets of moral imperatives. In making a decision to take to arms for Korea and to call on others to do the same, a course of action that they had neither experienced nor expected, they had to translate the basis of their individual moral choice into an activist moral imperative to be collectively shared by members of the entire community of Korea. In confronting their personal situation, they constructed and articulated a moral-national ideal.[67] I believe that provincial elites were compelled to link the moral to the national by their interpretation of popular sovereignty, that is, by their idea that it was their responsibility to carry on the functions of the state when nothing else was doing so. Now that the ruling body was incapacitated and could not safeguard the country, it was their responsibility as the one remaining group with the means to organize a resistance army to step temporarily into the vacuum and act. Insofar as "morality" and "civilization" were conceived in Confucian terms, the civilizational concept was placed in service to the polity. Likewise, the moral-national concept was also created by directing an individual's moral duty to the national community. That is, whereas previously an individual's duty as a member of Confucian civilization and as a member of a national community were conceived as coextensive, at this point the former was directly linked to the latter: a Korean Confucian's duty was to save Korea. This was to be accomplished by resisting and expelling the enemy and restoring the state to its former condition. Likewise, cultural tools and imagery that carried dual connotations were also put to use primarily for the sake of the nation. Literary Chinese, which was simultaneously the language of the Confucian canon and the lingua franca of the educated in East Asia and the language of governance for each state, was used to rally for the polity. Nowhere was this more clearly shown than in the lofty heights to which the image of dying for the country was thrust. Despite two hundred years of peace during which dying for the country (sun'guk) was a remote ideal rather than a possible choice for Koreans, it was seized on instantaneously as the ultimate enactment of dedicating one's body to the service of principle. There were many historical examples available for the late sixteenth-century Korean to draw from. Moreover, in the context of the Confucian system of values that prized earning a name for posterity above all else, dying for one's country offered the chance of fulfilling that goal and securing a place in memory for all posterity. The rhetoric quickly seized on this point. Martyrdom for Korea was a noble exit, writing a glorious end to one's life and earning immortality.

While the mode of executing one's moral duty may have changed, the cultural logic remained the same in making one's own choice or persuading others to make the right decision: one's body became the text on which one wrote one's own life story by making a series of autonomous decisions. Thus the writers of the letters of exhortation premised their arguments for rising against the invaders on the ideal of free and personal choice. They also conceded that, if an individual arrived at the decision, they did so for different reasons and from different motivations. Ko Kyŏngmyŏng's famous letter of exhortation described the scene in which volunteers joined the Righteous Army: "no one was forced; no one hesitated."[68] This envisions a spontaneous morally compelling choice. At the other extreme, personal morality is irrelevant; it is the shared objective that is stressed: "The extermination of the invaders, however, is something that not only loyal subjects or rightful scholars wish for, but something that even disloyal subjects and unfilial individuals also wish for." In this logic, moral-national is inverted to national-moral. It is posited that by accepting the responsibility of defending one's country, regardless of reason or motivation, one would become a full-fledged Korean and thus a moral being. And this awakening, as was the case with dedication to a moral-national community, was imagined as personal though the objective was a collective one.

The voluntary army became a successful national movement because by creating a national horizontal space, its organizers offered to all Koreans the choice to join it, as a free and personal one. The militarization of the people had to proceed on the basis of the "nationalization" of the people.[69] We have seen that the Righteous Army was initiated among the elite but soon expanded to include nonelite volunteers. It was not that distinctions between regions and classes were erased, but they were considered far less significant than the grave task of fighting the invaders. Thus all Koreans, presented as members of the Korean nation, were called on to take up arms to preserve their lives and their unique "civilized" way of life. If they were to die, then they would die as heroes, and their names would be eternally remembered in history. Various nonelite elements of the population, "the people (*min*)," as they were usually referred to, were important to the way in which popular sovereignty was reconstituted. All were transformed from objects of the government's beneficence into subjects who fought for and contributed to the survival of the country.

All Koreans, despite their differences, were imagined as persons who were capable of making the right decision. While there was an emphasis on the elite's special indebtedness toward the state, there was no sense in the rhetoric that the elite would have exclusive or even an inherently greater proclivity toward moral choice than the nonelite. We have seen one letter that explicitly disavows this notion: "When it concerns loyalty and the sense of justice, from the descendants of scholars to slaves in mangers, there is no difference; all possess the same." In this sense the discourse on nation that began during the Imjin War resonates with what Liah Greenfeld describes as the basis of all nationalism: "Every member of the 'people' thus interpreted partakes in its superior, elite quality, and it is in consequence that a stratified national population is perceived as essentially homogeneous, and the lines of status and class as superficial."[70]

Aftermath

After the Chinese Army of forty thousand led by Li Rusong arrived to assist Chosŏn toward the end of 1592, the volunteer army lost much of its significance as a military force. Unlike 1592, during which it was the only land force that kept Chosŏn alive, mainly by guerilla tactics, from 1593 the main battles were fought by the allied forces of Chosŏn and Ming, to which the volunteer army units functioned as auxiliary or service units.[71] By the fourth month of 1594, all groups of the Righteous Army were placed under the command of Kim Tŏngnyŏng (1567–1596), a charismatic twenty-eight-year-old leader from Chŏlla, and those who were unwilling to accept his leadership were to be disbanded.[72] In 1596 the government charged Kim with sedition and put him to death. The charge was so evidently false that even the official history quickly admitted to it,[73] turning him into a wronged martyr of unrequited loyalty.[74] The volunteer army movement faded. During the second Japanese invasion of 1597 the movement was revived, but as the allied forces of Chosŏn and Ming matched the Japanese forces in fighting capacity, the volunteer army's role was far less conspicuous. Its distinction as a symbol of activist loyalty, however, continued. At the time of its formation in 1592, the volunteer civilian army, organized and supported by local leaders, was not only historically but also conceptually new. The Righteous Army of the Imjin War set a precedent to which later Chosŏn people looked, and on the two occasions when the country faced crises, the same movement under the same name and rhetoric was attempted: during the Manchu invasions of 1627 and 1636–1637, and for several years after the Chosŏn became Japan's protectorate in 1905.

It was through its impact on Chosŏn political culture that the legacy of the volunteer army exerted its greatest influence. In postwar Chosŏn everything associated with the Imjin War, such as persons, locations, and battles, was turned into sacral sites on which discourse of nation perpetuated and expanded. The Righteous Army, especially some of its leaders, took a central place in the commemorative culture as symbols of "purity, through fatality." It did not, however, end with the addition of dead scholar-warriors to the pantheon of patriotic heroes. Participatory roles for civilians—local elites and ordinary people—had to be accommodated in political life. The activist concept of popular sovereignty was reformulated to rebuild the war-torn country. The state also recognized that the postwar reconstruction had to proceed, acknowledging the crucial contributions all constituent groups had made, and it negotiated with them for changes in their social and political roles. The most conspicuous example of this development was that all constituents coconstructed the commemorative culture of postwar Chosŏn. In this way each group competed and participated in the changing discourse of the imagined community of Chosŏn.

We have already seen in previous chapters that the Imjin War was fought not only in military battles with weapons but also in communicative media with the corresponding tools. For the Chosŏn government it was particularly urgent that it devise a communication strategy that would fulfill dual purposes: to send messages to the Korean population in a medium accessible only to them and not to foreign forces, and to do so in a medium with the potential of reaching the broadest of audiences and in the most affecting of rhetoric. Under these circumstances, the Chosŏn government adopted a radical language policy: to deploy Korean vernacular script as a means of communication among Koreans. Departing from the practice of exclusively using literary Chinese in public missives, royal edicts in Korean script were sent out to population at large either to be posted in conspicuous places where people gathered or passed or to be distributed among them. Edicts in Korean script were also delivered to Koreans held captive by the Japanese.[1] The government also received certain reports in Korean script, and it used the script in espionage against the enemy. This language policy of using vernacular Korean script in official missives was not formulated in a systematic fashion; rather, the royal court, in flight and under extreme pressure, adopted it as a desperate measure to reach the scattered, endangered, and embittered population in an attempt to restore its faith. Nor was this policy carried out consistently but on an ad hoc basis only when there was urgently felt need. No matter, a vernacular national space emerged, as this and the next chapter will show.

3

WAR OF WORDS

The Changing Nature of Literary Chinese in the Japanese Occupation

The creation of a vernacular national space was an epochal measure that redefined the geo-cultural-political entity of Korea. The step was taken in part as a response to the changed nature and use of literary Chinese during wartime. Before the war literary Chinese was a linguistic medium that connected a cosmopolitan cultural imaginary and the participating polities in the region, which shared its values and worldviews. Although much of public writing in inscriptional spaces in each of the East Asian countries was in literary Chinese during the Ming, direct communication among them was along the prescribed lines, either diplomatic exchanges between states[2] or occasional correspondence between the educated of these countries, mostly between China and Korea.[3] True, Japan deviated from the model in that the military men who were in power were not particularly proficient in literary Chinese, but many public records, including diplomatic correspondence, were in literary Chinese written by Buddhist clergy.

During the war the cosmopolitan cultural imaginary was reconfigured into feuding polities. The three countries writing literary Chinese that converged on Korea either as allies or enemies deployed such writing as a part of their military strategy. In considering the function of language in the rise of nationalism, Benedict Anderson groups literary Chinese with sacral languages that included Latin and Qur'anic Arabic and maintains that sacral languages, "as truth languages, imbued with an impulse largely foreign to nationalism," made larger transnational communities imaginable.[4] Literary Chinese functioned as the sacral language of East Asia to the extent that it was the language of the Confucian canon and other religious scriptures. However, the vision that the Confucian canon portrays was that of well-ordered polity, and literary Chinese was first and foremost the language of governance of secular states and of political ideology and all that is associated with it, including patriotism. We have already seen in the preceding chapters that literary Chinese functioned in Chosŏn as a linguistic medium of patriotic expression.

When the war broke out, a dizzying array of multidirectional communiqués in literary Chinese began to flow within and across national groups and between enemies and allies. The boundaries of communicative space along national lines vanished, and the Korean domestic communicative space of literary Chinese became permeable to others. It was alarming to the Chosŏn government that Japanese and Chinese authorities penetrated into the interior of the Korean communicative space by sending out public announcements and promulgations in literary Chinese to the Korean population. The Japanese approached the Korean population with a dual policy of terrorization and appeasement. Frequently when the Japanese Army massacred residents and looted villages, they also put up posters coaxing residents who had fled to return from their places of hiding and promising them safety. Even before they entered the war, the Chinese, from the emperor on down to the military strategists and generals, also bombarded Koreans with their messages. Literary Chinese became the medium through which the three countries competed for the attention and support or appeasement of Koreans.

When the Chosŏn government sent out royal edicts in the Korean script, as described in the next chapter, it was consciously creating a separate linguistic space apart from the transnational one of literary Chinese that Korea shared with its enemy as well as its ally, but it was also seeking an inclusive space open to all Koreans. A royal edict was a communication that, by virtue of the ruler's unique position, enabled the king to address all the people of Korea in a vertical line of communication and was reserved solely for his or his deputy's use. Even after civilian leaders and the soldiers of the Righteous Army created another nationwide discursive space of a more horizontal nature, royal edicts still provided the ruler with a privileged stage from which he could send messages of assurance. When the country was swarming with enemy soldiers and allied but alien troops, in the rhetoric of affectivity available to him alone as the father of the country (*kukpu*), the king could conjure up a vision of the ethnic community of Koreans, the inhabitants of a nation besieged by intruders all of whom had to be expelled. Sŏnjo's wartime edicts in Korean script powerfully penetrated the emergent horizontal national discursive space, and competed with and mutually reinforced the other strands of discourse. In this sense, the royal edicts in Korean breached the last barrier to the movement toward constructing a new ethnolinguistic national space of discourse. Sheldon Pollock maintains that literature "addresses, sometimes calls into being, particular sociotextual communities."⁵ I contend that the vernacular royal edicts that the Chosŏn government deployed called into being a community of "us" as opposed to "them," and that this was "national" in that it was bound by and inclusive of the Korean ethnolinguistic community.

The inauguration of a vernacular national communicative space also marked a milestone in reconstituting the interior writing space of Korea and the way in which the vernacular and the classical were characterized and positioned in relation to each other. Previously, while the invention of the *han'gŭl* script in the mid-fifteenth century had been based on a new concept of writing—accessibility to all and for daily use—and its promulgation ushered in a diglossic writing culture, the vernacular space grew under the overweening hegemony of the classical space. The result was that, rather than being evaluated on its own terms, the vernacular was perceived as the shadowy other of classical writing and endowed with qualities opposite the latter in binary formation. That is, the vernacular was local; the classical, universal (or transnational); it was temporary where the classical was eternal; feminine as opposed to masculine; private as opposed to public; secretive as opposed to open. During the war some of these very qualities, such as the "secretive" and "local" qualities of the vernacular script, were transformed in meaning to "ours" and "national."⁶

JAPANESE INFILTRATION INTO DISCURSIVE SPACE

It may not be an exaggeration to say that the encounter between the Japanese Army and Koreans during the Imjin War remains one of the most intense clashes recorded in East Asian history. It occurred in the context of a worldview wholly different from that of the present: that of the sixteenth century, when different assumptions of self and other prevailed. To begin with, for most of those involved on all sides, it was the first time they were encountering "foreigners" on a large scale. True, the leadership of the invasion probably had had some dealings with Westerners. In fact, two of the generals leading the campaign, Konishi Yukinaga and Kuroda Nagamasa, were Catholics, and a Spanish Jesuit priest, Gregorio de Cespedes (1551–1611), went to Korea as Yukinaga's chaplain on two occasions, 1593 and 1597, and spent some time there, becoming the first Western visitor recorded in Korean in history.[7] Nevertheless, no one in the Japanese leadership, not to mention common soldiers, had set foot on foreign soil before they landed at Pusan. What could have been their expectations as they crossed the sea?

There is no indication that they had given much thought to the "foreignness" of Korea except to think of the place as a country in which to wage battles. As for Hideyoshi, who was thinking of himself as a conqueror, it is questionable whether he even had a desire to acknowledge any difference. In discussing Christopher Marlowe's (1564–1593) *Tamburlaine*, which was based on the fourteenth-century Tamerlane (c.1336–1405), the Mongol conqueror, Virginia Mason Vaughan observes that "the desire to conquer goes beyond notions of exchange to imply the transformation of another sort, whereby the conquered territory or people loses its original identity, becoming instead a mirror image of the conqueror." She also says that "Tamburlaine's geography is not a respecter of difference. In his catalogue of the territories he has conquered, Tamburlaine makes few distinctions. Instead he flattens and conflates—all will become homogenized under his rule."[8] Like his fictional contemporary, Hideyoshi acted the conqueror, showing no inclination to take note of the distinctiveness of Korea or of other Asian countries. To him Korea was merely the first step toward constructing a vast Asian empire, which he wished to homogenize in the image of Japan. As he declared in his letter to Sŏnjo, "I have it in mind to introduce Japanese customs and values to the four hundred and more provinces of that country [China] and bestow upon it the benefits of imperial rule and the culture of the coming hundred million years."[9]

This indifference to difference does not eradicate the logistical problems of dealing with the other or the shock of discovery of their "difference." This was obvious from the very beginning. I have already mentioned that the Japanese began the invasion with the massacre of residents of Pusan, where they landed. It was clear even during this indiscriminate mass slaughter, an act that one might imagine requires no exchange of words, that the invaders and the local residents were discovering that they were separated by a gulf of language. It is vividly brought home by a description of the massacre in a memoir by one Yoshino, a member of the Japanese Army, written twenty-four years after the event:[10]

> When we landed in the early morning on May 23, we immediately attacked the fort at Pusan. They were waiting for us inside the walled town. Arrows from half-size bows flew and fell upon us like rain. Ignoring this, our force responded with mass firing of arquebuses. Noise shook Heaven and Earth ... shields, watch towers all tumbled down. No one stuck his head out. Climbing a stone wall 3 *hiro* high,[11] we all charged in. ... The enemy was running in search of hiding places. They hid between houses or under tables. Those who could not find places to hide ran to the east gate to escape. [When captured] they all put their hands together kneeling down and uttered words that we had never heard, incomprehensible words that sounded like "manō, manō!" It sounded as if they were pleading for mercy. Yet, our forces ignored these words, slashed them and trampled them to death. This was done in the spirit of making an offering to the god of war. The victims were both men and women, and even dogs and cats were cut to pieces. In all, as many as 30,000 people were slaughtered.[12]

It is noticeable that in recollecting this scene, the narratorial voice of the participant-memoirist shifts. Most of the time he narrates as a member of the troop that landed at Pusan. He refers to the Japanese Army as "our force" (*mikata*) and to Koreans as "enemy" (*teki*). For a brief moment, however, he changes to an individual who sees and hears the other—Koreans were hiding and making noises that he had not heard before, but that seemed to be pleas. Then personal perspective is again replaced by a collective one, referring to the Japanese as "our force." And yet, submerged in it, there is a personal voice that observes that "our force" ignored what seemed like pleading, trampling "them" to death, and massacring people and animals alike. This is a complex document that dramatically displays the shock of discovery of the other from the point of view of the attacker, probably suppressed at the time but remembered and narrated later.

The March to Seoul

As the Japanese went inland, there is no indication that they changed their approach, either in tactics of intimidation or in their indifferent methods of dealings with the other. The Japanese took three separate routes in their march toward the capital city. The first group, led by Konishi Yukinaga and Sō Yoshitoshi, took the middle route and conquered Yangsan on May 26, Miryang on May 28, Taegu on May 30, Indong on June 1, Sangju on June 3, Mun'gyŏng on June 5, and Ch'ungju on June 6, reaching Seoul on June 12. The second group, led by Katō Kiyomasa, took the eastern route, starting from Tongnae and then occupying Kyŏngju, Yŏngch'ŏn, Ch'ungju, Chuksan, and Yongin before arriving at Seoul on June 12. The third group, led by Kuroda Nagamasa, started from Kimhae and took Ch'angwŏn, Sŏngju, Kŭmsan, and Chuksan, arriving at Seoul on June 16.[13] All three groups left trails of burned towns and pillaged villages on their march north.[14] Nevertheless, as their objective was to occupy Korea and to collect taxes from Koreans, not just to ransack and leave, it was not enough just to intimidate Koreans. Many of the terrified Koreans abandoned their homes and took refuge in mountains and valleys. The Japanese had to find ways to persuade them to return to their homes, and they became aware of a problem caused by their inability to communicate with Koreans. Hideyoshi, however, was not on site. Contrary to his original plan, he did not personally join the campaign in Korea.[15] Instead his orders were conveyed to field commanders as they advanced inland into Korea. In his absence the commanders had to make ad hoc decisions.

The first and most consistently used method was to dispatch written orders in literary Chinese to Koreans. Each battalion of the Japanese Army had a Buddhist monk-recorder who kept a record of the war and could be called on to write missives in literary Chinese. The Japanese began to post them at various places. The first such order (*yŏng*) was posted when the army led by Yukinaga and Yoshitoshi entered the town of Indong, a little north of Taegu in Kyŏngsang Province, on June 1. The proclamation, sent out in the name of Yoshitoshi although written by Tenkei, one of the Buddhist monk-recorders,[16] read: "The scattered residents must immediately return to their homes: Men are to go back to farming and animal husbandry, and women to sericulture. All must continue with the work of their occupation, be it scholarship, agriculture, craft, or commerce. If any soldier of our army were to violate the law by interrupting your work, he will be punished."[17] The *Miscellaneous Record* confirms this posting. It also adds that many Koreans surrendered to the Japanese and received plaques of identification, and that the Japanese sometimes distributed to people grain that they took from the Chosŏn government granaries.[18]

On June 12 Yukinaga and Kiyomasa, whose rivalry and enmity toward each other were legendary, arrived at Seoul leading their respective troops within a few hours of each other. They entered the eerily quiet and deserted city with no resistance.[19] Just as the loss of the capital city was a catalyst for the Korean local elite, propelling them to mobilize the volunteer army, the capture marked a turning point for the Japanese estimate of whether Hideyoshi's project of building an Asian empire might become a reality.

Hideyoshi's Plans for Occupation

When Hideyoshi received the news that Seoul had fallen, he began to dash off plans for its occupation. On June 15 he sent his generals in Korea a stratagem consisting of nine items: one called for "a seat of governance" to be "established for Hideyoshi in Seoul"; a second required that "townspeople will be forced back to [urban centers], and that the peasants scattered throughout the country will be directed back to their villages and prohibition laws will be enforced."[20] On June 18 Hideyoshi issued a memo (*oboegaki*) consisting of twenty-five items, directed to his heir, the Regent Hidetsugu, giving a blueprint for constructing a grand East Asian empire. This addressed mainly questions of redistributing the ruling body to geographical posts he hoped to acquire. For example, the Japanese emperor would be relocated to Beijing.[21]

Hideyoshi again postponed his departure to Korea. Instead, on July 11 he dispatched Ishida Mitsunari as the governor of Korea with further instructions: the eight provinces of Korea were to be placed under Hideyoshi's direct jurisdiction and a bailiff (*daikan*) was to be stationed in each; the peasants in hiding were to be returned to their villages to farm and pay tax; new lodgings for Hideyoshi were to be built along the route to China.[22] In accordance with Hideyoshi's instructions, eight daimyos were appointed as bailiffs to each of the eight provinces, and the tax due from each province was calculated in precise amounts down to pennies.[23]

Hideyoshi also sent detailed instructions to different bailiffs. One sent to Kiyomasa included a directive concerning a curious item called *tsukai me*, which can be rendered as "service women" or "service concubines." The order required that the Japanese authorities should let it be known to Koreans that along with tax and other produce, they would be obliged to send in "service women." Kitajima explains that this order was sent so that the high-ranking Japanese officials, bailiffs, mayors, and other generals of responsibility would be provided with service women, who would render services that included sex.[24] In view of the political uproar over comfort women in World War II, this reference to "service women" is potentially an explosive topic. A fuller treatment of the issue would require a thoughtful investigation of available sources in the context of the sixteenth-century practices of a conquering army toward local women and the significations of these practices. Rape of local women was a common practice in time of war. What is noticeable is the institutionalization of "service women" directed from the highest authority. We do not know the extent of this practice, who were taken as "service women," whether and how deeply the practice penetrated into civilian families, or the extent of the coercion involved.

There is, however, evidence that many Korean women were taken as "service women" by the Japanese occupiers. There are also indications that when they were recovered, these women were not treated well by Korean men. The *Miscellaneous Record* reports an incident involving such women. Kim Myŏn, the leader of the Righteous Army, won a battle at Chirye and burned all the enemy soldiers to death. He found many "beautiful women" from Chŏlla Province who had been taken and kept by the Japanese. The women pleaded for their lives, but Kim burned them to death along with the Japanese soldiers.[25] The familiar gendered symbolism and psychology seem to be at work here: the defilement of women symbolizing the emasculation of the conquered men who could not protect their women, and male fury turned on defiled women. There was also a fear of miscegenation. The question of female purity for its symbolic and human implications would emerge as an important issue for individuals and the state not only during the Imjin War but also during and after the Manchu invasions of 1636–1637. Suffice it to say that embedded in this question are issues of ethnic and national identity.

Colonizing Korea

The Japanese launched a systematic campaign directed at Koreans to transform Korea into their "colony" and to turn Koreans into taxpaying "subjects." The first order of business was to convince Koreans that the old world in which they had lived was gone, that the new world order was in place, and that they had no choice but to surrender to it. The Japanese began with a symbolic annihilation of the Chosŏn state. They set fire to the Yi Royal Ancestral Temple (Chongmyo) in which the tablets of the Yi royal ancestors were normally kept.[26] Though the tablets had been taken by the royal family and carried with them to their place of refuge, the incineration of Chongmyo was considered the worst possible desecration of Yi royal monarchy. Within months the Japanese literally defiled dead royal bodies, despoiling two Yi royal tombs, Sŏnnŭng, the tomb of King Sŏngjong (r. 1469–1494) and his wife, Queen Chŏnghyŏn, and Chŏngnŭng, the tomb of King Chungjong (r. 1506–1544). The bodies were disinterred and the tombs dismantled.[27] Koreans viewed the destruction of the Yi Royal Ancestral Temple and the two royal tombs as unimaginably horrible violations of the Yi monarchical body, and the actions apparently strengthened the Korean resolve to fight the invader.

The Japanese launched a campaign to disseminate the message that there had been a change of regime and that the public had entered a new age of Japanese rule. Posters were posted at public places in Seoul and in cities and towns in the provinces. Tenkei mentions in *The Diary of the Western Campaign* that soon after they entered the capital, the Japanese conferred and decided to post documents on the four main gates announcing their arrival and ordering the residents to return to their homes.[28] The *Miscellaneous Record* records a pronouncement that was sent out in the name of several Japanese generals to the towns and villages of Kyŏnggi and Kangwŏn Provinces on June 29: "Your ruler has run away, and China has become a part of Japan. We are planning to govern Korea by sending deputies to each province. Scholars and the people of rural areas should submit to the rule of Japan as you did to the previous regime. You cannot object to this. All rice and grain, jade and valuables, silk and linen should be kept intact and undispersed. Governors, magistrates and people, male and female, should not leave their posts, and should serve our deputies. Beware of this point."[29]

A proclamation that Kiyomasa sent to the residents of Hamgyŏng Province immediately after he and Nabeshima Naoshige entered the province, the northeast border region, struck a loftier tone. Believed to have been written by the Buddhist monk Zetaku, it contained the following points: The purpose of the military campaign by His Highness (Hideyoshi) is the political reform of Korea; the king of Korea has fled from Seoul, but it is not our intention to punish him; we promise to provide protection to those who submit to us. Residents must return to their homes and devote themselves to farming; eight Japanese commanders have been assigned to rule each of the eight provinces and the person who is to rule Hamgyŏng is Kiyomasa. In accordance with the order of His Highness, Kiyomasa is determined to rule completely according to laws and regulations, and the residents should have no fear; residents must return to their homes and devote themselves to farming.[30] What is noteworthy is an attempt to present the Japanese invasion as having been motivated by Hideyoshi's desire for political reform in Korea. This was rhetoric challenging a regime in power, be it from a leader in rebellion or an invader. To mitigate their presence as outsiders, the Japanese attempted to project a better future for Koreans based on law and order.

The confident Kiyomasa built separate headquarters for himself and Naoshige, the second-in-command, in southern Hamgyŏng, had garrisons built throughout the province, and set about pacifying the whole province. Hamgyŏng Province was a distant border area to which the Chosŏn government sent criminals in exile, and its residents seem to have felt a sense of alienation from if not outright resentment for the central government, so the initial reaction to the Japanese promise does not seem to have been entirely negative. Korean officials, for example, cooperated with Japanese assessments of land and agricultural productivity. Naoshige collected the tax thus assessed, 244,360 *sŏk* in total.[31] It was also around this time that Kiyomasa captured two Korean princes, Princes Imhae and Sunhwa, a huge prize, especially since they were handed over by a disgruntled Korean. Buoyed, leading eight thousand Japanese soldiers and three thousand Koreans, Kiyomasa made incursions into Manchuria. Upon his return he triumphantly wrote to Hideyoshi, proudly reporting on his perfect stewardship of his domain.[32]

The meaning of a better future, however, remained debatable. It appears that any resemblance to order was achieved by force and coercion.[33] Tajiri Akitane records in *The Diary of the Campaign of Korea* (*Kōrai nikki*) that the way Naoshige collected tax was by taking hostages and releasing them one by one in exchange for the delivery of tax.[34] The report of the governor of Hamgyŏng Province, Yi Hŭidŭk, in the *Veritable Records of Sŏnjo* is more scathing: "The enemy's rule of this province is fiercer than in other provinces. Starting from Anbyŏn, they stationed generals in all six garrisons, each with 300 to 400 soldiers. They send soldiers to the residents every day and forcefully take from them their daily necessities. At strategic points, ambushes were installed making it impossible for people to travel. There is endless massacre and robbery. Our people are so enraged that they want to rise against them and eagerly await the arrival of the Chinese assistance army."[35] A Japanese sources shares this Korean assessment that cruelty by Japanese led to the Korean revolt. In *Korea Diary* (*Chōsen nikki*), the Buddhist monk Zetaku says: "Commoners at first complied with the Japanese orders and paid tribute in kind and tax. Later, however, they returned to the old Korean ordinances. They refused to remain in their regular abodes, hid in mountains and valleys, took up military weapons, and used bows and arrows."[36]

Alarmed by the escalating resistance among the Korean civilian army all over the country, a scenario they had not anticipated, the Japanese accelerated a propaganda campaign. Posters were disseminated more widely and frequently, and their rhetoric was sharpened with equal measures of persuasion and threat. Particularly noticeable is a portrayal of Japan's occupation as having been motivated by a lofty vision of a new world. For example, to the residents of Pian in Kyŏngsang Province on August 10, 1592:

> The objective of this Japanese official is to put into effect our Highness's goal of civilizing the world and establishing good governance for the people. The residents of this county who are in hiding or have taken refuge elsewhere should return to their abodes and live peacefully. We have arrested and are killing those Japanese who took wives from Koreans. Farmers should till the land, water the fields, get rid of weeds and await the harvest in the fall. If any in Chosŏn were to take up weapons and interrupt our activities, all will be killed. If any commoner has grievances, then come and report to our staff at our headquarters.[37]

Another was addressed specifically to the volunteer army in Kŭmsan, Chŏlla Province, on August 15, 1592:

> The great king of Great Japan wishes to establish a political reform in Korea to save its people. What is the reason for stopping us on sea and land and turning us into the enemy? This is comparable to an insect resisting the wheel of a chariot or a dayfly shaking a great tree. Because of resistance, foot soldiers and cavalry alike had to go into the streets and lanes of villages and towns, and under our flag we had to unsheath the sword. The gates of walled towns were thus burned and the noise of cannons rumbled through every house. We captured these rebels

and thought of decapitating them all. It is, however, difficult to evaluate the heaviness and lightness of each one's crime, and so, out of our pity for the parents, wives, and children of these criminals, we forgave them. We saved them from hunger and let them live. Anyone daring to fight us further will not be tolerated and will be killed at once. Those of you who have been roaming the fields in the resistance army, repent your crime and go home. The Japanese emperor and the Korean ruler will soon reach an agreement. You should know this. You should let this news be known to armed people hiding in the mountains. If they discard their bows and swords, and surrender to us, no one will be punished. If this order is disobeyed, we will come with several hundred soldiers and will again massacre the whole population.[38]

Still another to residents of Hwasan, Hwanghae Province, promises on August 19, 1592, a peaceful future of benevolent rule:

Japan is no longer the Japan of the past. It looks forward to a time when the whole world will enjoy peace. We will reduce corvée labor and lower taxes. There is no reason to be anxious. Return to your old life. When the great army of Japan passes through, adults and children alike should welcome and greet them. Those who flee to the mountains will be beheaded. Those who possess weapons must turn them in to the authorities. Anyone who disobeys this order will be beheaded. Even high ministers and officials who have taken refuge should not stay in hiding and should come to meet us. Slaves, both public and private, will become our subjects.[39]

One can clearly see a shift in rhetoric from invader to "colonizer": on a global scale, the emphasis shifted to the project of "civilizing" the world and bringing peace to it, and, on the local level, of reducing taxes and guaranteeing security. These Japanese attempts to mollify the fears of the local population, however, invariably were followed by the threat of death for disobedience. Situated as they were as occupiers who wanted to collect taxes in grain from the local population to feed their troops and finance their further campaign to China, there simply was no way the rhetoric could transcend the limitations imposed by the adversarial relationship. Nor could they successfully negotiate the problem of language. Various Japanese generals commented on the difficulties caused by the language barrier. Mōri Terumoto, the bailiff of Kyŏngsang Province, for example, stated that one of the greatest problems the Japanese faced was their inability to communicate with Koreans, and that even with the use of interpreters, incomprehension remained.⁴⁰ Written communication was believed to be somewhat better since the use of the cosmopolitan language ensured communication at least to a certain segment of the local population, and the use of posters in literary Chinese continued.

However, there is a suggestion that Japanese might have attempted to go beyond literary Chinese. Yi Chŏng'am, a leader of the Righteous Army of Hwanghae Province, mentions in his *Daily Record of the Western Campaign* that he obtained a copy of a promulgation written in a mixture of literary Chinese and *idu* posted by Kuroda Nagamasa, the bailiff of Hwanghae Province. *Idu* was a system of writing that used Chinese ideograms phonetically to inscribe Korean and was employed by clerks in Korean government offices to supplement writings in literary Chinese. Yi surmises that a Korean clerk in the governor's office must have written this poster.⁴¹ But this method was hardly more comprehensible to the Korean population who were not versed in literary Chinese. In the *Record of the Campaign Against Barbarians*, Yi T'aegyŏng states on August 17: "The enemy stationed at Koryŏng used a woman of our country to deliver a letter saying, 'Why do you kill those travelling on waterways or land routes? If you continued this way, we will send our well-trained army of several tens of thousands to exterminate everyone in your country.'"⁴² Though the woman is identified as a messenger, it is remotely possible that by identifying the gender of the messenger, Yi may be saying that the message was in her hand, namely, in Korean script. As Japanese scriptural culture consisted of writings in literary Chinese and in Japanese script, it is not impossible that the Japanese hit on the idea of penetrating into the Korean vernacular space.

The Massacre of Seoul

It was Seoul, the capital, in which the Japanese invested their most intense hopes in projecting their grand vision, even if they were accompanied by an equally sharp sense of disappointment. I mentioned that they entered the capital with such a sense of triumph and that they put posters at all four gates urging residents of the city to return. A considerable number must have returned. After a couple of weeks, however, the Japanese launched a mass killing of Seoul residents. The *Miscellaneous Record* reports the following in the entry of June 29:

> Upon being ordered that they should display their might by exterminating the people, the huge battalion of the Japanese Army stationed in Seoul massacred the residents of the capital. Within half a day, dead bodies filled the streets from the East Gate to the South Gate. Those residents who had surrendered to the Japanese could not flee, and the horrible sight of pools of blood and the mounds of piled human bodies was simply beyond words. After a full day's massacre, it was stopped. At every gate, they posted the announcements ordering that "men devote yourselves to farming, thus securing your livelihoods, and women to sericulture and weaving."[43]

This mayhem is reported to have been tactically motivated. What were the occupiers attempting to do through such a display of force?

There is an indication that this display of force was an overture to the Japanese initiation of a program to remake Koreans into Japanese. In a report to Hideyoshi dated July 16, Buddhist monk Ekei of Ankokuji discussed several items, the first concerning language: it was through written words that communication took place, and when it came to the sound of Chinese characters or spoken language, they were completely different from the patterns of Japanese language. He then asked permission to employ and attach translators to various offices so that Hideyoshi's laws could be disseminated widely. He volunteered to take charge of the operation. Then he reported what he did in Seoul: "As has been previously discussed in Japan, we have taught the Japanese syllabary (*Iroha*) to Koreans, shaved adults' heads bald, shaved boys' heads in the middle, and used them in subordinate positions. Unlike Japanese children, children here write prose and compose poetry. We order and collect things written in Korean characters (J. *Kōrai*, K. *Koryŏ muncha*). We leave them five or ten days and send them out to various places. At present I am employing two or three children, and they are quicker than Japanese."[44] When he says Korean characters, it is not clear whether he refers to writings done in Korean script or in literary Chinese. I have not come across any reference suggesting that the Japanese sent out their orders in Korean script, although one cannot completely eliminate the possibility. The program of imposing Japanese language and customs on Koreans, however, was part of an overall plan for a long-term occupation, and this seems to have been initiated in the capital city. Given the fact that the Japanese stayed in Seoul less than a year, one wonders how far the experiment went. It is most likely that the capital was the first place in which the program was put into practice.

The Retreat

Japanese dreams of turning Seoul into a mirror image of their own cities ended on a bloody note. By the end of 1592 the Japanese occupation was faring badly. They suffered guerilla attacks from the Righteous Army, which took back many key areas in various provinces, and naval victories led by Admiral Yi Sunsin—ten during the summer and early fall of 1592—which cut supply lines from Japan.[45] Food provisions that the Japanese took from Korean government granaries ran out. Korean farmers proved to be uncooperative. The winter was cold, especially in the North. According to the Jesuit priest Frois, a confidant of Yukinaga, of 150,000 Japanese soldiers and transport laborers who went to Korea in the first invasion, one-third died, mostly from exhaustion, hunger, cold, and disease.[46]

The long-awaited Chinese army of 43,000 under the leadership of Supreme Commander General Li Rusong (1549–1598) arrived on January 26, 1593.[47] Allied Chinese and Korean troops recaptured P'yŏngyang on February 8. The Ming, equipped with great fire power, especially great cannons, easily defeated the exhausted Japanese. The battle resulted in huge Japanese casualties—1,300 to 1,700 killed, another 500 dying in the flames, and about 6,000 more drowned in the Taedong River. Song Yingchang claimed that only 796 Ming soldiers died.[48] The Japanese Army began its retreat south in great disarray, with the allied forces in pursuit. In rapid succession the allied forces recovered P'yŏngan, Hwanghae, and Kangwŏn Provinces, and they took back Kaesŏng city on February 19.

If the Japanese march to south was dejected, it was also cruel. Kiyomasa in particular seems to have expressed his fury by destroying what he could on the way. The *Miscellaneous Record* describes Kiyomasa's desecration of the land on his retreat from Hamgyŏng: "Everything turned to red, even waters and mountains changed." The author then comments that Kiyomasa was the cruelest of Japanese, and the desecration of land and the massacre and looting of villages that his army inflicted could not be compared to what others did.[49]

The recapture of the capital proved to be more complex. The overconfident Li Rusong lost a battle at Pyŏkchegwan, from which he barely escaped. He returned to P'yŏngyang, and refused to fight.[50] As if to compensate for this, determined Koreans won the famous victory of Haengju in which, under the leadership of General Kwŏn Yul, an army of 2,500, in cooperation with the residents of the town, defeated an army of 30,000 Japanese led by such distinguished Japanese leaders as Konishi Yukinaga, Kuroda Nagamasa, Kobayakawa Takakage, and Ukita Hideie.[51] Coming after the loss at Pyŏkchegwan, this victory, which has since become a legend producing the term *Haengju ch'ima* (Haengju skirt) for apron, so named because local women carried stones in their aprons, signaled a stalemate between contending forces. Against Korean objections, the Chinese and Japanese agreed to halt the war and negotiate a peace. The Japanese evacuated Seoul and retreated farther south.

The capital city again became the site on which the Japanese inscribed their disappointed fury. When the Japanese evacuated the capital on May 18, 1593, they chose to decimate its people and to devastate the built city. A number of documents describe the brutal manner in which they left the city. Tajiri Akitane in *Korea Diary* describes the mayhem: the Japanese "killed all the Chinamen [Tōjin] to a man who were found in the capital and burned all the houses outside the [Japanese] fortifications."[52] The *Miscellaneous Record* simply says that "the enemy secretly ordered that all the residents be killed, and so all those who had not yet fled were killed."[53] The *Revised Veritable Records of Sŏnjo* offers a fuller description: "The enemy massacred the residents of the capital. Yukinaga was furious over his defeat at P'yŏngyang. Suspecting that our people were in secret communication with the Chinese, he killed every male in the city. Because women were not killed, some men disguised themselves as women and thus escaped death. They set fire to all the public building and private houses."[54]

When Li Rusong and Song Yingchang entered the city, they were horrified at the sight that greeted them: streets filled with dead humans and horses and survivors so starved and emaciated that they looked like ghosts. They ordered that the bodies be burned that very evening.[55] It is noteworthy that the chief perpetrator of the massacre was Yukinaga, the strongest proponent of peace talks. Could it be that he destroyed the city to gain an advantage in peace talks with the Ming? It is impossible to know. What is clear is that he was leaving behind a city that he had hoped to remake in the image of a Japanese city inhabited by a people speaking Japanese and wearing Japanese hairdos. The severity of the brutality may have been correlated to the acuteness of his disappointment.

When the Chosŏn court returned to the capital on October 24, 1593, one of Sŏnjo's first decrees was to purge the residents of Seoul of the Japanese language. The day after he returned to the capital, the king issued an order: "The residents of the capital have been under enemy occupation for a long time, and so some of them might have been infiltrated by Japanese language. Put up special posters strictly forbidding its use. If there are people who use Japanese, place strict restrictions [on their movements] within their respective neighborhoods so that no trace of the enemy's barbarian language is mixed into ordinary use."[56] To be decontaminated of the Japanese language was a first step toward regaining Korean identity.

The dispatch of the Chinese Army and its campaigns on the Korean peninsula further complicated the war of words initiated by the Japanese invasion. As an ally, the Chinese had an even more complicated communicative relationship with Koreans. A much larger radius of written communication was constructed with more points of contact between the two countries, and these points of contact changed with the arrival of the Chinese Army toward the end of January 1593.

Before the arrival of the Chinese Army, communication between China and Korea was still shaped by the ritualistic rhetoric of tributary relations. This was evident in a long series of exchanges of messengers and missives through which Korea and China negotiated the arrival of the Chinese troops. While the negotiation was not without tension, it was carried out in the language of mutual concern. After the arrival of the Chinese troops, however, the unequal relationship, evinced by Korean status as a Ming tributary state, was further accentuated by a situation in which Korea, as a recipient of Ming military assistance, was placed subordinate to the Ming in all matters related to war. Moreover a number of elements, such as rumors, suspicions of each other, their own internal dissensions, the separate pursuit of national interests, and most especially different positions on war and peace, affected them differently.

Chosŏn Koreans felt deeply discomfited at having to rely on the Ming. To begin with, they were apprehensive about the prospect of having a Chinese army on their soil, something that had not happened for almost a thousand years. Allied Silla-Tang troops conquered Koguryŏ in 668, but

4

LANGUAGE STRATEGY

The Emergence of a Vernacular National Space

the Tang attempted to stay and Silla went to war to expel the Tang Army from the peninsula in 676.[1] Though initially the Ming entertained suspicions that Chosŏn might have colluded with Japan in a campaign against China, they were promptly disabused of the notion. However, Ming was simultaneously engaged in a large-scale military pacification of the Mongol mutiny at Ningxia[2] and, as a first step, dispatched to Korea in late July the Liaodong Army of three thousand led by Zu Chengxun (fl. 1570–1600), along with weapons and 20,000 *liang* of silver.[3] The Korean Army joined the Liaodong Army in its attack on P'yŏngyang, but the allied forces were decimated by Konishi Yukinaga. Zu and the Koreans made charges and countercharges blaming each other for the defeat.[4] The Korean government dispatched a round of envoys to the commander of the Liaodong Army to defend itself. It was a particularly disheartening turn of events for the Korean court. Not only did the prospect of the recapture of P'yŏngyang seem more remote than ever, the court also became greatly concerned that this unfortunate initial foray might adversely influence the Chinese government's decision on whether to participate in the war.[5] On the contrary, Zu's defeat seems to have been a wake-up call for the Chinese government, which came to see the Japanese as a genuine threat to China's national security. The Wanli emperor decided on a massive expedition. He appointed Song Yingchang (1530–1606) military commissioner of Jizhen, Baoding, and Liaodong and ordered him to commence with full-scale preparations for the war.[6]

Chinese Communiqués

Wanli also sent the envoy Xie Fan to the Korean government. On October 6, 1592, Xie arrived with the following imperial edict promising a large army:

> The Emperor decrees to the king of Chosŏn as follows. Your country has for generations guarded the eastern periphery and served [us] with consummate propriety. Rituals and decorum, culture, and economy have prospered and so it was called a paradise [*naktʻo*]. We learned recently that Dwarf Slaves (*Waeno*)

have consolidated and invaded [your country]. They assaulted and captured the capital and attacked and occupied P'yŏngyang. The people are in chaos and misery; disorder prevails far and wide; the king has taken refuge on the western sea coast and is reduced to holding court in the wilderness. When we think that national territory has been taken away from you, and you are plunged into confusion, our heart is also deeply saddened. We have heard the urgent news and have already decreed to the officials in charge of outlying areas to assemble troops and to carry out a rescue mission.

We are sending the official Xie Fan to bring our special message to the king. You have been entrusted with a dynastic mission of fundamental importance that has been transmitted through many generations of your royal ancestors. How can you lightly discard it in one morning? You must wash away your humiliation, expel the evil enemy, and devotedly work at restoration.

We are also addressing our message to the officials and the people of your country. With a firm resolve to avenge your king, rise up with the righteous rage of revenge.

We have appointed two officials, one civilian and one military, with the sole task of facilitating this. We have ordered them to lead a well-trained army of 100,000 selected from garrisons of Liaoyang, to go and help vanquish the evil enemy. Make sure that the foot soldiers and cavalry of your country join forces with them before and behind, and cooperate to trounce the bloodthirsty savages, exterminating them to the last man.

In receipt of Heaven's brilliant mandate, we preside as the ruler of the Brilliant Center (*Chunghwa*)[7] as well as the barbarians of the north and south. Every country is at peace, and the four seas are in order. How dare that this ignorant people of small and ugly (*soch'u*) stature disturb the world! We will send imperial decrees to the garrisons on the southeastern coast. We will also encourage other countries such as Ryukyu and Siam to join [our endeavors], and to assemble an army of several hundred thousand. Together, our allied forces will make a punitive expedition (*zheng*) to Japan, directly attack the enemy's central command, and behead the chief of that evil rebellious mob. We will endeavor thus so that the storm will subside. We will not spare generous rewards to those who accomplish [meritorious deeds].

To restore the dynasty of one's ancestors is great filiality and to rescue the ruler-father from troubles is great loyalty. The ruler and the ministers of your country are well versed in propriety and righteousness. If, in consideration of my wishes, you were to recapture your ancestral land, let the ruler return to the capital, preserve the altars of the state, and guard [your corner] of the periphery; may our sympathy for your distant land and our care for that small country comfort you.[8]

The *Veritable Records* describes an emotional scene of the delivery of this edict: upon hearing this, Sŏnjo burst into a wail, joined by all the officials present. The imperial messenger was also moved.[9] Evidently the news was balm to Sŏnjo and his officials.

Unlike the Japanese infiltration into the communicative space of domestic literary Chinese, over which the Korean government had no control, the Korean court was able to mediate Chinese missives to the Korean people to a great extent. Xie Fan urged Sŏnjo to quickly disseminate the imperial edict to the whole country.[10] Sŏnjo needed no prompting. It does not appear that he, a practitioner of ruler-father rhetoric himself, found any objection to Wanli's universal claim. What mattered was Wanli's promise of a large force. He seems to have felt that Wanli's message not only reassured Koreans but also buttressed royal authority, which had plummeted very low. On October 8 Sŏnjo ordered that the Wanli emperor's edict be distributed to the whole country. What is interesting is that he also ordered it translated into Korean and disseminated throughout Hamgyŏng Province.[11] As far as I can tell, this was the only missive by a ruler of a foreign country that was translated into Korean under royal auspices. Sŏnjo must have felt that the wider dissemination of the edict enhanced his own image. I will discuss the sending out of public missives in Korean script later.

Xie Fan also dispatched his findings in Korea to the Ministry of War in Beijing. It is noteworthy that, whereas Wanli's edict was couched in the rhetoric of the universal ruler's benevolence and sympathy to the ruler and the people of a faithful tributary state, and the dispatch of the Chinese troops was promised as the universal ruler's duty to pacify all within the four seas, Xie's report, which urged the speedy dispatch of troops, is written with the logic of national security for China:

> What we have to be attentive to is that the current state is not with Chosŏn but with the problem of our borders. The point that worries me deeply is that this question does not end with borders, and that they might shake us even into our interior. Liaodong is like the arms of our capital, and Chosŏn is like Liaodong's fence. Yingping is the crucial area for the Imperial Court and Tianjin is the gate to the capital. Is it not true that for two hundred years, while Fujian and Zhejiang were constantly harried by Japanese pirates, these problems had not reached Liaoyang and Tianjin because Chosŏn protected them as a barrier? . . .
>
> If we campaign soon, we will be able to rely on the help [of Koreans]. If we do it late, the Japanese thieves, commanding Koreans, will confront us. Thus it is my opinion that we cannot delay the mobilization of our troops and vanquishing this enemy for even one day. . . . I sincerely hope that Your Majesty makes an astute decision and promptly orders the concerned ministry that soldiers and horses be dispatched as soon as possible so that it will bring fortune to our borders and the Imperial Altars.[12]

During his visit Xie Fan said that the Ming army would arrive within about a month.[13] Soon after Zu Chengxun's defeat, China had begun serious preparations for an expedition army, calling up officers and soldiers, apportioning 200,000 *liang* of silver, and accelerating the production of military weapons and supplies, including transport carts, large and small cannon, crossbows, bullets, and other miscellaneous arms and supplies,[14] but it took time to assemble a major expeditionary army. Meanwhile Katō Kiyomasa made forays into Manchuria.

The Wait

To stall the Japanese from taking further steps, the Chinese adopted a two-pronged strategy: to prepare for war but also to engage in peace talks. Minister of War Shi Xing (1538–1597) sent an envoy, Shen Weijing, to negotiate a peace with the Japanese general, Konishi Yukinaga. Both Shi and Yukinaga seem to have believed that peace negotiations were far superior to fighting, and, although to different degrees, they were willing to engage in deception of their respective governments to achieve this desired goal. At their initial meeting Shen Weijing and Yukinaga agreed to a fifty-day cease-fire.

The Korean government was deeply anxious over the evolving situation. The cold weather began, but the Chinese Army still had not come. On December 18, when, instead of the eagerly awaited Chinese Army, Song Yingchang sent an exhortation to the Korean king in which he reiterated the Chinese promise of a dispatch of troops, without mentioning any date, and rhetorically encouraged the king to gather the Korean forces so that when the Chinese forces arrived they could join forces "to cleanse the stench of blood, and to accomplish great deeds which would render the magical powers of Our Emperor visible, and to preserve the old territory of Kija,"[15] officials responded in a number of ways.[16] The Censorate memorialized the king declaring that it was impractical to idly wait for a Chinese force whose "real intention is unfathomable," and that rather than losing the winter, which, in view of the Japanese weakness to cold weather, would be the best time to wage battle against them, the Korean Army should attack on its own.[17]

Yun Kŭnsu, serving as minister of rites, sent another letter to Song Yingchang stressing that since the ice was already firm, it was urgent that they attack the enemy without delay. It is noteworthy that this letter shifts in logic from emphasizing the imperiled state of Korea to stressing the potential threat the ruin of Korea posed for China.

Yun pointed out that Korea was invaded because it refused a Japanese suggestion that it join Japan in invading China, and that the enemy's real intention was to attack Liaodong. The letter chastised China for interrupting their plans of war with futile peace negotiations. Yun then says: "If China really wishes to come to Korea with an army to save her, it should do so before the Japanese Army marches again, and before the Korean Army is completely decimated. Only by joining our forces can we succeed in our objective. If Korea were to be devastated and China had to face the enemy alone, it would require an effort a hundredfold greater. Our plea is not for the sake of Chosŏn alone but in consideration of China as well."[18] Sŏnjo declared that he was going to go to Liaodong to see Song in person to ask for the assistance of the army. This did not happen, and an official was sent instead.[19]

At the second round of peace negotiations between Japan and China in late December, each side's proposed terms were unacceptable to the other. One of the terms that the Japanese proposed was the division of Korean territory between them, with Japan possessing the east of Taedong River (territory south of P'yŏngyang) and China acquiring the northern territory (beginning with P'yŏngyang).[20] The Korean government had also been approached by Yukinaga for peace talks but found no base level to begin serious talks.[21] Greatly alarmed by the Japanese proposal of territorial division, the Korean government asked the Ming court to clarify its position on the matter. In response, on January 19, 1593, Song Yingchang sent a letter assuring Sŏnjo:

> Chosŏn has been China's external periphery in the Eastern Sea and has been sincere in its loyalty and fidelity. It has faithfully carried out the duties of a tributary state. When it was invaded and occupied by the Japanese thieves and could not preserve its territory, it has repeatedly dispatched official envoys asking for our help. In sympathy for the king in his plight, our sagacious emperor ordered this command to go to out with an army and vanquish [the enemy]. Just now, our huge army is about to cross the river to attack and recapture P'yŏngyang and the royal capital. These Japanese thieves are cunning, and they are scheming to play us against each other. For example, when Shen Weijing

went to their camp, they loudly shouted such things as "We will give P'yŏngyang to China, and not to Chosŏn." P'yŏngyang is Chosŏn territory. How could China take advantage of the crisis of another country to seize its land while rescuing the very same country? There certainly is no logic to this. I am sending this letter lest the king, at this time when the royal court is in refuge far away from the capital, might suspect us upon hearing such scheming words.

Please rest assured. Govern your country well, accumulate military provisions, assemble soldiers and, with the help of the Chinese Army, recapture your land. If P'yŏngyang is recaptured, then protect it with the army of your own country. If your army is found to be too meager to protect the city, and if you ask for help, we will cooperate with you temporarily, but when order is restored, all personnel and soldiers under this command will immediately evacuate the area. China will display the graciousness of raising up the country which is on the brink of ruin; our command will attempt to carry out the tasks that will preserve benevolence and straighten out righteousness. Please be assured, and do not be swayed by rumor.[22]

Here was a change in Song's rhetorical stance. He still adhered to the rhetoric of imperial benevolence, but he embedded his denial of China's ambitions for Korean territory and its desire to rescue Korea in the logic that Korea was China's outlier external periphery and thus Korea was China's national security concern, and that Korea's status as China's faithful tributary was of primary importance. In other words, he did not avoid implicitly acknowledging the self-interest of China, confirming mutual benefit as the basic premise of tributary relations.

Complexities of Dealing with the Chinese

With the arrival of the Chinese Army, a more complicated communicative relationship appeared. In addition to such points of contact as the Wanli emperor, Minister of War Shi Xing in Beijing, and Song

Yingchang, who stayed mostly in Liaodong, the on-site Chinese contingent consisting of Supreme Commander Li Rusong and other generals and officials stationed in Korea emerged as an important nexus of communications. True, though some Chinese written communiqués still addressed their messages to Koreans at large, unlike Japanese missives, they were neither solely addressed nor directly sent to them, enabling the Korean government to act as mediator. Thus it was their dealings with Chinese authorities in China and Korea that required the attention of the Chosŏn court.

That the Chinese came as an ally to help Korea expel the Japanese did not erase their cultural difference. It was a difficult situation for both parties, and it seems to have been particularly trying for Sŏnjo and his officials. The ceremonial decorum that had marked the exchanges between the two countries at a distance was replaced by disagreements and conflicts in day-to-day dealings with each other. As is often the case with people representing a stronger country aiding a weaker one, the Chinese often exercised their prerogatives. Sometimes this was provoked by what appeared to be remiss behavior on the part of Koreans. Supreme Commander Li Rusong, when greeted by Sŏnjo on his arrival on January 27, seems to have behaved with decorum. The Korean king expressed gratitude, and the Chinese general responded by declaring that he would not cease his efforts until he had driven the last Japanese from Pusan and assuring the king of imminent victory over the evil enemy.[23]

From the very next day, though, problems appeared. Enraged that food provisions for soldiers and fodder for horses were inadequately distributed, Li came close to hitting the Korean official in charge. Sŏnjo sent a royal secretary to Li to display concern, punished the responsible officials, and instructed that provisions be delivered without fail.[24] Supplying food provisions to troops required complicated logistics, and this problem would remain one of the main concerns of the Korean government. The cost of provisions for the Chinese Army was borne by the Chinese government, but it was Koreans who were responsible for transporting them and, very often, securing grain, an enormously difficult task.[25] We have seen that one of the reasons for the Japanese retreat was that supply lines for food were cut.

There are numerous anecdotes describing Li's imperious manner. He demanded whatever struck his fancy, including the Korean king's horse.[26] He casually castigated Korean ministers of state. For example, several days after the allied army recaptured P'yŏngyang on February 8, 1593, Li sent an official letter addressed to Koreans entitled, "To the Korean court: proclamations (*p'aemun*) to the officials and people of Chosŏn":

> We have come here from distant lands crossing ocean and mountain in order to save the endangered and the weakened. The head ministers of Chosŏn, Yu Sŏngnyong and Yun Tusu, have behaved entirely laxly. Instead of exerting themselves to wash away shame and exterminate the enemy, they have been feasting, and sitting comfortably in their rooms, drinking and enjoying themselves. This is not only a slight to the court of Heaven (*ch'ŏnjo*); it also invites ruin to their own country. Their discourtesy and bad manners are truly extreme.... Since we are truthful and generous, we will not find fault with small things. We will act according to discipline and lofty principle. We will station troops at P'yŏngyang, decide on military strategy, and, at an opportune moment, achieve victory to bring peace to your home and your country. After national affairs become orderly and the people are safe, we will send an imperial promulgation. Hereby I am sending this letter. Our hope is that officials of the Chosŏn state, high and low, will let all hear of this, and that high ministers shall come to our headquarters at once and try to put our policies into practice. Anyone who neglects or betrays our order will be punished by the heaviest of punishments.[27]

Li ended with a warning against Yun and Yu: "If they should be idle again, I will impeach them, and apply the law choosing the heaviest penalty. I certainly will not tolerate it." Yun Tusu had to go to apologize in person.[28] It is difficult to assess the basis of Li's criticism. Li was well-known for his arrogant manner toward civil officials of his own country, sometimes even slapping them.[29] The cultural difference might have abetted his anger. Nor is it easy to assess how widely

Li's letter was disseminated among Koreans. The letter is recorded in a number of works compiled by private scholars, including *The Trivial Matters*,[30] which suggests that even if the letter was not circulated right after it was written, it came to be known among officials and scholars.

If Li was behaving arrogantly, some of the generals under him seemed to have behaved with even less restraint. The entry of February 28 in the *Veritable Records of Sŏnjo* contains the report by the commander-in-chief of the Korean Army, Kim Myŏngwŏn, that Li had cautioned generals under him not to demand food and liquor from Koreans, pointing out that "Chosŏn was the country of ritual and righteousness," and had reprimanded Zu Chengxun for having beaten the magistrate of a town for failing to instantly produce liquor, which Li pronounced "unseemly behavior for a general."[31] Nor did Chinese troops display inhibitions in plundering and looting Korean property.[32]

Another difficulty for the Korean court was navigating between various Chinese camps that were in contention with one another. The Chinese were divided into complicated groupings—between hawks and doves, along regional lines, especially between southern and northern armies, and so forth. Li Rusong and Song Yingchang, for example, were fierce rivals. All imposed their will on Koreans to support their views, and Koreans were in no position to alienate any party. For instance, the Korean court was dragged into Chinese disputes regarding evaluations of merit in recapturing P'yŏngyang on February 8, 1593. This victory, won after three days of intense fighting, restored Korean hopes for their country, but it also was the occasion of intense competition for recognition among Chinese generals and soldiers.[33] The first concerned Li Rusong's performance. Several Chinese officials memorialized the Wanli emperor, saying that of the severed heads that Li Rusong produced, fully half were Korean, and that all ten thousand who died either by fire or drowning during the battle were Korean civilians, not Japanese soldiers. The Chinese court sent inspectors to P'yŏngyang and asked the Chosŏn court to make its own report. Beholden to Li Rusong, the Koreans had to defend him.[34] The second occasion involved Li's memorial in which he assessed the merits of different groups in the battle. He assigned higher credit to the northern army, asking the Korean court to second him. The Koreans are believed to have been much more impressed by the southern army, both in tactics and in bravery.[35] Yi Homin, who was commissioned with the task, however, evenly credited the northern and southern armies with merit.[36] These were but two examples of the delicate lines that Koreans had to tread between different interest groups all demanding support against other groups.

The greatest challenge facing the Koreans was their very different position from the Chinese toward war and peace. To begin with, the Koreans suspected that, unlike themselves, who were determined to expel the invaders by military means to prevent future incursions, the Chinese generals starting with Li Rusong were not as keen on fighting. Their difference was already visible during the battle for P'yŏngyang. Li was far less eager to pursue the retreating enemy than the Koreans were. He let Yukinaga's army escape, fearing that a genuine showdown would inflict far more Chinese casualties.[37] The Koreans also faulted the Ming armies for their unwillingness to fight at close quarters with the Japanese even though this was the most effective strategy, since Japanese muskets were inaccurate and less effective in close fighting.[38]

An unbridgeable rift emerged after Li Rusong lost the battle at Pyŏkchegwan, not far from Seoul. The contemporary consensus seems to have been that Li was too confident after recent victories at P'yŏngyang and Kaesŏng and approached the battle with a poorly prepared strategy and too few troops. In any case, the battle was a disaster for the allied forces, and Li barely escaped with his life. He retreated to P'yŏngyang and was reluctant to resume fighting. There seems to be consensus that the Ming defeat in the battle of Pyŏkchegwan was a turning point for the Chinese attitude toward the war. Yoshi Kuno maintains that Li "lost all hope and no longer had either military spirit or energy. He realized that the Ming army of China could not cope with the fighting power and the military spirit of the Japanese, and was convinced that China had no fighting chance against Japan."[39] Chinese sources also suggest that the defeat demoralized the Chinese Army and led to serious peace negotiations with Japan.[40] Taking advantage of this noncombative mood, the peace party, which believed that, having recovered the northern half of Korea it would be more beneficial to resolve the conflict through peace negotiations, swiftly pushed ahead with their plan.

The Chinese actively engaged in peace talks with the Japanese, without Korean participation. A completely different politics of war and peace unfolded. In China the peace policy was orchestrated by Minister of War Shi Xing in Beijing, Song Yingchang in Liaodong, and Shen Weijing as the on-site negotiator. In Japan Yukinaga headed the peace camp. The heads of both states also favored it. It appears that each one of these participants entertained his own vision of peace, which was starkly dissimilar from others. When these differences became clear, peace talks ended and the Japanese invaded Korea for a second time in 1597.

The period of peace negotiations in its own way was extremely trying for the Koreans. China and Japan were pursuing their own separate interests. The Chosŏn government was made to feel that ultimately it had to rely on its own people, whose support it needed more than ever. Its language policy was the product of an acutely felt sense of separateness from the other, first the enemy and then the ally, and a mechanism through which the government attempted to create and consolidate a sense of unity among Koreans.

The Emergence of a Korean National Vernacular Space

The Chosŏn government felt an acute need to shore up the support of its people from very early in the war. During the flight north the royal court vividly experienced popular anger. Indeed, narratives depict the Sŏnjo court's flight as at the least nightmarish. As the defense posts around Seoul fell rapidly, the royal court discussed fleeing to seek refuge in the North, but as something unprecedented in the two–hundred-year Chosŏn dynasty, it was simply too horrible to contemplate.[41] Hence the journey was taken only at the last moment, after the arrival of news of the disastrous defeat at Ch'ungju, the breakdown of the last of the capital's defense posts.[42] Leaving in haste with minimal preparation, the court seems to have been a pathetic sight: it crossed the Imjin River in torrential rain and complete darkness, the whole retinue, including the king, rain drenched and famished.[43] The entourage left Seoul on June 9, arriving at P'yŏngyang on June 13. On the following day an order was issued asking that royal table be adequately provisioned.[44]

In a monarchy, news of royal flight was always terrifying and the sight of the monarch in flight induced shock and horror. There are well-known instances of royal flight. Timothy Tackett describes the shock and confusion of the French residents of a country town when they discovered Louis XVI in flight in their midst.[45] In the case of the French king, it was the ancien régime that was endangered. With Sŏnjo, it signaled peril for the whole country and the entire population within it.

That the people were dismayed and frustrated at a government that had failed to protect them was understandable enough. What enraged them still more was the devious manner in which the government proceeded: it announced to the residents that the royal court would stay in place, then left the place surreptitiously when danger threatened. This tactic was employed in part to forestall mass flight and demoralization of troops while minimizing the risk of capture of the king. The populace, however, justifiably saw it as an ultimate government betrayal inflicted with no concern for the lives of its people, who were thus exposed to the capture by the invaders. We have already seen that in Seoul an angry populace and unruly mobs stormed the palace and burned a number of buildings.[46]

Yu Sŏngnyong describes the reaction of P'yŏngyang residents as follows. When it was rumored that the royal court was about to leave the city, the residents began to flee the city. Wanting to stop this flight by soldiers and residents in order to mount some kind of defense, Sŏnjo, accompanied by the crown prince, had to assure residents that the government would guard the city. When the Japanese Army was seen on the banks of the Taedong River, which flowed through the city, a certain portion of the royal entourage began to leave. Even women and children screamed: "If you were going to leave us behind, why did you deceive us by bringing us back within the walls to make of us food for the enemy?" Everyone is described as having some kind of weapon so that officials were frightened. Yu assured them that the government would guard the city.⁴⁷ The royal carriage left immediately afterward, while Yu and others remained to guard the city. In a few days the city fell and most officials escaped.

The *Veritable Records of Sŏnjo* also describes a riot of enraged soldiers and residents (*kunmin*) who poured into the streets. Palace servants were hit with sticks and fell to the ground, and Hong Yŏsun (1547–1609), the minister of taxation, was hurt. The queen's entourage was prevented from leaving the city. Only when the governor had several rioters beheaded did the crowd disperse.⁴⁸ It should be noted that only nine days previously the king had gone to a city gate and declared to a crowd who congregated there that the government would defend the city to the death.⁴⁹ Then, on the day of his departure, Sŏnjo met with the elders of the city and, without telling them of his imminent departure, "consoled and instructed" them. The *Veritable Records of Sŏnjo* says that the royal letter was read to them and that in consequence "all those present wept; the elders at once burst out wailing at full throat, and the whole city wept aloud."⁵⁰ This is the meeting, according to Yu, in which the king assured the residents that the government would guard the city, but the *Veritable Records of Sŏnjo* is silent on what Sŏnjo said or what the contents of his edicts were.

Sŏnjo and his officials were also having the worst of times. Sŏnjo seems to have been particularly affected. He had ascended the throne in 1567 at the age of sixteen, and for twenty-five years he ruled without particular mishap. In 1583 and 1587 Korea was even able to pacify disturbances by various tribes in the northeast border region. Sŏnjo seldom left his palace except for ritualistic outings, and he lived in a world of Confucian decorum and order. There was nothing in his reign or the history of his dynasty to suggest that he would not live out his life in an environment of peace as his royal ancestors had for two hundred years.

The record indicates that throughout the flight north, he was in a state of trauma. Particularly sharp was a sense of regret caused by equal measures of shame that he had failed his people and grief that he had been abandoned by them. When, in his edict dated June 4, after his acknowledgment that "this terrible state has all been caused by my mistake. I have no one but myself to blame and I feel nothing but shame," he cries out, "All you scholars! For generations, your grandfathers and your fathers before you, and you have been in the good graces of the state. Yet, the moment you face a crisis, you all forsake me. Though I do not fault you, you cannot possibly behave thus to me."[51] He does seem to have fallen into a state of plaintive despair.

The urgency of restoring popular good will was clear to the king and his officials. The king began to deploy royal missives, directly addressing the people with unusual frequency. He addressed his letters to all Koreans, to the people of specific provinces, to groups of provinces, and even to specific persons. Interestingly, though the *Veritable Records of Sŏnjo* mentions that these letters were sent, their contents are seldom recorded, such was the state of disarray in administrative function during the war. Some of the edicts as they were received are included in writings by private persons. Their tone of contrition and pleading intensifies with each reiteration.

In a letter to the scholars and the commoners (*samin*) of Chŏlla Province, Sŏnjo professes, "If I could, I would use my body as a sacrifice to apologize to the ancestral spirits and all the spirits between Heaven and Earth. My remorse is so acute. I ask scholars and commoners to allow me the chance to correct my mistakes and to search for new rule."[52] To the people of Kyŏngsang Province, he portrayed a vision of peaceful life that all of them could return to if only they were to redouble their efforts to vanquish the enemy and earn brilliant names for posterity.[53] To several leaders of the volunteer army, he praised their bravery and loyalty and presented himself as a man of sentiment who feels lonely and homesick, as anyone would in his situation, languishing as he was in a distant border region.[54]

While these edicts were clearly meant to reach as broad an audience as possible, they were written in classical Chinese and hence their accessibility to the nonelite population was questionable. True, they were often read aloud, and read in Korean pronunciation, but this secondhand access was not a comforting affair since he desired direct communication. If it were to be truly inclusive, a letter had to be written and sent out in Korean. This was, however, a leap into unimagined and untried territory. No official had ever broached the possibility. It was Sŏnjo who seized on it, and his officials, making no objections, complied.

SŎNJO'S LEAP: HAILING THE PEOPLE IN KOREAN

In the entry of the first of the eighth month (September 6), the *Veritable Records* says that the king pointed out that his letter to the people of Hwanghae Province has been written but that only scholars would understand it, and so volunteer army leaders and magistrates should see to it that "the letter gets translated into Korean script so that even people in rustic villages will be able to comprehend it."[55] This was done at arguably the worst moment for the Chosŏn, right after the Liaodong Army led by Zu Chengxun was defeated at P'yŏngyang.[56] As I noted, the court grew alarmed that this unfortunate initial encounter might adversely influence the Chinese central government's decision to participate any further in the war. Enemy troops were seen in the vicinity, and there was a real danger of capture. Confined to Ŭiju, the northwestern corner of Korea, the court, however, had no place to escape to.

Sŏnjo seems to have again been seized by terror. He reintroduced the possibility of leaving Korea and taking refuge in the Liaodong region of China, which he had discussed earlier. During the court's flight north from P'yŏngyang, he had declared that he would cross the Yalu into Liaodong and ordered that a formal request for permission to enter be sent to the governor of the province.[57] No sooner did the court arrive at Ŭiju than he instructed a messenger to issue a dispatch announcing his arrival in Liaodong.[58] In preparation for his departure, he transferred to his son the duties of the state and the royal house— governance and responsibility for the ancestral tablets.[59]

What he could not transfer was his symbolic role. He represented final authority in Korea, and his flight would jeopardize Korea's survival. Officials were aghast at the proposal and objected unequivocally and relentlessly—"the unconscionable act of deserting the people under his care, an act that would turn him into a cowardly little man (*p'ilbu*),"⁶⁰ as they termed it. Coupled with the information that his entourage would be received with scorn and shabby treatment in Liaodong, this caused the king to decide to stay on at Ŭiju.⁶¹ When Sŏnjo revived the possibility on several occasions in early September, his officials rebuffed him with even stronger warnings and sharper criticism: "He must not only not voice it but completely eradicate it from his mind as a possibility" (Chŏng Ch'ŏl, governor general of the three southern provinces); "once he crosses the Yalu, any hope for a restoration of the country would forever be extinguished" (Yun Tusu, minister of the left); "once he leaves for the Liaodong, he would become a cowardly little man" and "if the royal carriage were to cross the Yalu, all will end" (Sin Chap, royal secretary).⁶²

The moment of decision came: was he to remain king and do what was necessary to resist the enemy, and thus to regain his authority, or was he to run away to Liaodong and become a "cowardly little man"? Northward across the Yalu lay Liaodong; southward was the wartorn land of Korea. It appears that he gazed at the North one last time but finally accepted his destiny as the king with all it entailed. Sŏnjo would from this time on act with unflinching leadership and resolution. He must have felt he needed to reach all his people, every Korean, to make them understand his true feelings and to ask them to fight the enemy and rebuild Korea with him. And for this he had to use Korean script to ensure true inclusiveness. This is when he made a radical move: he ordered that his edict be translated into Korean and disseminated in that script among the ordinary people. It was as if Sŏnjo's kingship was reborn in Korean script. Within weeks Sŏnjo reconfirmed the use of the Korean script as a medium of addressing the people.⁶³ Korean script publicly entered the inscriptional space.

For a while Korean script was used to produce translated versions of literary Chinese missives and was deployed in a diglossic context. This symbolized the script's inclusivity of Koreans. There was of course another property of the script—its exclusivity to the other, that it was inaccessible to non-Koreans, or the perception thereof. Exploiting this special quality necessitated that the script be used alone, without any literary Chinese accompaniment accessible to the other.

The Korean government's independent use of the Korean script came during the period of peace negotiations, when the war entered into a quasi-truce.

The Peace Talks

The politics of the peace talks were enormously complicated. It was not just that each of the three countries pursued different objectives and were thus at cross purposes to one another. What was remarkable was that the representatives of Japan and China, the two countries negotiating the terms of peace, were willing to mislead and deceive not merely each other but also their respective central authorities. To conclude peace talks, they orchestrated elaborate schemes toward their own governments using miscommunication, falsification of documents, and outright deception.

There are scholarly treatments of the details of the various phases of peace talks that lasted three and a half years, though in spurts, and the extraordinarily complicated inter- and intra- national negotiations and maneuverings that contain some of the most baroque instances of treachery and sabotage.[64] I do not intend to repeat them here. Suffice it to say that the ineffective control of the diplomatic front by central authorities in both China and Japan was vividly illustrated by the fact that the peace negotiations irrevocably collapsed not when the two parties realized that they could not agree on terms of peace but when the terms of peace as they were dictated by the Ming central government could no longer be concealed from the Japanese authorities.

It is amazing how close the doves in both parties came to deceiving their governments. The Wanli emperor's investiture ceremony for Hideyoshi as king of Japan, for instance, held on October 22, 1596, at Osaka Castle, proceeded peacefully, as its recipient did not suspect that he was being invested as the king of Japan. On October 25, just as the Ming envoys were about to depart, Hideyoshi asked the Buddhist monk Seishō Shōtai (1548–1607) to translate Wanli's edict of investiture. Only then did he learn that there had been no concessions on any of the seven conditions whose fulfillment he required and which he had been led to expect were being honored—including Korean territorial concessions and the hand of a Ming imperial princess in marriage—and that instead he was being invested as "the king of Japan." He flew into a rage and immediately broke off the talks, foreswearing further negotiations.[65]

It is difficult to believe that Hideyoshi was completely duped by the peace negotiators. It is commonly assumed that, having realized the futility of the invasion, Hideyoshi sought a way out of the predicament in some face-saving manner, but that in the end he could not accept the terms offered to him.[66] Ronald P. Toby and Kenneth R. Robinson showed instances of diplomatic negotiations between East Asian states in which various parties were engaged in knowing acquiescence to deliberate deception as a means of concluding talks without challenging the face-saving measures of the other party.[67]

In what Ray Huang has termed "one of the greatest diplomatic blunders of all time,"[68] the Chinese central government was deceived a little longer. Seeing the wisdom of controlling Japan through diplomacy, the Wanli emperor had set the terms of peace on three conditions: first, the withdrawal of Japanese troops from Korea and even Tsushima; second, Hideyoshi's acceptance of investiture as king of Japan without demanding the restoration of trade, the usual privilege granted to a tributary state; and third, a pledge that Japan would not invade Korea again. The document detailing these conditions was relayed to Konishi Joan, an envoy sent by Yukinaga, when he arrived in Beijing in January 1596. Joan behaved completely in accordance with what would have been expected of the envoy of a country seeking to enter a tributary relationship with the Great Ming Empire.[69]

Thus when the Ming sent envoys with the paraphernalia of investiture for Hideyoshi, it had been led to believe that Hideyoshi would be content to receive such investiture and ratify the peace. Even after the fiasco at Osaka Castle, the Ming envoys continued in their deception. Upon their arrival in Seoul they presented a false report to the Korean king and later to the Chinese emperor that Hideyoshi had accepted the Ming investiture, and they presented supposed gifts from

Hideyoshi that they themselves had procured. Their deception was soon uncovered. The representatives of the peace party were punished; Shi Xing was imprisoned and died in prison, probably under torture;[70] and Shen Weijing was executed.[71]

If the details of the Japan-China peace negotiation sound bizarre and outlandish, we can also view it in the larger context of conflicting worldviews—China was operating from the Sinocentric view that its proper mode of relating to the world was tributary relations, while Hideyoshi, unversed in the intricacies of the diplomacy of this Sinocentric world, was advancing an alternative new vision of the world based on power. As such, as Swope states, the talks were "doomed from the start."[72] The war resumed in August 1597 and ended by late December 1598.

Heightened Awareness of Self-Reliance for Korea

The years of peace talks were a trying time for the Korean government. Despite the fact that the stakes were highest for Korea, the government was excluded from the decision-making process. Sŏnjo was adamantly opposed to peace negotiations, and in the first half of 1593 he thrice conferred with the Chinese personnel in charge of Korean affairs—twice with General Li Rusong and once with Vice Minister of War and Chief of Policy for Korea Song Yingchang—in unsuccessful attempts to argue against peace negotiations with Japan.[73] Both Japan and China believed it advantageous for them to conclude the war without further fighting. Agreeing to a mutual withdrawal from Korea, the Japanese Army evacuated Seoul in late May 1593 and withdrew to the coastal region, although it attacked and occupied Chinju in Kyŏngsang Province on the way.

Left out of the negotiations for the most part, Korea had to be vigilant against two possible outcomes. One was the resumption of mass-scale fighting without the benefit of Chinese troops. Thus the Korean government expressed great concern with the timing of the withdrawal of troops. The Chinese troops departed from Korea in September 1593, leaving behind a force of sixteen thousand, which also left in the February 1594, whereas the Japanese Army evacuated, though not completely, only in the middle of 1595.[74]

Even more worrisome was the possibility that a peace might be ratified making territorial concessions of the southern provinces of Korea to Japan. Caught between differing Chinese factions and constantly shifting policies and yet dependent on China, the Korean government had to endure intimidating tactics from various Chinese officials. Intent on executing his peace plans and fearing that Sŏnjo might pose an obstacle to his tactics of deception, Song Yingchang, for example, prohibited all direct diplomatic contact between the Chosŏn and Ming governments. Only when he was recalled upon the discovery of his deceitful schemes was a direct channel between the two governments reestablished. Time and time again the *Veritable Records of Sŏnjo* mentions growing convictions on the part of Koreans about the unwillingness of the Chinese to fight for Korea and about Japanese territorial ambitions.[75] While this assessment led to different strategic formulations—the Sŏin faction proposed fighting by relying on the Korean Army while the Namin faction stressed the tactical necessity of peace negotiation as a way of buying time while strengthening the army—all seem to have been made aware of the importance of self-reliance.[76]

A New Linguistic Typology: Parity of Chinese and Korean Script

It appears that during this period royal edicts and official missives written in Korean script alone, not as translated versions of ones in literary Chinese, were sent out and distributed. One such missive dated the ninth month of 1593 survives. The text says:

> The King duly instructs the people. After you were captured by the Japanese army, you have been following them contrary to your will. Because you are afraid that you might be killed by them if you were to be caught escaping, and are also afraid that since you have joined the Japanese, you might be killed by our

government, you are not leaving the enemy camp. Do not harbor such suspicions. Persuade each other and return. Not only will you not be punished, but anyone who renders meritorious service—who returns with captured Japanese personnel, who offers detailed information about enemy operations, or returns with many captured people or any other worthy task—will be rewarded with an official post appropriate to their status. I urge you to banish your suspicions and to return at once. We have instructed every general and commandant of this order. Have no fear and come back all.

There is no one among you who does not have a parent, a wife, or children. Wouldn't it be wonderful to return to your old village and to resume your old life? If you do not return now you will be killed by the Japanese. How you will regret it after peace and order are restored. The Chinese Army has been rejuvenated; Pyŏngan Province is filled with them and they are also everywhere in Kyŏngsang and Chŏlla Provinces. The Japanese have hastened in retreat to their land, our joint army with the Chinese will vanquish them in Pusan and Tongnae; the Chinese Navy and the navy of our country will enter the sea side by side and will destroy and burn each and every enemy ship. If you linger there among the Japanese, you will not avoid getting killed. Come quickly before that happens.[77]

Ninth month, Wanli 21st year (1593)

The *Veritable Records of Sŏnjo* records in the entry of October 3 Sŏnjo's order to send out what must be this edict:

Among our people who reside in the Pusan area, many have surrendered to and joined the Japanese army. There must be those who wish to return but hesitate because they are afraid of punishment. We should put up posters for these people assuring them that if they leave the enemy camp not only will they be spared of death they will also be exempted from corvée labor for the remainder of their lives and they may even be rewarded with official posts. Let the Agency for Border Affairs (Pibyŏnsa) take care of this matter.⁷⁸

It is noteworthy that the *Veritable Records of Sŏnjo* neither records the contents of the edict nor specifies which language it was promulgated in. We know that it was circulated in the Korean version because a copy survives. I hazard a guess that this was written and circulated only in Korean because of its content and its intended recipients. The Korean script was deployed here as a self-conscious tool of communication among Koreans, intending to exclude others. This was done when multidirectional communiqués among the three countries were at their most active. The edict above displays linguistic exclusivity among Koreans accompanied by an appeal to a shared past evoked in the phrase "to return to your old village and resume your old life." Unlike the bright future that outsiders might have flaunted, this shared past belonged only to insiders. In conjuring up a shared past, it also reminds the receiver of a shared destiny. Thus the exclusivity of the script also signified an exclusivity of shared history and destiny.

With the autonomous appearance of Korean script untethered to any Chinese text in the public space, linguistic typology changed. Literary Chinese and vernacular Korean, which had been in strict hierarchy, were now seen as complementary. The use of the Korean script was not at the expense or exclusion of literary Chinese. Rather the two languages were deployed strategically, almost with equal value, their use determined only by circumstance.

The royal edicts of this period display this new parity quite clearly. These edicts were written in several modes: some were written in literary Chinese, translated into Korean and transmitted in both languages; others were written exclusively in one language, either Korean or Chinese. The key question to consider is whether a particular edict was written in one language and translated into another or written solely in one language. In the case of the former, the original version seems to have functioned as a principal or more visible version. Each language seems to have reinforced the role of the other in delineating and strengthening the notion of ethnic exclusivity. It was almost as if not only the Korean script was nationalized but literary Chinese was as well. Edicts of all categories, in the affective language of a ruler-father, increasingly evoked the vision of the Korea's peaceful and unsullied existence before the war and appealed for the people's active cooperation in reconstructing their country.

The Language of Affect

Nowhere was the rhetoric of national affect more vividly displayed than in Sŏnjo's "edict of heartfelt pain" (*aet'ongsŏ*) sent out in mid-February 1599 soon after the war ended. The edict begins with the terrible trial of the war and the heavy burden of taxation on the people that resulted from its expenses: "The smallest thing had to be provided by no one but the people, pushing them into the abyss of poverty." It elaborates on the depth of royal sympathy for the plight of the people. Then it shifts to the somber tasks that awaited them. Now that Hideyoshi had died, the disaster of war had passed, but Sŏnjo pointed out the enfeebled state to which the country had been brought: "When I think of what lays ahead it hardly looks different from the dangers we endured. The situation is comparable to a person who passed [the crisis of] a great illness but is so sapped of energy that it takes extreme caution to administer acupuncture or medicine, and to a big tree that, though alive, has been shaken to its roots and loosed from its foundation so that it would take a great effort to make is stand again."

After this display of sympathy and concern for their plight, the king goes on to ask for cooperation in rebuilding the country:

> The people are a lovable yet fearful entity; if not for you on whom can my state rely? . . . My heart aches with pain [at the thought of your plight]. I believe the government's tasks are to reduce what can be reduced and eliminate what can be eliminated of taxes and levies carefully considering what is more urgent and what is not; to mourn the dead and to comfort the living; and to induce the dispersed population to return home and to be together again. This is the beginning of reconstruction, and it will signal a new start. I request that everyone in this

country endeavor to make our rivers and lands (*kangt'o*) beautiful again and to regain our easy and peaceful way of life.⁷⁹

Like many edicts disseminated during the war, this one was recorded in the *Miscellaneous Record* but not in the *Veritable Records of Sŏnjo*. We do not know in which script it was circulated. By this time it does not seem to have mattered. The Korean script, as did literary Chinese, functioned either solely or as the translated half of a principal message in the public sphere. What mattered was that both scripts were deployed to evoke a vision of the ethnic community of the Chosŏn.

THE POSTWAR INSCRIPTIONAL SPACE

For the duration of the war, the government actively explored and utilized various aspects of the vernacular for its qualities—it was the "national" script, exclusive of the other, inclusive of Koreans. It is not that vernacular writing dominated the inscriptional space or that the activity of vernacular writing was conspicuously shifted to the inscriptional space. Even during the war, literary Chinese continued to be used in the inscriptional space, and the vernacular was much more actively used in the noninscriptional space. The postwar trajectory of the vernacular became rather complex. During the seventeenth century, during Chosŏn's conflict with the Manchus, and afterwards in its self-appointed role as the carrier of Confucian civilization, the government seems to have returned literary Chinese to prominence in the inscriptional space. It was in the eighteenth century during the reigns of Yŏngjo (r. 1724–1776) and especially Chŏngjo (r. 1776–1800) that the vernacular returned to the inscriptional space.⁸⁰

The induction of vernacular writing into the inscriptional space, however, fundamentally changed its role and function. Released from its position as the inferior other of literary Chinese, vernacular Korean gained autonomy, legitimacy, and, most particularly, visibility. The vernacular became an integral part of larger discourse. Discourse was carried out in various combinations of linguistic spaces and languages, and the discourse in literary Chinese referred to and even quoted from discourse in the vernacular more frequently. Through intertextuality, fragmentary portions of discourse in the vernacular that might have been otherwise lost to us are made visible in the classical language, even if distantly. The vernacular offered, on its own, a discursive field in which disparate discourses of ethnicity cohered. It created an alternative discursive space, especially in the fictional mode, in which such topics as nation and ethnicity were contemplated, as will be shown in the next chapter.

Dead bodies as metaphors for the wounded political body of the Chosŏn state occupied a prominent place in the postwar discourse of identity in seventeenth-century Korea. The fifty-year period beginning with the Imjin War, the six-year Japanese invasions of 1592–1598, and ending with the Manchu invasions of 1627 and 1636–1637 was one of the most politically and socially challenging periods of Korean history. Chapters 1 and 2 have conveyed the trauma and destruction that Korea suffered from these military encounters as well as the emergent discourse of the nation that ensued.

The Manchu invasions presented the Korean court, elites, and common people with a crisis of a different type. Although the duration of the confrontation had been much shorter and the carnage less severe, the Korean capitulation in 1637 to the Manchus, whom they regarded as "barbarian," and the subsequent Manchu conquest of China in 1644 profoundly challenged the Korean sense of cultural identity.[1] To begin with, the ascendancy of the Manchus and their demand that Korea cooperate in their bid to challenge the Ming for supremacy in China had presented an extremely agonizing dilemma to the Chosŏn state. Koreans felt not only a deep ideological and cultural bond to the Ming—whom they regarded as the leaders of Confucian civilization, membership in which was the kernel of their identity—but also felt indebted to the Ming for the military assistance that they had received during the Japanese invasions.

Indeed, the Manchu question caused profound political upheavals internally, including a coup d'état and a rebellion. King Kwanghae (r. 1608–1623), who adhered to an even-handed policy

5

THE AFTERMATH

Dream Journeys and the Culture of Commemoration

between Ming and the Manchus, was deposed and his nephew Injo enthroned by the pro-Ming faction.[2] In the following year Yi Kwal (1587–1624) rebelled against the new regime and briefly occupied the capital. After pacifying the rebels, Injo's court resisted Manchu pressure until Hong Taiji, leading an army of 100,000, invaded Korea to demand capitulation.

Besieged in Namhan Fort on a mountain near Seoul in a bitterly cold winter, with little hope for provisions, the Injo court withstood the siege as long as it could but capitulated on the forty-seventh day and was forced to perform a ritual of surrender in accordance with a protocol imposed on it. Injo and the crown prince, wearing the blue garb of commoners, bowed three times and kowtowed nine times on bare earth to Manchu leader Hong Taiji, who was resplendent in imperial symbols—clad in a golden dragon robe and seated on a throne draped with cloth embroidered in golden thread, atop a podium of nine steps. Afterward Hong Taiji departed with Korean hostages, including the crown prince, the second oldest prince, and many of the Korean officials who had been most vocally opposed to the Manchus.[3] The shame of the Korean king in performing this ritual of surrender to a foreign ruler, the only such occasion recorded in Korean history, seems to have extended far beyond the person of the king to the entire political body of the Chosŏn state.

Fighting for personal survival and that of their country in the face of an alien other, Koreans had to confront many of the elements of what Anthony Smith calls "ethnies," such as the sense of ethnicity, territoriality, and language,[4] and an intense discourse of identity emerged. The trajectory of this discourse continuously evolved in response to the changing political and social life of Korea and to events outside, such as the establishment of the Tokugawa shogunate in Japan,[5] the Manchu conquest of China,[6] and the resulting transformation in the topography of culture and power among the countries of East Asia.

How to characterize this discourse of identity poses a certain conceptual problem: contemporary scholarship in Korea is bifurcated. Historical scholarship stresses the impact of the Japanese invasions on the economic, military, political, and social structure;[7] diplomatic relations with China and Japan;⁸ and the ideological change resulting from Manchu supremacy.⁹ Literary scholarship concentrates on postwar works that deal specifically with the war.¹⁰ Scholarship in both disciplines tends to take as a point of departure the deepening of national consciousness, but neither provides a theoretical underpinning or a systematic analysis for this position.

Commemoration and the Postwar Discursive Field

Throughout this book I have emphasized that the seventeenth-century discourse of identity and nation is composed of many interwoven strands. Instead of analyzing each strand, my goal in this chapter is to identify the cultural grammar of the discursive field in which the postwar discourse took place. I show that a genre of fictional accounts called "dream journeys" is particularly evocative of the texture of posttraumatic memories.

The cultural grammar that provided emotional subtext and ideological structure to the discursive field is what I call the culture of commemoration. Commemorating the war dead is a universal phenomenon. Postwar discourse is where the past and the present, and the dead and the living, are conjoined. The past, which contains many tragedies, must be laid to rest in order to move forward into the future. The war dead must be properly taken care of—buried, remembered, given honors, or put into a pantheon of "national" heroes when appropriate. Mourning the dead thus functions as the fulcrum in creating "common glories in the past" and remembering "the sacrifices to which one has consented."¹¹

The questions of who is mourned and how and which agencies are involved in the activity, however, are both culture and time specific. Depending on cultural elements such as religious and philosophical notions of life after death, funerary practices, and ideas of who deserves attention, different modes of commemorative activities are produced.¹² Commemorative activities are a revealing site of the discourse of the communal identity because they indicate the evolving changes concerning the scope and category of subjects of commemoration, the concept of the community, and the relationship between the war dead and the community.

Commemorative activities for the dead of the Imjin War began during the war, expanded in scope in the postwar years, and gradually escalated into a pervasive and long-lasting phenomenon in the subsequent centuries.[13] This phenomenon, the "culture of commemoration," was a huge and extensive enterprise involving multiple agencies in the realms of ritual, oral performance, and literary production. At one extreme the central government performed public sacrifices, conferred honors, and placed personal names of commended heroes in official histories; at the other extreme local populations nationwide, even in remote provinces, orally narrativized war heroes according to their own visions.[14] Many regional and familial agencies between the central government and the local population engaged in their own modes of remembering and honoring the dead.

Confucian ideas and practices concerning the dead in Chosŏn society were conducive to producing a culture of commemoration. Although Confucian societies did not have an especially strong cult of the dead, Confucians believed that the welfare of the dead and that of the living are inextricably intertwined. With no specific conception of the length or autonomy of the afterlife of an individual, the dead attained immortality only through remembrance by the living. The popular belief in the power of the spirits of the dead—that they might bestow blessings or wreak havoc on the living—seems to have reinforced the interdependence. This idea is embodied in the importance of activities such as funerary and mourning rituals, ancestral sacrifices in the family, public sacrifices to the worthy, historical writing, and other commemorative writing. These elements constituted an ethos in which, in interaction with hugely traumatic historical events such as the Imjin War and the Manchu invasions, the culture of commemoration grew.

At the heart of commemoration are dead bodies. Dead bodies in myth and literature, as much as living bodies, are culturally produced and gendered, and they are inscribed with marks of a specific place and time. In this chapter I analyze three fictional narratives that focus on dead bodies. In interpreting the meaning of these works,

I find inspiration in Mikhail Bakhtin's concept of heteroglossia, the idea that "all utterances are heteroglot in that they are functions of a matrix of forces practically impossible to recoup."[15] Therefore when reading these narratives one should be mindful of the intertwining matrix of forces present in them. The symbolic meaning of dead bodies in the political discourse of a particular time must be decoded in several steps. It requires an examination of specific constituents, such as what category of dead bodies is recalled, how and under what circumstances, and the genre and the media in which they are deployed. In the sections that follow, I first discuss the genre of dream journeys in which these narratives are written and then analyze the categories of dead bodies that each narrative recalls and their meanings, intertextualizing with other literary works whenever appropriate. In conclusion I assess the nature of subversion in the texts by examining the relationship between literary production and the culture of commemoration.

Dream Journeys and Subversion

The three narratives are written in a genre known as *mongyurok* (records of dream journeys). Two narratives, *Talch'ŏn mongyurok* (Dream journey to Talch'ŏn) by Yun Kyesŏn (1577–1604)[16] and *P'isaeng mongyurok* (Master P'i's dream journey),[17] are about dead bodies left by the Imjin War. The third, *Kangdo mongyurok* (Dream journey to Kanghwa Island), is about the Manchu invasions. *Dream Journey to Talch'ŏn* is believed to have been written in 1600. The other two are transmitted anonymously and hence their dates are unknown. The emotional rawness of these tales and their intertextuality with other works seem to indicate that they were written soon after the war with which each narrative deals. Both tales about the Imjin War recall dead male bodies, while the tale about the Manchu invasions summons dead female bodies. Although dead bodies were discussed extensively in historical texts during and after the wars, of the known fictional treatments, tales of dream journeys represent them most vividly.

In appearance dream journeys closely resemble *chŏn'gi* (more commonly known by their Chinese counterpart, *chuanqi*, often rendered as "strange tales"), but the relative lack of fictionality expressed by a proclivity toward historical events and personages has led scholars to place these narratives into a separate genre distinct from, although closely associated to, *chŏn'gi*.[18] There are about a dozen extant dream journeys.[19] Early dream journeys seem to date from the fifteenth century, which makes them contemporaneous with Kim Sisŭp's (1435–1493) *Kumo sinhwa* (New tales of the golden turtle), the earliest extant collection of *chŏn'gi* in Korea.

Dream journeys are stories written in classical Chinese by elite males for the same audience. In terms of subject matter, linguistic space, as well as the gender and class of both producers and consumers of the genre, they fall within the boundaries of well-established traditions. Yet the nontraditional way in which the three dream journeys deploy the familiar dream trope sets them apart. In Korean literature, just as in Chinese literature,[20] dream motifs have occupied a prominent place in many genres. Works centering on dreams range from stories included in Kim Sisŭp's *New Tales of the Golden Turtle* to Kim Manjung's (1637–1692) *Kuunmong* (A nine-cloud dream), one of the earlier vernacular novels,[21] and many works influenced by *A Nine-Cloud Dream*. In these texts the dream is connected to either a Daoist or a Buddhist space, and, as Judith Zeitlin says of Chinese literature, the dream trope is often used to evoke the indistinctiveness and ambiguity between reality and dream.[22]

Dream journeys in time of war, however, display different properties. In general, dream journeys can be divided into two groups, based on the mode of narration, marked by the relationship between the dreamer and the dreamed. In the first group, the dreamer-narrator is the observer of the scene unfolding in front of him, and center stage is given to the dead characters whom the dreamer-narrator encounters. In the second, the dreamer-narrator is either a protagonist or a major participant in the unfolding drama, and the dream sequence focuses on the dreamer's interiority, which is transformed through the experience.[23] All three dream journeys of war are told by a dreamer-observer, and it is this mode of narration that sets these texts apart from the usual preference for a dreamer-protagonist in the established genre.

Of previous dream journeys, only one was in the dreamer-observer mode.[24] The explosion of stories adopting the dreamer-observer mode in the aftermath of the Imjin War and the Manchu invasions thus amounts to an emergence, if not the invention, of a new genre.[25] This phenomenon requires explanation, since there is a conspicuous disjunction between the subject matter and the generic form. In these postwar tales, social and political issues become articulated, unlike in earlier dream narratives that focused on the dreamer's interiority.

The device of alternating between the real and the fantastic in these dream narratives offers an opportunity to present dead bodies in two modes: as they are—rotting bodies—and as they are being imagined—dead persons who retain subjectivity. This transformation from silent bodies to speaking ghosts provides a satisfying subject for the reader's imagining. In the beginning of each of the three narratives, the dreamer-observer arrives at a deserted field where he comes upon piles of discarded and unburied bodies, parts of them eaten by wild beasts and predatory birds. In discussing the representation of the authentic in modern China, Prasenjit Duara remarks that the most effective symbols of authenticity are passive ones without agency,[26] which seems to apply to seventeenth-century postwar Korea as well. One cannot imagine more authentic symbols of the victimhood of war than these unburied bodies. These fragmented bodies constitute a stark imagery embodying the atrocities of war but also a sharp indictment of the survivors' neglect of the dead.

The pathos of these anonymous bodies is magnified when they are imagined as individual ghosts with emotion. The dead speaking in their own voices, using an existing or invented genre, is a common literary occurrence, especially in the aftermath of particularly devastating wars. Noting the preponderance of supernatural or ghost characters in postwar Japanese plays, David Goodman explains that ghost characters had disappeared from drama during the Meiji period, when Japan was eager to modernize, but they returned in abundance after World War II because of the national psychic need to deal with atom-bomb victims.[27] Similarly, dream journeys seem to have been adapted to create a space for the dead to speak directly of their unrequited grievances. In this sense the device is reminiscent of shamanic ritual, in which suppressed grievances of the dead are heard through the medium of the shaman, and the fear or guilt of the living is sublimated.[28]

Beyond their strategic suitability for the appeasement of the war dead, the generic properties of dream journeys require further articulation. Can we define them generically, and, if so, can we evaluate whether their common properties are deployed as integral constituents of the narrative to render specific meaning? As a genre these stories defy easy categorization either by traditional Korean definitions or by Western theories of dream literature. I have already mentioned that dream journeys are placed in an ambiguous relationship to *chŏn'gi* in the development of narratives in Korea. An attempt to place them in a scheme accessible to Western categorization also brings difficulties. If we apply Tzvetan Todorov's definition, the way in which these narratives straddle the marvelous and the uncanny seems to place them in the "fantastic."[29] Nonetheless, Todorov places the fantastic in opposition to the real and insists that the reader ultimately must make a clear-cut generic distinction.[30]

Zeitlin points out that in Chinese dream literature the fantastic and the real seem to converge.[31] In most dream literature produced in Korea, this also seems to apply. In war narratives of dream journeys, however, the center of gravity tilts more toward the real, and the fantastic is used as an alternative space in which social and political issues are reenacted. The two spaces, the real and the fantastic, are clearly demarcated, as they appear sequentially but never simultaneously. In all three narratives the dreamer-observer's entry into dreamland takes place in a neutral zone, temporally and spatially, between the living and the dead: on a journey, the observer arrives at a lonely field with piles of dead bodies and later dreams of them on a bright moonlit night.[32]

The moment of entry into the dream space is usually marked by a sudden strange noise that breaks an eerie quiet. P'adamja of the *Dream Journey to Talchŏn* notes that "without warning, a great angry loud wind swirled around. Ominous and dreadful air filled the field, which was quickly covered with complete darkness. Then he saw at a distance a group of men carrying torches marching toward where he was. There were many of them and they created pandemonium."³³ The Buddhist monk Ch'ŏngho of the *Dream Journey to Kanghwa Island* hears "a faint noise which sounded like singing, or laughing, or crying. It was indeed singing, laughing, and crying, and all came from a group of women."³⁴ The moment of the dreamers' exits is clearly marked by their realization that they have just dreamed. Thus, although the dreamer travels between the real and the fantastic, he returns to the real.

In one way, however, dream journeys seem to share the properties of the fantastic. Rosemary Jackson discusses the subversive function of fantasy literature.³⁵ These narratives utilize this function. The question that they raise about the mound of dead bodies is not merely whether the living have the physical capacity to bury them. The question is a more profound and pointed one: Are the living good enough, in a transcendental, cosmic sense, to offer burial to the dead? Will the dead accept the burial offered to them? Confucian mortuary and funerary practices specify an elaborate set of rules governing who can bury and mourn whom according to a calibrated scale of kin affinity.³⁶ What is called into question in these narratives is not consanguineous or relational tightness but the moral fitness of the living and the agency responsible. The question of the (un)buriability of dead bodies is thus a subversive one; it brings to the fore questions with profoundly moral and political implications.

What these tales place under scrutiny is the hegemonic order, represented in two ways: the Confucian cultural order and the political order of the Chosŏn state/patriarchy, although sometimes the two converge as the established order. In them a question is raised over whether the Confucian order, as a religious or philosophical system, is able to cope with the enormity of postwar trauma. An even more pointed question is the restorability of the moral legitimacy of the Chosŏn state. The dream journeys present as a given the degraded state of the political body, which is represented by the dead bodies that are evoked as they are at the moments of their deaths. In the scene in which P'adamja encounters the dead in *Dream Journey to Talch'ŏn*, he watches, hiding in terror behind a tree, a long line of people bearing torches marching toward him: "Some had no head, some no right or left arm, some were missing a right or left leg. Some had the middle part of their body but no legs, some had legs but no torso, some had bellies swollen so badly that they could hardly walk, appearing to have drowned. All of them had disheveled hair that covered their faces, and their arms and legs bled profusely."[37]

The female ghosts in *Dream Journey to Kanghwa Island* appear to the monk Ch'ŏngho in a similar manner: one had a yard-long rope dangling from a strangled neck, one had a huge knife stuck in her back, one bled profusely from a sharp object, one had a completely shattered head, and another had a belly swollen from swallowed water.[38] Can the political body be cleansed of contamination and regain its moral fiber? Can it be made whole? This will be possible only if these frightening apparitions of the dead can be buried and laid to rest. Thus the (un)buriability of these different groups of dead bodies in these narratives becomes the signifier for hope or despair.

BATTLE-UNCONSUMMATED BODIES

Dream Journey to Talchŏn contemplates the war dead who died on the battlefield and consists of two parts. The first part discusses anonymous soldiers who died in the infamous battle by the Talch'ŏn River in Ch'ungju city. Upon hearing of the invasion by the Japanese army, the Korean court had appointed the civil official Sin Ip (1546–1592) as military commander of Ch'ungch'ŏng Province and expressed the hope that he would guard Ch'ungju city and prevent the Japanese Army from marching northward. As recounted in chapter 1, the Korean Army, hastily gathered and inexperienced in the art of war after two hundred years of uninterrupted peace, could offer no resistance to the well-trained and well-equipped Japanese vanguard of seven thousand led by the warrior-general Konishi Yukinaga. The defeat of the Korean Army was swift and total: the entire unit was decimated, and every soldier met a miserable death, including Sin Ip, who took his own life. The Japanese capture of this last defense post for the capital only two weeks after they had landed in the port city of Pusan sent the Korean court fleeing to the northern border.[39] This battle, which displayed the inadequacy of the Korean Army, became a signifier of Korea's humiliation, and Sin Ip became a synonym for the incompetent official.

The question that the narrative raises is how—or whether one is able—to console those soldiers sacrificed in battle. Two issues are involved here. The first is the manner of their death. As soldiers they were prepared to die in battle. They met their deaths, however, with no opportunity to fight. Due to the ineffectual strategies of their commander, their deaths seem to have been in vain, the cause of lasting regret and unending shame. This sentiment is articulated very early. When the ghosts first appear, they sing in chorus: "When we were alive, we were not used properly; what are we now that we are dead? It is our parents who gave us birth; who was it that killed us? Indebted to our sovereign who nurtured us, we do not begrudge the country our dying. Our regret is our commander who spoke too easily and left us in this terrible plight."[40]

The second issue is the anonymity of these soldiers. Is there some way to offer remembrance to these faceless, nameless soldiers? The way in which P'adamja's role is imagined in the endeavor to valorize their lives is interesting. His distinguishing attribute is his ability to write movingly. The ghosts tell him how moved they had been by the poems that he had written and recited for them on the occasion of his passage through this former battlefield a few months previously. The craftsmanship, the beauty, and the emotional power of the poems were such that they could "make even ghosts weep."[41] Then they request that he listen to their tales of woe and transmit them to the world. What is evoked is a connective power of language that transcends the barrier between the living and the dead: since they were moved by his poems, the living will be moved by his rendering of their fates. P'adamja is chosen as a messenger because he possesses the power of affective language based on his ability to traverse the space between written and spoken language. Hence language is conceived in the form of writing but imagined as spoken word. The poems that he wrote were composed and then vocalized. He is supposed to render into writing the spoken words of these ghosts.

Soon an inquest of Sin Ip ensues. A number of soldiers who died at Talch'ŏn, one by one, come forward to accuse Sin of irresponsibility and bad judgment and to express their bitterness at dying without even the chance of a good fight. Sin's humbled ghost offers an abject apology. He then states that momentous events such as defeats in battle cannot be attributed solely to human error. The Talch'ŏn defeat should be seen ultimately as Heaven's will—there is no use blaming anyone for it. Sin's trial concludes with a statement by a third party to the effect that, since Sin's misconduct has been acknowledged and since the ultimate outcome of the event depended on fate, no further discussion is in order. This pronouncement is rooted in the concept of a separation between the realm of fate and the realm of human endeavor. That Sin was in error is not in dispute. At the same time, the pronouncement also acknowledges the rationality of his explanation, thus freeing him from total responsibility for the deaths of so many soldiers.[42] This separation also makes it easier for the ghosts to accept their inglorious deaths. It acknowledges their bitterness, yet it also reminds them of a cosmic force at work, something beyond human control. Nothing but this vague philosophical view is offered to these soldiers, thus leaving them unburied.

In the second part, the narrative moves from anonymous soldiers' lamentations to famous war heroes' presentations of their own lives and deaths. No sooner does the inquest of Sin Ip end than a commotion announces the arrival of twenty-seven historical personages who died somewhere else during the war. Unlike anonymous soldiers who march on foot, these ghosts arrive by various modes of transportation, such as cart and ship, indicative of their status when alive. Indeed, their manner of arrival is reminiscent of Daoist immortals coming to the Kunlun Mountain to attend the celebration hosted by the Queen Mother of the West every three thousand years when the peaches of immortality ripen.[43] They take their seats in accordance with their presumed hierarchical status. The identities of these persons are hinted at in the dream but revealed only after P'adamja awakens. This assemblage is seated in two files. In the most honored position, at the head of the file on the right, is Admiral Yi Sunsin (1545–1598), hero of the Imjin War. Ko Kyŏngmyŏng (1533–1592), the leader of the volunteer army, is next at the head of the file on the left.[44] The Buddhist monk Yŏnggyu (d. 1592), a militia general, takes the lowest seat, the last on the right-hand file. P'adamja is invited to take the lower seat. Then, beginning from the lowest and moving to the higher end, except the monk general, who speaks last, each of the twenty-seven narrates his life and death and composes a poem.

This long section is devoted to the question of how to assess meaning in life and death. This question is probed from several angles and pursued through constant shifts of perspective, not only from the perspective of one ghost or another, which is explicit, but also from that of the speaker (dead) and the reader (living). Individuals' narratives offer a forum in which the dead speak directly to the living and are thus empowered to present their own cases. This direct appeal is constructed in full awareness that the living can rescue the dead from being objectified as war victims and endow them with subjectivity and hence meaning.

This section begins with a personal view. Each of the twenty-seven ghosts fought the invading army in the way required of his particular station in life, and as they encompass the whole spectrum of Korean upper-class society, their actions illustrate a variety of modes of courage and integrity imaginable in that society. They display to the reader twenty-seven different ways of facing crises. These are demonstrated by militia leaders such as Ko Kyŏngmyŏng, one of the first private scholars who recruited a volunteer army and whose two sons (present in the lower seats) also died in the same cause; Kim Simin (1554–1592), the magistrate of Chinju, who directed the famous battle of Chinju in which he, leading a small army, was able to mount a successful defense against the attack of an enemy army of much greater size but died by a bullet; Song Sanghyŏn (1551–1592), the magistrate of Tongnae, who valiantly resisted the Japanese until the end and whose dignified demeanor in death so moved the Japanese that they gave him a generous funeral; Kim Yŏn'gwang (1524–1592), who, as a scholar untrained in military arts, offered resistance by refusing to flee and by guarding his home and his books and was captured and killed;

and Kim Yŏmul (1548–1592), who, released from prison and ordered to assist Sin Ip, jumped into river along with Sin when the Korean Army suffered an irreversible defeat.

The self-assessments of the lives and deaths of these ghosts also vary widely, but they are constructed on two axes of duty and fate. Ko Kyŏngmyŏng believes that, since he has done his duty, he can accept his fate without regret; his two sons believe that, although they did what they could, they did not accomplish their objective and so are deeply regretful. Kim Ch'ŏnil (1537–1593), another leader of a volunteer army, believes that his failure to accomplish his objective was not for lack of plans and strategies, which he had, but because Heaven did not come to his aid. Cho Hŏn (1544–1592), yet another leader of a volunteer army, attributes his defeat to his underestimation of enemy strength and is deeply ashamed of the humiliation that he has inflicted on his country. A few, including Sim Tae (1546–1592), Kim Yŏn'gwang, and Kim Yŏmul, profess gratitude for the opportunity to express their devotion to their country by dying with integrity.

The story then moves on to consider the question of the military and social implications of individual action. One might be privileged to construct a narrative of one's own life, but what about the consequences of one's action on others and on society? Because many prominent persons in responsible positions were seen as having failed to discharge their duties effectively, this question must have loomed large in the postwar period. Sin Ip is a case in point. He is included in the assemblage of twenty-seven men. Despite his presumed error, he is not denied the opportunity to present his own version of what happened—that he had enjoyed great fame, but his one great error at the Talch'ŏn River has earned him lasting ignominy and existence as a lonely ghost. This statement is immediately countered by Yu Kungnyang (d. 1592): heroes do not begrudge their dying, but they do regret dying in vain, and Sin's misguided strategy caused thousands to die in vain. The question raised is whether these contradictory evaluations can be reconciled and, if so, how.

Sin Ip's intentions here are juxtaposed to his social responsibility. Sin's remorse, established in the inquest into his role in the earlier portion of the story, is also considered. In Confucian Korea, in judging one's "criminal" actions, intentions and remorse, on the one hand, and the social consequences of one's acts, on the other, constitute elements of equal weight. In assessing Sin, another perspective is introduced: individual accountability in the context of irresistible historical force. A dream journey with the same title as Yun Kyesŏn's but by Hwang Chungyun (1577–1648), for example, also contemplates Sin's defeat but attributes it mainly to the deficiencies of the military system of the Chosŏn government. Questions involving Sin's defeat ultimately become questions about the Korean Army during the war. Why had it been so ineffectual? Why had it suffered so many defeats and casualties? The ambivalent manner in which Yun's dream journey treats Sin may have been an attempt to consider the complexities involved in judging great events. This qualification, however, is not applied to all failed warriors. The story unqualifiedly condemns Wŏn Kyun (d. 1597), who has emerged in history as the antithesis to Yi Sunsin, a symbol of corrupt opportunism as opposed to the latter's selfless heroism. The begrudging forgiveness of Sin may have been grounded in a sense of the futility of holding him responsible. Sin, too, is dead. He cannot save the others from their present state of neglect and oblivion.

This question gives rise to the third issue. Can these warriors acquire meaning for their sacrifice and, if so, how, and who can confer it? A recurring refrain is individual valor in the face of insurmountable obstacles. These ghosts are presented as having fought to the death, undeterred by the bleakest of circumstances. Achieved in the absence of government support, their valor seems particularly poignant. As much as individuals are portrayed as heroic, the government is depicted as deficient. Not only did it fail to provide necessary provisions, it even obstructed individual warriors. This failure is exemplified by the way the government treated Admiral Yi Sunsin. His heroic career is well known: his construction of iron turtle ships, his superior defense strategy, the slander by his rivals, his subsequent imprisonment and replacement by Wŏn Kyun, the complete destruction of the Korean Navy under Wŏn and Yi's resumption of the admiralship, the final battle at Noryang Strait during the retreat of the Japanese Army, and Yi's death by a bullet, kept secret from his troops until the conclusion of the battle. Some of the elements of this hagiography may have been supplied later, but Yi's ghost narrates almost the same tale. What is conspicuous is the way in which Yi's life is presented—all his achievements are attributed to his prescience; all the impediments, including his demotion and the destruction of the entire fleet, are attributed to the shortsightedness of the government.

These considerations culminate in an obvious question: if the state was unable to protect these warriors when they were alive, can it console them in death? An urgent need to render meaning to the dead is summed up in the concluding lines of Admiral Yi Sunsin's poem: "A soldier died before the battle ended / Can the warrior's tears be dried?"[45] Perhaps they should seek redemption elsewhere. The possibility of an alternative redemption, however, is flatly denied. That the ghost who speaks last is a Buddhist monk induces the reader to anticipate a Buddhist solution, but monk Yŏnggyu's speech is used for the opposite effect. He does not deny his religion but justifies his life by a patriotic cause. He declares that he was extremely fortunate to have been able to use his Buddhist self to fight for his country, to earn glorious death in battle, and to prove wrong the common myth that monks have no sovereign. He then refutes the Buddhist concept of reincarnation. His poem concludes: "Oh, people! Speak not of reincarnation / Imprisoned in the netherworld, I am unable to release the bitterness." Hope for a Buddhist salvation is shattered. Admiral Yi Sunsin commends him: "This monk truly endorses us!"[46]

Having come full circle, the story concludes: ultimately the state must confer meaning on war heroes by honoring and commemorating them. It confirms the Confucian worldview that individuals acquire immortality through historical remembrance and that the state is the most authoritative agency for this task. Once this role of the state is affirmed, its deficiency in military planning and government affairs takes on a different meaning. The criticism is not a condemnation of the state but a wish for a stronger and more competent one. This desire is underscored in the parting messages of the dead to the dreamer: the country should shore up two components, the civil and the military, in order to prosper. While civil culture brings brilliance, military prowess protects the country from invasions. The Chosŏn state should not neglect the affairs of national security any longer. The urgent need for reform and strengthening of the military must have been a major component in postwar discourse. Hwang Chungyun's *Dream Journey to Talchŏn* also stresses the same message. In this sense the dead are dual signifiers: they are reminders of past negligence by the state but also its protective guardians. The dreamer also brings dual messages to the living: the state should remember the war dead, and in so doing it should remember the importance of national security to protect the living.

Upon waking, P'adamja performs a commemorative act. He offers a sacrifice to the dead, accompanied by a eulogy in which each of the twenty-seven men is valorized. It begins with a paean to royal virtue that is so sagacious that it produced twenty-seven scholars who fought the "barbarians," so that, "though their physical bodies perished, their names shall remain forever." The ceremony concludes with a lamentation to Heaven: "Why have you sent them to the world and why did you take them back so soon?"[47] Through this ritual, these neglected ghosts are transformed into historical heroes etched in national memory, the ultimate honor and the only immortality available to Confucians. That P'adamja, the dreamer and the officiant of the sacrifice, is a royal official signifies that these twenty-seven people who fought separately have been together subsumed into a pantheon of national heroes. Thus a literary war memorial has been constructed for these twenty-seven warriors.

How are we to interpret the two contradictory solutions offered in this text: the construction of a virtual war memorial to the famous warriors versus the vague philosophical commemorations offered to the anonymous dead whose unrequited state is only made more vivid by the contrast to the definitive solution offered to the famous? It may help to compare these fictional solutions with the way in which the state handled these issues in its commemorative activities. The Chosŏn government began to perform official sacrifices to the war dead in the summer of 1593. On September 2, 1593, the Ministry of Rites requested and received royal approval that a sacrifice be performed for those who died defending Chinju city and that the eulogy be dedicated not only to the six who were identified but also to all of the dead whose identities could not be easily verified.[48] Eventually an altar, Chŏngch'ungdan, was constructed by the Ch'oksŏk River in Chinju, at which the state offered sacrifices twice a year, spring and autumn, to all those who died in battle during the Imjin War. The central government sent incense and a eulogy on each occasion.[49] The date of the construction of the altar is unknown, but the sacrifices continued until 1908, when they were discontinued by a royal edict.[50]

One may view the construction of the literary war memorial in this text as a parallel activity converging with that of the state. When these twenty-seven people assume their historical identities in the story, they are presented as the people whom the dreamer has always admired. The story thus does not attempt to conceal the author's sleight of hand, nor does it contest the list compiled by the state. Although the list is incomplete and excludes some names, all twenty-seven have come down in history as war heroes. Extensive commemorative activities to them were performed by both public and private agencies.

In the treatment of anonymous soldiers, however, the narrative diverges from the actions of the state. Rather than paralleling the state in offering sacrifices to them, it leaves them unburied. This problematizes the issue concerning anonymous soldiers. To my knowledge, before this story was written, the fate of anonymous soldiers had rarely received prominent attention in Korea. This, however, is not unique to Korea. Historically the death of anonymous soldiers, perhaps with the exception of ancient Greece, had been glossed over in most cultures. Two issues are involved in this: class and the problem of individual identity of the soldiers. Both these issues have been resolved in many countries through changing notions of the relationship of the citizen to the state and the technology and practice of individuating the army, but they were resolved only over long periods of time.

We, of course, know of the inscription of individual names on the famous Vietnam Memorial. Only in 1868, however, with the establishment of the cemetery at Gettysburg in which bodies of soldiers were transferred from random, mass graves into individual graves in a collective cemetery, did the first "national" cemetery that recognized the war dead individually appear in the United States. Likewise, only in 1927, when Britain erected at Ypres a memorial arch on which are inscribed the names of each of the dead and the missing at the battle fought there during World War I, were individual names remembered.[51] Thomas Laqueur terms this the beginning of the new era of remembrance—"the era of the common soldier's name or its self-conscious and sacralized oblivion."[52]

The seventeenth-century Korean narrative addresses the contradiction between remembrance and anonymity. Perhaps we should view this as belonging to a liminal space between the author's recognition and his inconclusive search for resolution. The most striking image from the story, however, is that of the long line of anonymous soldiers, each maimed and bleeding, marching on foot under torchlight, the image rendered more powerful and pathetic as they remain unburied.

Anonymous Civilian Bodies

The (un)buriability of the anonymous dead is again the subject of *Master P'i's Dream Journey*, but this time the bodies are those of unclaimed civilian war casualties left in the path of the invasion. Supposedly, if implicitly, the bodies of anonymous soldiers were in the domain of the state, but civilian dead belonged to their families. When discarded dead bodies are imagined as members of a family, their anonymity takes on a greater poignancy. They signify the total breakdown of order, the failure of that fundamental requirement of civilized life—that the living should tend to their own dead. Despite the fact that a proper burial for loved ones was a central concern in Confucian Korea, the realities of war, in which so many died far from home in unknown places, did not allow the luxury of fulfilling this duty. *Master P'i's Dream Journey* explores alternative systems of thought beyond the hegemonic order for ways to cope with this most basic disruption. It attempts to overcome the anonymity of the dead by imagining them as individuals and to conceptualize the meaning of death in such a manner as to permit the living to find closure.

The opening of *Master P'i's Dream Journey* is similar to the opening of *Dream Journey to Talch'ŏn*. A private scholar, P'i Tal, who is fond of traveling, arrives at a lonely field somewhere in Kyŏngsang Province at twilight and finds moss-covered bodies, partly eaten by vultures, strewn as far as the horizon. Moved by this sight, he composes a poem. A monk appears and informs him of the horrors and atrocities that the people of the region suffered at the hands of the Japanese invaders. He tells P'i that, of thousands upon thousands of dead bodies lying there, only one was claimed and buried: a Master Yi, after ten years of neglect, came from the capital and, after making desultory inquiries concerning the circumstances of his father's death, selected a body and gave it a generous funeral. The monk, who remains anonymous, plays the role of a Greek chorus exposing the horrors of the war and venality of humanity. He intimates that Master Yi chose the wrong body and that he buried his "father" for ulterior motives. This burial, the only burial in all those years, merely accentuates the terrible state of disorder. P'i then crosses a hill and, in a lonely village, finds lodging. As soon as he falls asleep, he is inducted into the dream world.

In the dream space this self-same burial is transformed into a site on which mounds of anonymous bodies are individuated and resolutions for the forgotten dead are sought. Rather than numerous ghosts, *Master P'i's Dream Journey* concentrates on one case. Like the Unknown Soldier buried in Arlington National Cemetery to represent all unknown soldiers who died in World War I,[53] this one, a random although specific example, represents all the anonymous dead. In this case, Yi Kuksin, the son, indeed chose the body of someone other than his father. The dream takes the form of an inquest over which P'i presides. It is a dispute between the ghost of the father and that of the person who received burial, and it is resolved in several stages. The first stage concerns who has the prior claim. Yi Hŏn, the father, acting as plaintiff, states his case. His lonely ghost, suffering from rain and wind, waited for a long time to be claimed by one of his three sons. His oldest son, Kuksin, has passed the examination and has attained a high official post. Fearing the criticism of others, he decided to give his father a proper burial, but he chose the body of Kim Kŏmson, a petty clerk, instead. Although the son learned of his error, fearful that he might be held in ridicule, he refused to attempt another burial.

Then Kim Kŏmson, with his long, flowing beard, enters and defends himself. Basing his defense on karmic theory, he says that he had been Yi Kuksin's father in a previous life and that this was why Heaven let Yi Kuksin choose his body. He advises Yi Hŏn to give up his claim and to seek the help of his other sons. P'i sides with Yi Hŏn, declaring that, since Yi fathered and raised his son in this world, it was a terrible mistake to bury someone else. At this point the inquest becomes a debate between Confucian and Buddhist views that is resolved with the triumph of Confucianism. The main function of the Confucian-Buddhist debate, however, does not seem to establish a superior doctrine but to introduce the notion that there are multiple views and that each is relative. In other words, it seems to be saying that if one happens to bury someone other than one's parent by mistake—a terrible thing for all involved in the context of Confucian society—then perhaps there was some cosmic reason for this.

In the second stage another notion is introduced: that the appearance of fortune and misfortune is deceptive. This emerges through the revelation of Yi Kuksin's corrupt nature. Both Kim Kŏmson and Yi Hŏn agree that Yi Kuksin is evil. In due course he will commit a crime for which his entire family, including his dead relatives, will be punished. Their bodies will be exhumed and dismembered. Thus Kim Kŏmson's fortune and Yi Hŏn's misfortune are not what they appear to be. Indeed, both of them conclude that it is better to remain unclaimed than to be buried by someone like Yi Kuksin. Buried or not, neither wishes to have accepted the offer of burial, and in this sense the story implies their unburiability.

What is the meaning of their unburiability? Does the story suggest that human beings are too venal to offer burial to their own kin? Does Yi Kuksin's extreme evil represent the condition of humanity?[54] The psychological focus of the story does not seem to be the exposure of human weakness but rather the liberation of the dead from the living. This notion is suggested by P'i Tal, whose given name, Tal, means "the one who has attained the Way." P'i says that after death, nothing really matters. Thus there is nothing wrong with being left in the wilderness, nor is there any real advantage in being properly buried. This consoles Yi Hŏn, but it also comforts Kim Kŏmson for his anticipated dismemberment. The problem of unburiability is resolved by the irrelevance of burial. As the dead are liberated, by extension, the living too are liberated from their guilt. This resolution is redolent of the essentially Daoist concept of the relativeness of views. Moreover the Confucian patriarchy, represented here by a son's symbolic need to bury and mourn his father, is also rendered irrelevant. Is this, then, a dissent from Confucian order?

Master P'i's Dream Journey differs in many ways from *Dream Journey to Talch'ŏn*. The latter views the war in terms of military victory and loss and seeks to define the relationship between the state and its subjects. The former, on the other hand, conceives of war in terms of disruption and destruction of ordinary lives. It recognizes lives lost by confronting the enormity of individual tragedies. It mourns the ordinary by refusing to accept anonymity and massification and by individuating ordinary victims. The main focus of the story is a search for a way to accept the unacceptable and so to heal the wounds of war. In representing Daoist worldviews that were available in the eclectic religious Chosŏn culture of the time, the story seems to affirm that healing is possible, even if the process is long and arduous.

Unburiable Female Bodies

Confucian patriarchy and the Chosŏn state come squarely under attack in *Dream Journey to Kanghwa Island*. While the Imjin War affected almost all Koreans, those who suffered most during the Manchu invasions were the members of the ruling elite. When news of the approaching Manchu Army reached Korea, the royal court divided into two parties, which took refuge in separate locations. The king's party went to Namhan Fort while the crown prince's went to Kanghwa Island. Earlier, in the thirteenth century, Kanghwa Island had been a haven for resisting the invading Mongols, but the seventeenth-century Manchu Army landed on it with ease. In principle, people believed that capture by or surrender to the "barbarian" enemy was a fate worse than death. Although this applied to men as well as women, when Kanghwa Island fell in early 1637, it was mostly women, especially elite women wishing to avoid physical violation, who took their own lives. The *Dream Journey to Kanghwa Island* is about these women.

In this story, the dreamer, Ch'ŏngho, is a Sŏn monk. Unlike P'adamja and P'i Tal, who happened to come upon fields with mounds of unburied bodies, he has gone to Kanghwa Island specifically to bury the bodies strewn about. In contrast to Confucian literati whose medium of connection to the world of the dead is their poems, Ch'ŏngho enters it through compassion. In his dream fourteen women of all ages appear—a courtesan and thirteen aristocratic women, two related to the royal family. In a similar manner to the hero warriors of the *Dream Journey to Talchŏn*, the story consists mainly of fourteen individual narrations of lives and the circumstances of deaths. All are proud that they rose courageously to the challenge of defending their honor. This conviction is summed up by the final speaker, the courtesan: "Heaven is moved and people are overwhelmed by the nobility of integrity and the beauty of faithfulness. Though we died, we still live on. How can we regret it!"[55]

Their pride is juxtaposed against stinging criticism of the male establishment: high officials who were in charge of the central government and the defense of Kanghwa Island, and male members of these women's families. These officials are named by historical aliases, but the identities of the women and their male relatives are only hinted at and not revealed either in the dream or after Ch'ŏngho awakes. One by one these women expose the cowardice, corruption, and hypocrisy of the officials and of their own husbands, sons, fathers, and fathers-in-law. Some fled disguised as servants, and some surrendered without fighting. In one instance a son had urged his mother to take her life long before the island fell, so that the family would receive a red gate from the government and he could receive the privileges due to the son of an exemplary woman.[56] One woman laments that although she kept her honor, because of her husband's miserable failure to perform any of his public duties despite his exalted post she received from the Great King of Underworld the verdict of eternal damnation with no hope of ever being reincarnated as a human.[57]

The leitmotif of these women's narrations is that the members of the male establishment, high officials as well as their relatives, deserted the country at its crucial moment of need to preserve their own lives, thus committing the crime of disloyalty (*pulch'ung*). The courtesan again contrasts female integrity to male cowardice: "Among ten thousand men there is not one who can be said to be a loyal minister who preserved his integrity. Virtue and faithfulness can be found only in the women who died to preserve them."[58] This provokes loud lamentations from the other women. Just as the monk Yŏnggyu, an outsider, has the final word in *Dream Journey to Talchŏn*, the person making this statement is an outsider, a lowly courtesan. Yŏnggyu, however, affirms the Confucian order, while the courtesan exposes the bankruptcy of the patriarchy.

This utter distrust of the Confucian male is illustrated by the fact that a Sŏn monk rather than a literatus is chosen as the dreamer. Ch'ŏngho's role, however, is limited to that of custodian of female honor. In the dream he merely witnesses the female soliloquies. P'adamja and P'i Tal communicate with the dead and bear messages from them, but Ch'ŏngho has no interaction with them. After he awakens, the story ends abruptly. There is no mention of burying or commemorating these women. Unlike the other dreamers, he can neither mediate between the living and the dead nor offer meaningful supplication. He can only bear witness to the tragedies of the women. They remain unburied, drenched in blood, bloated with water.

What is notable is that not only is the Confucian patriarchy indicted, but this is also done through unburiable female bodies. Duara points out that in the discourse of modernity in Asia, women's bodies are often employed as representations of authenticity in support of national patriarchy. He cites as examples historical models of self-sacrificing, frugal women as symbols of economic growth in Meiji Japan and raped women as symbols of the defiled purity of the nation in the discourse of wartime China.[59] The bodies of these seventeenth-century Korean women are also evoked as representations of authenticity in that they possess virtue and purity, but, contrary to those of Japanese or Chinese women, they underscore the bankruptcy of patriarchy. That is, the patriarchy has collapsed because, of the two axes of gendered virtue that buttress it—the loyalty (*ch'ung*) of men and the faithfulness (*yŏl*) of women—one has given way. In this most political of dream narratives, women are profoundly disturbed at men's desertions of their places, but the gender barrier prohibits them from appropriating the virtue abandoned by men. These women cannot expand their female faithfulness to include male loyalty.

In *Pakssi chŏn* (The Tale of Madam Pak), a vernacular story of anonymous authorship written in Korean script and probably dating from the same period, a different solution is offered. Madam Pak, married to Yi Sibaek (1592–1660), a historical personage, crosses the gender boundary. Unlike her husband, who is an ordinary person, she possesses superhuman talent in political acumen and military strategy. She guides her husband in his career at each point. During the Manchu invasions she steps into the male role and helps the royal court weather many crises, all the while playing the role of a virtuous wife. The king confers on Madam Pak the honorary title Ch'ungnyŏl Puin, or "Lady of Loyalty and Faithfulness."[60] This contradicts the historical record. Ch'ungnyŏl is a posthumous title that the Chosŏn state conferred on meritorious men but never women.[61] In this vernacular narrative the living female body is made to represent publicly both male and female virtue. Patriarchy is upheld and the woman nominally stays within it, but as she appropriates male virtue and occupies male space, the male is erased.

In contrast, the gendered division of virtue in *Dream Journey to Kanghwa Island* leaves the male space intact. Unlike Yi Sibaek, who lives under the administration of his wife in public life, men remain empowered as they retain a monopoly of political space and the virtue associated with it. In this sense, even the disintegration of patriarchy affirms rather than negates male power. It implies that, although men caused its disintegration, men can cause it to recover. One may interpret the use of mutilated female bodies as a clarion call to men. In discussing the role of raped women in the historiography of the 1857 Indian Mutiny against the British, Jenny Sharpe points out that the trope of sexually brutalized English women was used to campaign for the British counterinsurgency and subsequently to justify violence used against mutineers.[62] Could it be that, in the *Dream Journey to*

Kanghwa Island, the trope of wounded female bodies is used for a similar end: to arouse Korean men into vengeful rage and shame that they have failed to protect their women?

In fact the sharp yet mournful tone of the criticism seems to be more like self-accusation than the reproach of others. True, dead female bodies and living male bodies are dichotomous signifiers: faithfulness and courage versus disloyalty and cowardice, respectively. Also true, the criticism of men is spoken by female voices. The assumption of a female voice by the male authors, however, as in the famous *kasa* poem "Hymn of Constancy" (*Samiin kok*) by Chŏng Ch'ŏl (1536–1593),[63] was not an uncommon device in Korean literature, especially in political allegory. What the female narrators articulate in this story is purely political, conceived of and expressed in male language: the male failure to protect the country.

Unlike dead bodies in *Master P'i's Dream Journey*, whose unburiability breaks the mutual dependence between the dead and the living, the unburiability of these female bodies underscores male responsibility. Their deaths were caused by men's desertion of virtue; these bodies remain unburied until men resume virtue. These women attain a kind of immortality as stern guardians of conscience. As one woman proclaims, they are dead but they live on; on the contrary, although men live, they are dead. Left in their disheveled, untidy rage, these women wait for their men to awaken to virtue so that they can be laid to rest.

Literary Production and the Hegemonic Order

Literary production in the private sector such as these dream journeys was a major component of the postwar discourse of identity in seventeenth-century Korea. Shaping and being shaped by the construction and evolution of the culture of commemoration, literary production maintained complex relationships with other constituencies, particularly the state. It shared the power of writing with the state and competed with it for audience and influence. As Mark Edward Lewis points out, writing derives its power not merely from the fact that it is able to connect the moment of its inscription to a reader across great distances in time and space but also because the voice within the texts retains potency to command the reader's attention.[64]

The Chosŏn state, with its bureaucratic apparatuses, was by far the most active producer of written texts and public pronouncements. From the postwar period, however, literary production in the private sector expanded greatly in both quantity and variety. Personal memoirs of war experiences, histories of war years, and commemorative biographies of war heroes poured out. People began writing prose fiction in vernacular Korean, and poetry and prose fiction in both languages (literary Chinese and vernacular Korean) explored new genres and reshaped the old. Literary culture was no longer the exclusive domain of the upper-class yangban male. New groups of people, men of humble social status, began to assume roles of cultural arbiters, while women emerged as major, although by no means sole, contributors to written culture in Korean.[65] The readership of fiction and other similarly noncanonical genres also increased.[66]

The increased literary production in the private sector can also be, in part, attributed to a relatively benign government policy. Although the government did have a public position on "correct" texts—and the texts under discussion here were beyond the pale by its standards—and although there were occasional instances of state intrusion into "private" writing, by and large the state refrained from exercising censorship.[67]

The relationship between the various groups of producers and consumers in this multilayered diglossic literary culture seems to have been quite complex. One cannot assume that readership was clearly demarcated by genres and languages. Queen Insŏn's (1618–1674) letters to her married daughters, for instance, show that they were borrowing one another's copies of works of fiction, including *Shuihuzhuan* (Water margin), novels that were usually regarded as being popular among male readers.[68] Although these novels presumably were versions translated into Korean, this borrowing was an example of the crossing of gender boundaries between reader and product. Within acceptable boundaries, works seem to have circulated widely. Yun Kyesŏn's *Dream Journey to Talch'ŏn*, for example, is included in its entirety in the *Miscellaneous Record*, which includes a wide variety of documents pertaining to the war. Both were written in classical Chinese by private male scholars.

Of various strands of literary production in the private sector, fiction in classical Chinese displayed a particular penchant. It frequently dealt with political issues; certain genres, such as fantasy or satire, took up issues subversive to the dominant order. The state deployed the power of language to perpetuate its vision of the ideal state. In commemorative activities, for example, the state used writing, whether in recorded texts or performance, to conceal the weakness and to proclaim the glory of the state. In the fictional space of fantasy literature, the language highlights what is hidden and problematizes what is glossed over. In the three dream journeys, unburiable bodies are used to represent metaphorically the deficiencies in the hegemonic order.

How to interpret the nature of subversion in these texts, however, presents problems. Each story uses a different category of unburiable body to raise different questions. Can all be interpreted in the frame of hegemony and antihegemony? *Master P'i's Dream Journey*, for example, evaluates the Confucian order as a religious or philosophical system. In proposing the unburiability of civilian dead bodies, the story denies the possibility of finding solutions for victims of the Imjin War within the Confucian order and searches for a resolution in alternative systems. One should remember, however, that postwar discourse was conducted in a culture in which several religious or philosophical systems coexisted, if in hierarchy, and many people commonly subscribed to a certain mixture of these systems.[69]

Jackson articulates a relationship between literary fantasy and the hegemonic order: while the fantastic reveals what is hidden and repressed in culture, "since excursion into disorder can only begin from a base within the dominant cultural order, literary fantasy is a telling index of the limits of that order."[70] Because alternative religious systems belonged to the order, although they occupied less prestigious positions in Korean society,[71] it does not seem appropriate to use the dichotomy between hegemony (Confucian order) and antihegemony (other religious systems) to trace the anguish expressed in these narratives. Rather than challenging the Confucian order, *Master P'i's Dream Journey* exposes its incompleteness. In this sense, it seems to be more suitable to use as an interpretive frame Jean-Paul Sartre's philosophical distinction between the thetic (propositions [theses] that are supposed to be real and rational) and the nonthetic (unreal).[72] What the narrative conveys is more nonthetic than antihegemonic in that what is desired is that which is absent in the Confucian order rather than a refutation of what is present within.

Can we apply the Sartrean scheme to interpret the narratives' positions on the state/patriarchy? Through the two wars the Chosŏn state suffered a terrible erosion of its moral authority. Because the Chosŏn state managed to survive for almost another three hundred years, unlike the political regimes in Japan and China, which were replaced in the seventeenth century, the impact of the wars on the Chosŏn state has hardly been examined. During the Japanese invasions people saw the state as having failed to protect the land and the people. In the first month of the first Japanese invasion, as Sŏnjo and his entourage fled north, they encountered angry mobs and left a trail of towns falling into complete disorder and chaos. Symbols of the royal house also suffered; the severest instance of this was the burning of the Yi Royal Ancestral Temple by the Japanese Army soon after it entered the capital city.[73]

Sŏnjo suffered an additional humiliation when Chinese generals accused him of disloyalty to the Ming court, after which he had to await their verdict.[74] Haunted by the example of the Tang emperor Xuanzong (r. 713–756), who had to abdicate the throne to his son after the An Lushan Rebellion,[75] King Sŏnjo repeatedly declared his wish to abdicate to his son during his stay in the North and after he returned to Seoul. "I am seriously ill . . . no one in my condition has ever stayed on the throne," he declared at one point.[76] Although he stayed, he must have felt compelled to atone publicly. When he returned to Seoul after an absence of eighteen months, he took up residence in a temporary palace outside the city wall.[77] At the time it looked as though he was staying at a temporary palace because his main palace had been destroyed, but he continued to reside there until he died fifteen years later.

The diminution of the authority of the Chosŏn court that was brought on by the Japanese invasions paled in comparison to what happened to it when it surrendered to the Manchus in 1637. The humiliation inscribed on the royal body of Injo seemed to envelop the whole political body of the Chosŏn state. When the Ming fell in 1644—which Koreans saw as the beginning of "barbarian" domination of the center of civilization—Koreans found a new mission for Korea as the last bastion of Confucian civilization and a new role for the Chosŏn state as its guardian. Despite the Korean hostility and contempt for the "barbarian" Qing, the Chosŏn state was forced to render regular diplomatic rituals that recognized the Qing as its superior. Thus the shame of surrender was endlessly reenacted, never to be forgotten.[78] It continued to be a point of deep anguish for the educated population, and it seems to have contributed to the sense of alienation that a large number of intellectuals felt toward the state, as well as to the fragmentation within the scholar community.

The unburiable bodies in *Dream Journey to Talch'ŏn* and *Dream Journey to Kanghwa Island*—anonymous soldiers and women who died by their own hands to keep their honor—imagined at their moments of death represent the scarred political body of the Chosŏn state and the bankrupt patriarchy. These two groups of dead were among those included in public commemoration. They were either sacrificed to or given honors. Seeking to fulfill its role as the agency that appeased communal sorrows and thus to repair its scarred image, the state vigorously engaged in these activities. In insisting on the unburiability of these dead, the dream narratives contest the resolution adopted by the state. Presumably composed in different postwar periods, the two narratives embody different "contemporary structures of feeling."[79] The unburiable bodies of the anonymous soldiers signify a search for a resolution that remains elusive and thus indicative of a Sartrean sense of the nonthetic. The unburiability of mutilated female bodies underscores a much more urgent crisis of identity. Nevertheless, the criticism directed at the state and the patriarchy seems to have been embedded in an acute sense of humiliation and self-reproach that was pervasive among the male elite after the Korean capitulation to the Manchus.

Unburiable dead bodies are sites of revelation not only of the way in which the postwar discourse of the Imjin War and that of the Manchu invasions differ but also, after the Manchu invasions, of the way in which the two discourses interacted, especially the way in which images of the Imjin War were transformed. The choice of the monk Ch'ŏngho as the dreamer in *Dream Journey to Kanghwa Island* illustrates how a historical event from one era acquires a different signification in another in the evolving discourse of identity. Ch'ŏngho is a nom de plume of Hyujŏng (1520–1604), the eminent monk who led the monk soldiers during the Imjin War.[80] Although he was a principal Buddhist intellectual leader noted as the proponent of the synthetic vision of Buddhism,[81] he is immortalized for his role in defending the country in a time of crisis despite the fact that, as a monk, he was not obliged to fight.[82] Hyujŏng's disciple Yujŏng (1544–1610), who fought as effectively as his teacher, had twice conferred with the Japanese general Katō Kiyomasa during the war,[83] went to Japan in 1604 as a special royal envoy to negotiate with the newly established Tokugawa shogunate for the repatriation of Korean prisoners of war and brought back 3,500 with him.[84] By the time of the Manchu invasions Hyujŏng was long since dead, and thus the presence of Ch'ŏngho, who is among the few identified by name in the narrative, is not historically accurate. Nevertheless, it seems to express a wistful longing for the legendary Hyujŏng and perhaps Yujŏng, who successfully fought to defend the country and capably attended to the postwar tasks.

The post-Imjin stories only tentatively suggest the possibility of healing and express ambivalence toward the hegemonic order. In the period after the Manchu invasions, the Imjin War, which ended with no compromise to the integrity of the Chosŏn state, came to be crowned with a nostalgic halo of victory, and the Imjin War heroes seemed to glow with invincibility. Interestingly enough, in narratives written after the Manchu invasions, an Imjin hero outside the hegemonic order such as Ch'ŏngho became the metaphor for nonthetic desires. In this sense *Dream Journey to Kanghwa Island*, the narrative among the three dream journeys most critical of the state, also expresses a nonthetic rather than antihegemonic sentiment in that it evokes unreal wishes and elusive hopes.

Beyond their specific historical significations, each type of dead body, especially an unburiable body, viewed in terms of the poetics of literary works, expresses a humbling sense of inadequacy that the living feel toward the war dead. This seems to echo Abraham Lincoln's words: "But in a larger sense we cannot dedicate, we cannot consecrate, we cannot hallow this ground. The brave men, living and dead, who struggled here have consecrated it far above our poor power to add or detract."[85] In full cognizance of a similar limit, these tales attempt to immortalize the dead in remembrance or to release them to oblivion. This is done in a culture in which language is imagined as having magical power.

What is distinctive in these narratives is that, however they choose to treat their dead, either with remembrance or oblivion, they refuse to consign the anonymous dead to a collectivity and are determined to treat the unnamed as individuals just as the named are treated. In this sense the true poetics of these tales is their construction of an "imaginary memory," which Wolfgang Iser saw as "essential to the aesthetic attitude; it is no mere passive registration of events, but [it] actively selects impressions and transforms them."[86] In this fictional space they "preserve" and "adapt to the requirements of the imagining, remembering individual." In constructing an imaginary memory and in imagining the dead, named as well as nameless, as individuals, these narratives create their own autonomous commemoration. Perhaps in this function, literary production in the private sector was most powerfully subversive of the state.

In an attempt to individuate the anonymous dead as well as to mourn and preserve their memory, these narratives, especially *Dream Journey to Talch'ŏn* and *Dream Journey to Kanghwa Island*, place the dead in a context we may rightly call "national": they become the emblems of "a long past of endeavors, sacrifice, and devotion" and the embodiment of moral consciousness, which, by the strength of their sacrifices, "demand the abdication of the individual to the advantage of the community."[87] The memories of their suffering, on the other hand, unify all of those who remember them, and the living's grieving becomes "national memories." In this way the culture of commemoration that began in the sixteenth century, be it state-sponsored or privately initiated, ultimately serves to perpetuate the discourse of the nation unto the modern era, long after the war dead in the Imjin War and the Manchu invasions were laid to rest.

PUBLICATIONS OF JAHYUN KIM HABOUSH

Compiled by Gari Ledyard

Books

1985 *The Rise of Neo-Confucianism in Korea.* Coeditor. New York: Columbia University Press.

1988 *A Heritage of Kings: One Man's Monarchy in the Confucian World.* New York: Columbia University Press.

1996 *The Memoirs of Lady Hyegyŏng: The Autobiographical Writings of a Crown Princess of Eighteenth-Century Korea.* Berkeley: University of California Press.

1999 *Culture and the State in Late Chosŏn Korea.* Coeditor. Cambridge, Mass.: Asia Center, Harvard University.

2001 *The Confucian Kingship in Korea* (paperback edition of *A Heritage of Kings* with an added preface). New York: Columbia University Press.

2003 *Women and Confucian Cultures in Pre-modern China, Korea, and Japan.* Coeditor. Berkeley: University of California Press.

2009 *Epistolary Korea: Letters from the Communicative Space of the Chosŏn, 1392–1910.* New York: Columbia University Press.

2013 *A Korean War Captive in Japan, 1597–1600: The Writings of Kang Hang.* Coedited and translated with Kenneth R. Robinson. New York: Columbia University Press.

Articles

1985 "The Education of the Yi Crown Prince: A Study in Confucian Pedagogy." In *The Rise of Neo-Confucianism in Korea*, ed. Wm. Theodore de Bary and JaHyun Kim Haboush, 161–222.

1985 "Confucian Rhetoric and Ritual as Techniques of Political Dominance: Yŏngjo's Use of the Royal Lecture." *Journal of Korean Studies* 5:39–61.

1987 "The Sirhak Movement of the Late Yi Dynasty." *Korean Culture* 8, no. 2:20–27.

1987 "Confucianism in Korea." In *The Encyclopedia of Religion*, ed. Mircea Eliade. New York: Macmillan and Free Press, 4:10–15.

1987 "Song Siyŏl," "Yi T'oegye," "Yi Yulgok," "Yun Hyu." In *The Encyclopedia of Religion*, ed. Mircea Eliade, 13:415–16; 15:517–18; 15:518–19; 15:543–44.

1988 "Tonghak," "Kim Ok-kyun," "Son Pyŏng-hŭi." In *The Encyclopedia of Asian History*, ed. Ainslie T. Embree. 4 vols. New York: Charles Scribner's Sons.

1991 "The Confucianization of Korean Society." In *The East Asian Region: Confucian Traditions and Modern Dynamism*, ed. Gilbert Rozman. Princeton: Princeton University Press, 84–110.

1991 "Women in Traditional Korea." In *Women's Studies Encyclopedia*, ed. Helen Tierney. 3 vols. New York: Greenwood.

1992 "Dual Nature of Cultural Discourse in Chosŏn Korea." In *Contact Between Cultures, East Asia: History and Social Science*, ed. Bernard Hung-Kay Luk. Lampeter, Dyfed, UK: Edwin Mellen Press, 4:194–96.

1992 "The Text of the Memoirs of Lady Hyegyŏng: The Problem of Authenticity." *Gest Library Journal* 5, no. 2:29–48.

1993 "The Censorial Voice in Chosŏn Korea: A Tradition of Institutionalized Dissent." *Han-kuo hsueh-bao* 12:11–19.

1993 "Perceptions of Korean Culture in the United States." *Korea Focus* 1, no. 2:72–86. Translated as "미국내의 한국 문화: 그 존재와 인식. (Representation and of Korean Culture in the United States). *Kyegan Sasang* (March): 149–75.

1993 "Public and Private in the Court Art of Eighteenth-Century Korea." *Korean Culture* 14, no. 2:14–21.

1993 "Rescoring the Universal in a Korean Mode: Eighteenth Century Korean Culture." In *Korean Arts of the Eighteenth Century: Splendor and Simplicity*. New York: The Asia Society Galleries, 23–33.

1994 "Academies and Civil Society in Chosŏn Korea." In *La société civile face à l'État: Dans les traditions chinoise, japonaise, coréenne et vietnamienne*, ed. Léon Vandermeersch. Paris: École Française d'Extrême-Orient, 383–92.

1995 "Dreamland: Korean Dreamscapes as an Alternative Confucian Space." In *Das Andere China*, ed. Helwig Schmidt-Glintzer. Wiesbaden, Germany: Harrassowitz, 659–70.

1995 "Filial Emotions and Filial Values: Changing Patterns in the Discourse of Filiality in Late Chosŏn Korea." *Harvard Journal of Asiatic Studies* 55, no. 1:129–77.

1997 "시공을 넘나든 만남" (Encounter beyond space and time), *Readers' Today* (December): 22–25.

1999 "Constructing the Center: The Ritual Controversy and the Search for a New Identity in Seventeenth-Century Korea." In *Culture and the State in Late Chosŏn Korea*, ed. JaHyun Kim Haboush and Martina Deuchler. Cambridge, Mass.: Asia Center, Harvard University, 46–90, 240–49.

2001 "In Search of HISTORY in Democratic Korea: The Discourse of Modernity in Contemporary Historical Fiction." In *Constructing Nationhood in Modern East Asia*, ed. Kai-wing Chow, Kevin Doak, and Poshek Fu. Ann Arbor: University of Michigan Press, 189–214.

2002 "Gender and the Politics of Language in Korea." In *Rethinking Confucianism: Past & Present in China, Japan, Korea, and Vietnam*, ed. John Duncan, Benjamin Elman, and Herman Ooms. Asian Pacific Monograph Series, University of California at Los Angeles, 220–57.

2003 "Conference on Historiography of Korea—Methodologies and Strategies." In 한국사 연구 방법의 새로운 모색, ed. 한국사학회. Seoul: Kyŏngin munhwasa, 1–8.

2003 "조선시대 문화사를 어떻게 쓸 것인가—자료와 접근 방법에 대하여" (How to write the cultural history of Chosŏn Korea—sources and approaches). In *Han'guksa yŏn'gu pangbŏp ŭi saeroun mosaek*, ed. Han'guksa sahakhoe. Seoul: Kyŏngin munhwasa, 173–96.

2003 "Dead Bodies in the Postwar Discourse of Identity in Seventeenth-Century Korea: Subversion and Literary Production in the Private Sector." *Journal of Asian Studies* 62.2 (May 2003): 415–42.

2003 "Private Memory and Public History." In *Creative Women of Korea*, ed. Young-Key Kim-Renaud. Armonk, N.Y.: M. E. Sharpe, 122–41.

2003 "Versions and Subversions: Patriarchy and Polygamy in the Vernacular Narratives of Chosŏn Korea." In *Women and Confucian Cultures in Pre-Modern China, Korea, and Japan*, ed. Dorothy Ko, JaHyun Kim Haboush, and Joan Piggot. Berkeley: University of California Press, 279–312.

2004 "Filial Emotions and Filial Values: Changing Patterns in the Discourse of Filiality in Late Chosŏn Korea." Reprinted in *Religion and Emotion: Approaches and Interpretations*, ed. John Corrigan. Oxford: Oxford University Press, 75–113.

2005 "Contesting Chinese Time, Nationalizing Temporal Space: Temporal Inscription in Late Chosŏn Korea." In *Time, Temporality, and Imperial Transition*, ed. Lynn Struve. Honolulu: University of Hawai'i Press, 115–41.

2005 "효의 감성과 효의 가치: 조선 후기 효 담론의 변화" (Discourse on filiality during late Chosŏn Korea). *Kungmunhak yŏn'gu* (June): 155–203.

2006 "Introduction." In *And So Flows History*, ed. Hahn Moo-Sook, trans. Young-Key Kim-Renaud. Honolulu: University of Hawai'i Press, 1–7.

2007 "우리는 왜 임진왜란을 연구합니까?" (Why do we study the Imjin War?) 임진왜란: 동아세아 삼국 전쟁. Seoul: Humanist Books, 23–39.

2008 "The Vanished Women of Korea: The Anonymity of Texts and the Historicity of Subjects." In *Servants of the Dynasty*, ed. Anne Walthall. Berkeley: University of California Press.

2010 "Yun Hyu and the Search for Dominance: A Seventeenth-Century Korean Reading of the Offices of Zhou and the Rituals of Zhou." In *Statecraft and Classical Learning: The Rituals of Zhou and East Asian History*, ed. Benjamin Elman and Martin Kern. Leiden: Brill, 309–29.

Scholarly Translations

1996 "King Yŏngjo: Eliminating Factions," "Lady Hyegyŏng: Two New Factions," "Literature, Music, Song," "Chŏng Naegyo: Preface to *Chŏnggu yŏngŏn*—The Emergence of the Chungin Patronage of Art." In *Sourcebook of Korean Civilization: From the Seventeenth Century to the Present*, ed. Peter Lee. New York: Columbia University Press, 39–43, 240–42.

2001 Chapter on education in *Sources of Korean Tradition*. Vol. 2. New York: Columbia University Press, 34–69.

Reviews

1988 Review of *Unforgettable Things: Poems*, by Sŏ Chŏngju, trans. David McCann. *Journal of Asian Studies* 47, no. 3:667–68.

1989 Review of *The Life and Hard Times of a Korean Shaman: Of Tales and the Telling of Tales*, by Laurel Kendall. *Korean Studies* 13:146–50.

1989 Review of *Tongsŏ munhwa kyoryusa yŏn'gu—Myŏng Ch'ŏng sidae sŏhak suyong* (A study of East-West cultural contact: The reception of Western Learning in the Ming-Qing period) by Ch'oe Soja. *Journal of Asian Studies* 48:130–31.

1991 Review of *Modern Korean Literature: An Anthology*, ed. Peter H. Lee. *Journal of Asian Studies* 50, no. 3.

1991 Review of *Pine River and Lone Peak: An Anthology of Three Chosŏn Dynasty Poets*, trans., with an introduction, by Peter H. Lee. *Journal of Asian Studies* 50, no. 4.

1994 Review of *Sourcebook of Korean Civilization: Early Times to the Sixteenth Century*. Vol. 1, ed. Peter H. Lee. *Journal of Asian Studies* 53, no. 1: 242–44.

1995 Review of Briefing 1993, Briefing 1994, ed. Donald N. Clark. *Korean Studies* 19:183–86.

2001 Review of *My Very Last Possession and Other Stories*, by Pak Wansŏ. *Journal of Asian Studies* 59, no. 4: 1055–57.

INTRODUCTION

1. Such an extensive empire had never existed in Asia. The East Asian khanates of the Mongol Empire attempted but failed to include the Japanese archipelago.
2. The list includes such familiar titles as Benedict Anderson, *Imagined Communities: Reflections on the Origin and Spread of Nationalism* (New York: Verso, 1983); Ernest Gellner, *Nations and Nationalism* (Ithaca: Cornell University Press, 1983); Eric J. Hobsbawm and Rerence Ranger, eds., *The Invention of Tradition* (Cambridge: Cambridge University Press, 1983); Anthony D. Smith, *Theories of Nationalism*, 2nd ed. (Boulder: Holmes & Meier, 1983); E. J. Hobsbawm, *Nations and Nationalism Since 1780: Programme, Myth, Reality* (Cambridge: Cambridge University Press, 1990).
3. Gellner, *Nations and Nationalism*.
4. Ibid., 6–13.
5. Ernest Renan, "What Is a Nation?" in *Nation and Narration*, ed. Homi K. Bhabha (New York: Routledge, 1990), 8–22.
6. David A. Bell, *The Cult of Nation in France: Inventing Nationalism, 1680–1800* (Cambridge, Mass.: Harvard University Press, 2003), 13, 34, 108–25, 145.
7. Anthony D. Smith, *The Ethnic Origins of Nations* (Oxford: Blackwell, 1986), 6–13.
8. Patrick J. Geary, *The Myth of Nations: The Medieval Origins of Europe* (Princeton: Princeton University Press, 2003), 1–40.
9. Gellner, *Nations and Nationalism*, 8–11.
10. Liah Greenfeld, *Nationalism: Five Roads to Modernity* (Cambridge, Mass.: Harvard University Press, 1993), 14.

11. Kenneth Pomeranz, *The Great Divergence: China, Europe, and the Making of the Modern World Economy*, rev. ed. (Princeton: Princeton University Press, 2001). [ED]
12. Andre Gunder Frank, *ReOrient: Global Economy in the Asian Age* (Berkeley: University of California Press, 1998), 220–57.
13. Michael Rogers, "Medieval National Consciousness in Korea," in *China Among Equals*, ed. Morris Rossabi (Berkeley: University of California Press, 1983), 151–72.
14. Both stemmed from the realignments of power in East Asia. One was in the seventh century, when the Silla, in alliance with Tang China, conquered its two neighboring states, Paekche and Koguryŏ, to turn Korea into one polity, and Japan unsuccessfully attempted to attack Silla in 661 to resurrect Paekche. The other came after the Koryŏ, overcome by the Mongols, were forced to join the unsuccessful Mongol campaign to conquer Japan in 1274 and in 1281. Neither resulted in full-fledged war.
15. JaHyun Kim Haboush, "Creating a Society of Civil Culture: Early Chosŏn, 1392–1592," in *Art of the Korean Renaissance, 1400–1600*, ed. Soyoung Lee (New York: Metropolitan Museum of Art, 2009), 3–14.
16. Many believe that this term originated after the Manchu invasions of Korea, but it long predates it. For the use of the term during the Imjin War, see Kim Myŏn's exhortation in Cho Kyŏngnam's *Nanjung chamnok* [The miscellaneous record of the war], 4 vols., in *Kugyŏk Taedong yasŭng* [The translation of the unofficial narratives of the Great East] (Seoul: Minjok munhwa ch'ujinhoe, 1972), 1:358, 2:557.
17. *Sŏnjo sujŏng sillok* (hereafter *SSS*), 25:3a–b [24/3#4#5]. Mary E. Berry, *Hideyoshi* (Cambridge, Mass.: Harvard University Asia Center, 1982), 208, quotes the same passage based on Kuwata Tadachika, *Toyotomi Hideyoshi kenkyū* (Tokyo: Kadokawa Shoten, 1975), 239. I believe it to be incorrectly translated.

The *Revised Veritable Records of Sŏnjo* (*Sŏnjo sujŏng sillok*) is cited in these notes according to fascicle and page (i.e., 26:5a) followed by the entry number in brackets (i.e., [26/5/#5]). The date is in the order of reign year and lunar month. The entry number reflects the organization of individual daily records in the *Veritable Records*

1. THE DISCOURSE OF NATION   161

of the Kings of the Chosŏn Dynasty (*Chosŏn wangjo sillok*) provided by the Kuksa P'yŏnch'an Wiwŏnhoe (National Institute of Korean History) at http://sillok.history.go.kr/. Date numbers are omitted for SSS entries (i.e., [26/5#5]) because records are organized by month, not by date. [ED]

18. SSS 25:4a–11a [24/3#7]; Jurgis Elisonas, "The Inseparable Trinity: Japan's Relations with China and Korea," in *The Cambridge History of Japan*, ed. John Whitney Hall (Cambridge: Cambridge University Press, 1991), 4:265–66.
19. Yoshi S. Kuno, *Japanese Expansion on the Asiatic Continent: A Study in the History of Japan with Special Reference to Her International Relations with China, Korea, and Russia* (Berkeley: University of California Press, 1937), 1:175.
20. Ibid., 1:173.
21. Anderson, *Imagined Communities*, 67–82.
22. Paul Connerton, *How Societies Remember* (New York: Cambridge University Press, 1989), 6–13.

1. THE VOLUNTEER ARMY AND THE DISCOURSE OF NATION

1. Kyŏngsŏng taehakkyo hyangt'o munhwa yŏn'guso, ed., *Non'gae sajŏk yŏn'gu* [A study of Non'gae from historical perspective] (Pusan: Sinji sŏwŏn, 1996).
2. Yi Sungju, Kim Chŏnggyu, and Han Chunsŏ, *Pulmyŏl ŭi Yi Sunsin* [Immortal Yi Sunsin] (South Korea: Korean Broadcasting System, September 4–August 28, 2005). [ED]
3. In practice, the army was not a unitary movement but consisted of dispersed groups with their own leaders. Nevertheless, in this study the groups are discussed together under the term "Righteous Army." The groups did not operate under a unified command, but for simplicity the term is used in the singular throughout this book. [ED]
4. Benedict Anderson, *Imagined Communities: Reflections on the Origin and Spread of Nationalism* (New York: Verso, 1983), 144.
5. For some of major studies this study relied on, see Ch'a Munsŏp, *Chosŏn sidae kunsa kwan'gye yŏn'gu* [A study of military affairs during the Chosŏn period] (Seoul: Tan'guk University Press, 1996); Chang

Pyŏngok, *Ŭibyŏng hangjaengsa* [History of the volunteer armies' fighting] (Seoul: Hanwŏn, 1991); Cho Wŏllae. *Imjin waeran kwa Honam chibang ŭi ŭibyŏng hangjaeng* [The Imjin War and the fighting of the volunteer armies in the Honam region] (Seoul: Asea Munhwasa, 2001); Ch'oe Hyosik, *Imjin waeran'gi Yŏngnam ŭi ŭibyŏng yŏn'gu* [A study of volunteer armies in Yŏngnam during the Imjin War] (Seoul: Kukhak charyowŏn, 2003); Ch'oe Yŏnghŭi, *Imjin waeranjung ŭi sahoe tongt'ae* [Social movements during the Imjin War] (Seoul: Han'guk yŏn'guwŏn, 1975); Samuel Dukhae Kim, "The Korean Monk-Soldiers in the Imjin Wars: An Analysis of Buddhist Resistance to the Hideyoshi Invasion, 1592–1598," (Ph.D. diss., Columbia University, 1978); Kim Tonghwa et al., "Hoguk taesŏng Samyŏng taesa yŏn'gu" [A study of the great patriotic Buddhist monk, Samyŏng], *Pulkyo hakpo* [Journal of Buddhism] 8 (1971): 13–205; Song Chŏnghyŏn, *Chosŏn sahoe wa Imjin ŭibyŏng yŏn'gu* [A study of the Chosŏn society and of the volunteer armies during the Imjin War] (Seoul: Haggyŏn munhwasa, 1998); Yi Sŏngnin, *Imjin ŭibyŏngjang, Cho Hŏn, yŏn'gu* [A study of a volunteer army leader, Cho Hŏn] (Seoul: Sin'gu munhwasa, 1993). [ED]

6. Raymond Williams, *Marxism and Literature* (Oxford: Oxford University Press, 1977), 128–35. [ED]

7. Yi Sangbaek, *Han'guksa: Kŭnse chŏn'gi p'yŏn* [History of Korea: Early modern period] (Seoul: Ŭryu munhwasa, 1962), 601–3.

8. For discussion of the misunderstanding concerning Korea's position toward Hideyoshi's request, see Kitajima Manji, *Chōsen nichinichiki, Kōrai nikki: Hideyoshi no Chōsen shinryaku to sono rekishiteki kokuhatsu* [Daily record in Chosŏn, Korea diary: Hideyoshi's invasion of Chosŏn and its historical judgment] (Tokyo: Soshiete, 1982), 19–38.

9. SSS 25:3a–b [24/3#4]; Wm. Theodore de Bary and Donald Keene, eds., *Sources of Japanese Tradition* (New York: Columbia University Press, 2002), 1:166–67. For a different translation, see Mary Elizabeth Berry, *Hideyoshi* (Cambridge, Mass.: Harvard University Press, 1982), 208. The letter had already been a subject of dispute between the Korean ambassadors of the mission, who saw it while they were in Japan, and Hideyoshi's intermediaries. Finding it full of suspicious and insolent passages, the Koreans had protested to Keitetsu

Genso, the mediator, who apologized and made a few cosmetic changes. SSS 25:3b [24/3#5].

10. The Korean response was sharp. One official demanded the execution of Genso. SSS 25:4a–11a [24/3#7]; Jurgis Elisonas, "The Inseparable Trinity: Japan's Relations with China and Korea," in *The Cambridge History of Japan*, ed. John Whitney Hall (Cambridge: Cambridge University Press, 1991), 4:265–66.

11. *Han'guksa: Chosŏn chunggi ŭi woech'im kwa kŭ taeŭng* [History of Korea: An outcry and its response of mid-Chosŏn] (Seoul: Kuksa py'ŏnch'an wiwŏnhoe, 1995), 29:24–26.

12. The preparations were opposed by the local elite, and resented by the people conscripted for construction of the fortresses for military training. SSS 25:18b [24/7#6]; also Yu Sŏngnyong, *Chingbirok* [The book of corrections], cited in *Han'guksa*, 29:25–26nn.8, 9.

13. Kenneth M. Swope, "The Three Great Campaigns of the Wanli Emperor, 1592–1600: Court, Military, and Society in Late Sixteenth-Century China" (Ph.D. diss., University of Michigan, 2001), 180.

14. During the early Chosŏn, Pusan was a small port town whereas Tongnae was a county of Kyŏngsang Province. [ED]

15. Korean sources intimate large-scale killings but do not give specific numbers. For example, see Cho Kyŏngnam, *Nanjung chamnok* [The miscellaneous records of the war], in *Kugyŏk Taedong yasŭng* [The translation of the unofficial narratives of the Great East] (Seoul: Minjok munhwa ch'ujinhoe, 1972), 3:330–31, which describes someone hiding under the pile of dead bodies.

16. Yoshino Jingozaeon, *Yoshino Jingozaeon oboegaki* [Yoshino Jingozaeon's memoir] (Tokyo: Zoku Gunsho Ruijū Kanseikai, 1931), 23:379. Another number cited was 8,500. Samuel Jay Hawley, *The Imjin War: Japan's Sixteenth-Century Invasion of Korea and Attempt to Conquer China* (Seoul: Royal Asiatic Society, Korea Branch, and Berkeley: Institute of East Asian Studies, University of California, 2005), 138.

17. These figures are given by Tenkei, the Buddhist monk who accompanied Konishi Yukinaga as a recorder, in his *Saisei nikki*. Quoted in Kitajima, *Chōsen nichinichiki*, 13.

18. There were surely occasional displays of brave martyrdom by loyal officials—for example, the martyrdom of Shin Kilwŏn, the

164   1. THE DISCOURSE OF NATION

   magistrate of Mun'gyŏng (*Nanjung chamnok*, 1:343)—but no effective resistance.
19. *Han'guksa*, 29:29; Kitajima, *Chōsen nichinichiki*, 12.
20. *Sŏnjo sillok* (hereafter SS) 26:1a [25/4/17#1]; SSS 26:3b–4a [25/4#8]; *Nanjung chamnok*, 3:343.

   The *Veritable Records of Sŏnjo* (*Sŏnjo sillok*) is cited in these notes according to fascicle and page (i.e., 26:5a) followed by the date and entry number in brackets (i.e., [26/5/12#5]). The date is in the order of reign year, lunar month, and day. The entry number reflects the organization of individual daily records in the *Veritable Records of the Kings of the Chosŏn Dynasty* (*Chosŏn wangjo sillok*) provided by the Kuksa P'yŏnch'an Wiwŏnhoe (National Institute of Korean History) at http://sillok.history.go.kr/. [ED]

21. SS 26:1b [25/04/17#4]; SSS 26:5a–5b [25/4#16]; *Nanjung chamnok*, 3:344–45.
22. Clifford Geertz, *The Interpretation of Cultures: Selected Essays* (New York: Basic Books, 1973), 332.
23. SS 26:2a–b [25/4/28#4]; 26:2b [25/4/29#1]; 26:3a [25/4/29#4]; SSS 26:12a [25/5#21]; 26:6a [25/4#23].
24. SS 26:3a [25/4/30#1;#3]; *Nanjung chamnok*, 3:348.
25. SS 26:1b–2a [25/04/28#1;#3].
26. SS 26:2b [25/4/29#2].
27. SSS 26:7a [25/04#28].
28. *Nanjung chamnok*, 1:347–48.
29. SS 26:3a [25/5/3#5]; 27:3b [25/6/10#1]; 27:4b [25/06/11#1]; *Han'guksa*, 29:33–34.
30. Ch'a Munsŏp, *Chosŏn sidae kunsa kwan'gye yŏn'gu*, 1–38.
31. Yi I proposed a creation of army of 100,000 men on active duty, with 20,000 in the capital and 10,000 in each province. James B. Palais, *Confucian Statecraft and Korean Institutions: Yu Hyŏngwŏn and the Late Chosŏn Dynasty* (Seattle: University of Washington Press, 1996), 76.
32. Their capture is first reported in the *Veritable Records* on October 8, 1592. See SS 30:3a [25/9/4#3].
33. Kuk Kyŏng'in was a native of Hoeryŏng, Hamgyŏng Province. SS 36:20b–21a [26/3/11#2].

1. THE DISCOURSE OF NATION 165

34. The two princes were released in the summer of 1593, after a year of captivity. SS 41:48a–b [26/8/23#4]; [26/8/24#2].
35. O Hŭimun, *Swaemirok* [The records of trivial and insignificant matters] (Seoul: Kuksa p'yŏnch'an wiwŏnhoe, 1962), 7.
36. For a critical assessment of this practice, see Yu Sŏngnyong's remark in *SS* 48:33–33b [27/02/27#1].
37. It is not clear when the edict was sent out. The *Veritable Records of Sŏnjo*, in an entry of 5/3 (June 12, 1592), says that the king wrote an edict addressed to the scholars and people of the capital city, but because the city fell to the enemy, the person in charge of delivering the message could not do it (*SS* 26:4b [25/5/03#8]). This was when the court was staying at Kaesŏng. The *Revised Annals*, in an entry for the fifth month, says that the king promulgated the edict and sent it out to eight paths, and sent officials with his message that the people should mobilize into a volunteer army (*SSS* 26:9a [25/5#9]). The entries in the revised annals are made by months, not specific dates, but this entry comes after one that reports that the capital city fell. Hence this edict must have been written at the earliest on the fourth of the fifth month (June 13, 1592).
38. Chŏng T'ak, *Yongsa ilgi* [The diary of the dragon and snake war] (9/15/Imjin year) (Pusan: Pusan University, 1962), 189–94. Chŏng T'ak's *Yongsa ilgi* indicates that nonelites would be allowed to take the state examinations or be granted degrees. [ED]
39. Chosŏn society was based on four different hereditary social status groups. At the top was the aristocracy, known as *yangban*, a small group of governing aristocrats who comprised less than 10 percent of the total population. Another small group just below this elite stratum was known as "middle people" (*chungin*)—government technical specialists, administrative functionaries, and some illegitimate sons (*sŏŏl*) of aristocratic fathers and concubines (*ch'ŏp*). Next were the commoners, who were mostly peasants but also artisans and merchants. These people made up the majority of the population and carried most of the burden of taxation, military service, and corvée labor. At the bottom were the low-born, known as *ch'ŏnmin*, who were mostly slaves but also included those with debased occupations such as butchers, tanners, shamans, and female entertainers. [ED]

40. Kim Su instructed the residents to hide. *SSS* 26:3b–4a [25/4#8]. Some officials are reported to have taken things from the state treasury. *SSS* 26:2b–3a [25/4#3].
41. In his memorial Kwak Chaeu puts the date as June 1 (4/22), but his first identifiable military action is set at June 3 (4/24). Ch'oe Hyosik, *Imjin waeran'gi*, 130.
42. Kwak's and his wife's families were supposed to have been affluent. Ch'oe Hyosik, *Imjin waeran'gi*, 125–26.
43. *Nanjung chamnok*, 1:339–40.
44. Kim was the deputy ambassador on the mission to Japan in 1590. Contrary to Ambassador Hwang Yun'gil who reported that Japan was likely to attack Korea, Kim maintained that he did not see signs of planned invasion and that it was unlikely. It is said that the new appointment was due to Yu Sŏngyong's defense of Kim. *SSS* 26:4b [25/4#12].
45. Yi No says that this was 5/8 (Yi No, *Yongsa ilgi*, 46–58) while Cho Kyŏngnam places it in the entry of 5/5 (*Nanjung chamnok*, 1:359–64).
46. *Nanjung chamnok*, 1:339–40.
47. Although the *Revised Sŏnjo sillok*, like all *Sillok*, was compiled after the death of the king who bears its title, it heavily consulted the documents produced during the time that it describes and attempted to represent the views of that time.
48. This entry is included in the sixth month of 1592, which corresponds to July 9 to August 6. *SSS* 26:19b [25/6#32].
49. The *Miscellaneous Record* states that Kwak took great care in safeguarding the river so that the inhabitants of many villages could farm no differently from the time of peace. *Nanjung chamnok*, 1:341; *SSS* 26:19b [25/6#32].
50. Yi Hyŏngjong, ed., *Cho Chŏng sŏnsaeng munjip* [The literary collection of Cho Chŏng] (Seoul: Cho Chŏng sŏnsaeng munjip kanhaeng wiwŭnhoe, 1977), 144.
51. *Nanjung chamnok*, 1:390, 393–95. *Nanjung chamnok* also states that Chŏng Inhong was the first one who formed the Righteous Army, but because he did not wish to claim the military merit, he was not awarded this distinction (1:390).
52. "Kyo Chŏng Inhong, Kim Myŏn tŭng sŏ," in *Swaemirok*, 259–61.

53. *Nanjung chamnok*, 1:367, 351. The court stayed at Kaesŏng. On June 12, the day the Japanese Army took the capital city, Governor Yi wrote to Ko Kyŏngmyŏng, a local elite and a former official who enjoyed a reputation as a good writer, asking him to compose a letter exhorting people to rise as a volunteer army. On June 30 Yun Ansŏng, magistrate of Namwŏn, sent out an open letter addressed to the scholars of the locality in which, after reporting that Kwak Chaeu had risen in the occupied region, he lamented that "no Righteous Army yet emerged in Chŏlla despite the beautiful custom of the province that was second to none." Ibid., 1:383.
54. *Swaemirok*, 30–36.
55. Yi's rationale was that the royal court had moved on and, not knowing its whereabouts or even its survival, it was pointless to keep marching north. Yi Kŭngik, *Kugyŏk Yŏllryŏsil kisul* [The translation of the narratives of *yŏllryŏsil*], ed. Kim Yungyŏng (Seoul: Minjok munhwa ch'ujinhoe), 4:89.
56. Kim Ch'ŏnil, "Yŏnbo," 12b–13a; Cho Wŏllae, *Imjin waeran*, 115–16.
57. About ten letters were sent out. Ko Kyŏngmyŏng, *Kugyŏk Chebong chŏnsŏ* [The translation of the anthology of Chebong] (Sŏngnam: Chŏngsin munhwa yŏn'guwŏn, 1980), 2:31–48.
58. Letters of exhortation were employed in different ways. For instance, rebel leaders used the genre to mobilize people for their cause. For various uses of the letters, see JaHyun Kim Haboush, "Open Letters: Patriotic Exhortations During the Imjin War," in *Epistolary Korea: Letters in the Communicative Space of the Chosŏn, 1392–1910*, ed. JaHyun Kim Haboush (New York: Columbia University Press, 2009), 121–40.
59. Yi Kwang sent a letter to Ko Kyŏngmyŏng urging him to compose an exhortation: "The royal entourage has left for the West, and we could not guard the capital city. Now that the affairs of our country have reached this, this is truly lamentable. If there is one thing we could do, it is to write a letter of exhortation of sorrow and urgency, to disseminate to like-minded colleagues wherever we can, and to hope that they will raise an army to blot out our heaven-searing rage. However, if words [in the letter] are not passionate, it won't be able to move people's hearts, and one should not compose it roughly or carelessly. Dare I ask you to please compose it, and show it to me?"

Nanjung chamnok, 1:351. The Japanese occupation of Seoul is recorded on the same day.
60. Anthony D. Smith, *The Ethnic Origins of Nations* (Oxford: Blackwell, 1986), 153–208.
61. According to Smith, the goal and the content of the national imaginings were to "to present a vision of ethnic fraternity of elites and masses through a historical drama in which a unified past is uncovered and re-presented, in the fashion of a museum, and thereby to evoke deeper meanings of collective destiny and community in the face of the dangerous fragmentation and alienation that modern industrialization and science unfold." Ibid., 173.
62. Kim Sŏng'il, *Hakpong chŏnjip* [The complete anthology of Hakbong] (Seoul: Hakpong sonsaeng kinyŏm saŏphoe), 141–43; *Kukyŏk Hakpong chŏnjip* [The translation of the complete anthology of Hakbong] (Seoul: Hakpong sŏnsaeng kinyŏm saŏphoe), 364–69. For a discussion and English translation of this exhortation, see Haboush, "Open Letters," 121–24, 126–30. Yi No says the date was 5/8 (Yi No, *Yongsa ilgi*, 46–58) while Cho Kyŏngnam places it in the entry of 5/5 (*Nanjung chamnok*, 1:359–64).
63. The author of the *Miscellaneous Record* comments, after quoting this letter, that Kim Sŏng'il let another scholar compose it but did not like it, so he rewrote it himself. His words came out of his heart and he was so moved that he barely had the time to wet his brush in ink. *Nanjung chamnok*, 1:364.
64. A *li* is a unit of measure equal to approximately 449.17 meters (a third of a mile).
65. T'oegye and Nammyŏng were two of the most renowned Neo-Confucian scholars of the sixteenth century.
66. Ko passed the higher civil service examination (*munkwa*) in 1558 at the top and served in both the central and local governments. He retired from service and mobilized a volunteer army as a private person.
67. "So passionate and heartfelt that when anyone reads it, his hair stands on end and tears began to roll down his cheek" (preface by Yi Chŏnggu, in Ko Kyŏngmyŏng, *Kugyŏk Chebong chŏnsŏ*, 2:25).

1. THE DISCOURSE OF NATION 169

68. Ko Kyŏngmyŏng, *Kugyŏk Chebong chŏnsŏ* 2:33–36; *Swaemirok*, 130–31. For a discussion and English translation of this exhortation, see Haboush, "Open Letters," 124–25, 130–32.
69. Ko Kyŏngmyŏng, *Kugyŏk Chebong chŏnsŏ*, 2:37–38.
70. Anderson, *Imagined Communities*, 144.
71. *Nanjung chamnok*, 1:472–73. See also Cho Wŏllae, *Imjin waeran*, 183–86.
72. Yi Sŏngnin, *Imjin ŭibyŏngjang*, 144–57.
73. The letter is undated but must have been written early in the seventh month of 1592. *Nanjung chamnok*, 1:91–93 (49–50). For a discussion and English translation, see Haboush, "Open Letters," 125–26, 132–35.
74. This exhortation is undated, but from context it can be located sometime in the twelfth month of 1592, just before Chinese Army arrived. Yi Hyŏngjong, ed., *Cho Chŏng sŏnsaeng munjip*, 454. For an English translation, see Haboush, "Open Letters," 137.
75. Ko, *Chonggirok*, 13a–14a. For an English translation, see Haboush, "Open Letters," 135–37.
76. From the first circular letter signed by the residents of Yŏngdong city, Chŏlla Province, dated 5/13/1592, *Swaemirok*, 17–18.
77. From an exhortation signed by private scholars Kim Hyŏn, Kim Hŭn, Kim Sŏm, and others residing in Kobu of Chŏlla Province around 5/27/1592. This letter is not dated but was written before July 6 (5/27). Ibid., 20.
78. Song Chemin's exhortation, in *Nanjung chamnok*, 1:91–93 (40–49).
79. From the exhortation of Yi Kwang, governor of Chŏlla, sixth month of 1592, *Swaemirok*, 18–19.
80. Kim Sŏng'il to Kwak Chaeu, 5/20/1592, *Nanjung chamnok*, 1:376–77.
81. From the circular letter that Cho Chongdo, the former magistrate, and Yi No, former petty officer, sent to Kyŏngsang Province, 5/5/1592, ibid., 1:365.
82. Chŏng Kyŏngse's memo (*kye*) to Kim Sŏng'il, 5/24/1592, ibid., 1:389.
83. From the exhortation of Governor Yi Kwang of Chŏlla, written sometime during the fifth month of 1592. *Swaemirok*, 18–19.
84. Two Ho refers to Chŏlla and Ch'ungch'ŏng Provinces.

85. From Yu P'aengno's circular letter, Ko Kyŏngmyŏng, *Kugyŏk Chebong chŏnsŏ*, 2:37.
86. From an exhortation by Ko Chonghu, ibid., 2:53–54. Also *Nanjung chamnok*, 1:399–400.
87. *Chunghwa* refers to China, but also it was used as metaphor for civilization. When Koreans referred to their country as *sojunghwa*, they meant an entity that was a territorially smaller than but culturally equal to China.
88. Kim Myŏn's exhortation, 10/20/1592, *Nanjung chamnok*, 2:557.
89. From Chŏng Kyŏngse's letter to the chief recruiter, 7/3/1592, ibid., 1:387.
90. From the commander of the Royal Army, Kim Myŏngwŏn's exhortation to eight provinces, 7/13/1592, ibid., 1:409.
91. From the exhortation of Yi Kwang, governor of Chŏlla, *Swaemirok*, 18–19.
92. From Chŏng Kyŏngse's letter to the chief recruiter, 7/3/1592, *Nanjung chamnok*, 1:387.
93. From the governor of Kwangju Kwŏn Yul's exhortation to all the gentlemen of all the counties of Chŏlla, 8/3/1592, *Swaemirok*, 31–33.
94. From the exhortation to all the gentlemen of all the counties of Chŏlla by Kwŏn Yul, mayor of Kwangju, 6/26/1592, ibid.
95. From the circular letter of Cho Chongdo and Yi No, 7/14/1592, *Nanjung chamnok*, 1:365.
96. From Kim Chibok's exhortation "ŭibyŏng kyŏngmun," in Yi Hyŏngjong, ed., *Cho Chŏng sŏnsaeng munjip*, 302, 454.
97. From Ko Kyŏngmyŏng's letter to Ch'oe U, Ko Kyŏngmyŏng, *Kugyŏk Chebong chŏnsŏ*, 2:46
98. From Yi Kwang's exhortation sent to the soldiers of Kyŏngsang, 6/12/1592, *Nanjung chamnok*, 1:357.
99. From a circular letter by the residents of Yŏngdong, Chŏlla, 6/22/1592, *Swaemirok*, 17–8.
100. From Yu P'aengno's circular letter to the magistrates and superintendents of county schools of Ch'ungch'ŏng, Kyŏnggi, Hwanghae, and P'yŏngan Provinces, Ko Kyŏngmyŏng, *Kugyŏk Chebong chŏnsŏ*, 2:37–39; *Nanjung chamnok*, 1:400–3.

101. From Kim Tongnyŏng's letter to the villages in Chŏlla, 11/2/1593, *Swaemirok*, 390–91.
102. From the first letter by the residents of Yŏngdong, Chŏlla, ibid., 17–18.
103. From Ko Chonghu's letter sent to monks secluded in temples, Ko Kyŏngmyŏng, *Kugyŏk Chebong chŏnsŏ*, 2:52–53.
104. From Ko Chonghu's exhortation, ibid., 2:55.
105. From the exhortation by Kim Hyŏn, Kim Hŭn, Kim Sŏm, and other private scholars of Kobu of Chŏlla, *Swaemirok*, 20.
106. Kim Yŏng's circular letter to Andong, Kyŏngsang, *Nanjung chamnok*, 2:613–14.
107. From Song Chemin's exhortation, ibid., 1:91–93 (40–49). [ED]
108. From the circular letter of Cho Chongdo and Yi No, 6/14/1592, ibid., 1:365.
109. From an exhortation by Cho Chongdo et al. *Nanjung chamnok*, 1:366, reports that Cho died at the walled city of Hwangsŏk in 1597.
110. This is reminiscent of early sixteenth-century France in which patriotism was equated with its image as the most Christian of kingdoms. Liah Greenfeld, *Nationalism: Five Roads to Modernity* (London: Blackwell, 1992), 102–3.

2. The Volunteer Army and the Emergence of Imagined Community

1. The editors added the chapter title and the transitional sentence from chapter 1 to chapter 2. [ED]
2. See, for example, an exhortation by the residents of Yŏngdong, Chŏlla, and O Hŭimun, in *Swaemirok* [The records of trivial and insignificant matters] (Seoul: Kuksa p'yŏnch'an wiwŏnhoe, 1962), 17–18.
3. For example, *Nanjung chamnok*, after recording a letter of exhortation, says that this was sent to all villages. See Cho Kyŏngnam, *Nanjung chamnok* [The miscellaneous record of the war], in *Kugyŏk Taedong yasŭng* [The translation of the unofficial narratives of the Great East] (Seoul: Minjok munhwa ch'ujinhoe, 1972), 1:453.
4. See Yu P'aengno's circular letter, no. 210.

5. Yi Hyŏngjong, ed., *Cho Chŏng sŏnsaeng munjip* [The literary collection of Cho Chŏng] (Seoul: Cho Chŏng sŏnsaeng munjip kanhaeng wiwŏnhoe, 1977), 169–71; Kim Sŏngu, *Chosŏn chunggi kukka wa sajok* [The state and the elites in mid-Chosŏn dynasty] (Seoul: Yŏksa pip'yŏngsa, 2001), 343.
6. *Swaemirok*, 31–34.
7. Ibid., 22.
8. Ibid., 33–35.
9. Ibid., 16–17.
10. *Nanjung chamnok*, 1:367. The court was staying at Kaesŏng at the time of the edict.
11. The *Veritable Records of Sŏnjo*, in an entry of June 12 (5/3), says that the king wrote an edict addressed to the scholars and people of the capital city, but because the city fell to the enemy, the person in charge of delivering the message could not do it (SS 26:4b [25/5/3#8]). This was when the court was staying at Kaesŏng. The *Revised Annals*, in an entry for the fifth month, says that the king promulgated the edict in which he took responsibility by blaming himself and sent it out to eight paths, and sent officials with his message that the people should mobilize into volunteer armies (SSS 26:9a [25/5#9]). The entries in the revised annals are made by months, not by specific date, but this entry comes after an entry that the capital city fell, and hence the edict must have been written at the earliest on June 13. The *Miscellaneous Record* also says that the king sent out a sad edict on June 7 (4/28) (*Nanjung chamnok*, 1:347).
12. For example, see the circular letter sent by the residents of Yŏngdong on 6/22/1592, *Swaemirok*, 22.
13. Jean-François Gilmont, "Protestant Reformation and Reading," in *A History of Reading in the West*, ed. Guglielmo Cavallo and Roger Chartier (Amherst: University of Massachusetts Press, 1999), 179–237, esp. 224–33.
14. For a discussion of the social setting in regard to art and literature, see Joseph Grigely, *Textualterity: Art, Theory, and Textual Criticism* (Ann Arbor: University of Michigan Press, 1995), 122.
15. See Yi Kwang's letter to Ko Kyŏngmyŏng, *Nanjung chamnok*, 1:351.

2. THE EMERGENCE OF IMAGINED COMMUNITY 173

16. For example, one circular letter specifically talks about appealing to those illiterate people who would be listening to the letter. See "Yŏngdong t'ongmun," in *Swaemirok*, 17–18.
17. This preface was written by Yi Chŏnggu in 1601. Ko Kyŏngmyŏng, *Kugyŏk Chebong chŏnsŏ*, 2:25.
18. "Yŏnbo," in ibid., 2:207.
19. Joseph McDermott, "The Ascendance of the Imprint in China," in *Printing and Book Culture in Late Imperial China*, ed. Cynthia J. Brokaw and Kai-wing Chow (Berkeley: University of California Press, 2005), 55–104, esp. 90–91.
20. For a survey of printing in Korea, see Pow-Key Sohn, "Early Korean Printing," *Journal of the American Oriental Society* 79, no. 2 (1959): 96–103.
21. For a discussion of the power of manuscript culture, see Sheldon Pollock, ed., *Literary Cultures in History* (Berkeley: University of California Press, 2003), 21.
22. Kim Tonguk, "P'anbon'go–Han'gŭl sosŏl panggakpon ŭi sŏngnip e taehayŏ" [The rise of woodblock-print vernacular novel], in *Ch'unhyang chŏn yŏn'gu* [A study of The Tale of Ch'unhyang], 3rd ed. (Seoul: Yŏnsei taehakkyo, 1983), 385–99; William Skillend, *Kodae sosŭl: A Survey of Korean Traditional Style Popular Novels* (London: School of Oriental and African Studies, University of London, 1968).
23. E.g., letters by Kim Sŏng'il, Yu P'aengno, and Kim Su in the following section.
24. Jurgis Elisonas, "The Inseparable Trinity: Japan's Relations with China and Korea," in *The Cambridge History of Japan*, ed. John W. Hall (Cambridge: Cambridge University Press, 1991), 4:276–77.
25. *Nanjung chamnok*, 2:577.
26. By the late sixteenth century the government had much relaxed its original anti-Buddhist stance and now welcomed the monks' contribution to fighting the Japanese. [MD]
27. *Nanjung chamnok*, 2:578; Samuel D. Kim, "The Korean Monk-Soldiers in the Imjin Wars: An Analysis of Buddhist Resistance to the Hideyoshi Invasion, 1592–1598" (Ph.D. diss., Columbia University, 1978).

28. Ch'oe Yŏnghŭi, *Imjin waeranjung ŭi sahoe tongt'ae* [Social movements during the Imjin War] (Seoul: Han'guk yŏn'guwŏn, 1975), 60.
29. On September 12, 1592, in a royal conference to discuss the deployment of troops, Yun Tusu, the minister of the left, proceeded from the assumption that Kim Ch'ŏnil's army was superior to the royal army, based on its being a Righteous Army. SS 29:8a [25/8/7#1].
30. SS 34:15a–17b [26/1/11#15].
31. Ch'oe Yŏnghŭi, *Imjin waeranjung*, 63.
32. Examples of this activity include Kim Sŏng'il, chief recruiter of Kyŏngsang Province, and Kyŏn Yu, governor of Naju, who recruited a large number of volunteers. Cho Wŏllae, *Imjin waeran kwa Honam chibang ŭi ŭibyŏng hangjaeng* [The Imjin War and the fighting of the volunteer armies in the Honam region] (Seoul: Asea Munhwasa, 2001), 7.
33. One example often cited for this category is Paek Kwang'ŏn, who mobilized several hundred men and fought under Yi Kwang, governor of Chŏlla, and was killed in the battle at Yongin. Ibid.
34. One case was Pyŏn Ŭnjing, the magistrate of Haenam, who joined Cho Hŏn, and died at the battle at Kŭmsan. Ibid.
35. Ch'oe Yŏnghŭi, *Imjin waeranjung*, 49–51; Ch'oe Hyosik, *Imjin waerani'gi Yŏngnam ŭi ŭibyŏng yŏn'gu* [A study of volunteer armies in Yŏngnam during the Imjin War] (Seoul: Kukhak charyowŏn, 2003), 468–94.
36. Ch'oe Hyosik, *Imjin waerani'gi*, 206–13.
37. Kenneth M. Swope, "Crouching Tigers, Secret Weapons: Military Technology Employed During the Sino-Japanese-Korean War, 1592–1598," *Journal of Military History* 69, no.1 (2005): 27–28.
38. *Swaemirok*, 17–18.
39. Cho Wŏllae, *Imjin waeran*, 142.
40. J. L. Boots, "Korean Weapons and Armor," *Transactions of the Korea Branch of the Royal Asiatic Society* 33, no. 2 (1934): 4.
41. For a discussion on this point, see Song Chŏnghyŏn, *Chosŏn sahoe wa Imjin ŭibyŏng yŏn'gu* [A study of the Chosŏn society and of the volunteer armies during the Imjin War] (Seoul: Hagyŏn munhwasa, 1998), 58–61.
42. *Nanjung chamnok*, 1:467.
43. Ch'oe Hyosik, *Imjin waerani'gi*, 134–38.

2. THE EMERGENCE OF IMAGINED COMMUNITY

44. Cho Wŏllae, *Imjin waeran*, 216.
45. *Nanjung chamnok*, 2:623–29.
46. Ch'oe Yŏnghŭi, *Imjin waeranjung*, 25–26; Cho Wŏllae, *Imjin waeran*, 216–21.
47. *Nanjung chamnok*, 2:562–72.
48. Kitajima Manji, *Chōsen nichinichiki, Kōrai nikki: Hideyoshi no Chōsen shinryaku to sono rekishiteki kokuhatsu* [Daily record in Chosŏn, Korea diary: Hideyoshi's invasion of Chosŏn and its historical judgment] (Tokyo: Soshiete, 1982), 249–50.
49. Cho Wŏllae, *Imjin waeran*, 86–88.
50. Ch'oe Hyosik puts it at 8,000 (*Imjin waeran'gi*, 93), while Cho Wŏllae estimates around 15,000 (*Imjin waeran*, 140).
51. *Nanjung chamnok*, 2:647; Ch'oe Hyosik, *Imjin waeran'gi*, 102; Chang Pyŏngok, *Ŭibyŏng hangjaengsa* [History of the volunteer armies' fighting] (Seoul: Hanwŏn, 1991), 116.
52. Chang Pyŏngok, *Ŭibyŏng hangjaengsa*, 118–31.
53. Cho Wŏllae, *Imjin waeran*, 144.
54. JaHyun Kim Haboush, "Dead Bodies in the Postwar Discourse of Identity in Seventeenth-Century Korea: Subversion and Literary Production in the Private Sector," *Journal of Asian Studies* 62, no. 2 (2003): 428.
55. *SS* 32:14b [25/11/16#2].
56. *SSS* 26:19a–b [25/6#31].
57. Liah Greenfeld states that popular sovereignty was interpreted either as actual sovereignty of individuals or as the theoretical sovereignty of the people, that whereas in the case of actual sovereignty the idea was inspired by the practice, in the case of theoretical sovereignty the imported idea initiated the changes of the political structure, and that these views led to either individualistic-libertarian or collectivistic-authoritarian nationalism. Greenfeld, *Nationalism: Five Roads to Modernity* (London: Blackwell, 1992), 10–11.
58. The first recorded announcement of this concept appears in the "Announcement by Tang" (Tang gao) in the *Book of History*. See Clae Waltham, ed., and James Legge, trans., *Shu Ching: Book of History, a Modernized Edition of the Translations of James Legge* (Chicago: Regnery, 1971), 72–73.

176 2. THE EMERGENCE OF IMAGINED COMMUNITY

59. *T'aejo sillok* 1:43a–45a [1/7/28#3]; English translation is in Peter Lee and Wm. Theodore de Bary, eds., *Sources of Korean Tradition: From Early Times Through the Sixteenth Century* (New York: Columbia University Press, 1997), 1:272–74.
60. Sŏnjo's edict of the twenty-fifth of the fourth month (6/4/1592) addressed to "officials, men out of office, older subjects, soldiers, and the people" pleaded that "the soldiers and people of all provinces forgive my mistakes and, in consideration of my sincere wish, rise in passionate determination and exterminate the enemy so that we can live in peace as before." See "Sŏnjo kyosŏ," in *Swaemirok*, 21–22. The *Revised Veritable Records of Sŏnjo* records another edict of the same type in the entry of the first of the fifth month. SSS 26:9a [25/5#9].
61. Martina Deuchler, *The Confucian Transformation of Korea: A Study of Society and Ideology* (Cambridge, Mass.: Council on East Asian Studies, Harvard University, 1992), 12–13.
62. Tu Wei-ming, "Yi T'oegye's Perception of Human Nature: A Preliminary Inquiry into the Four-Seven Debate in Korean Neo-Confucianism," in *The Rise of Neo-Confucianism in Korea*, ed. Wm. Theodore de Bary and JaHyun Kim Haboush (New York: Columbia University Press, 1985), 261–81.
63. Young-chan Ro, *The Korean Neo-Confucianism of Yi Yulgok* (Albany: State University of New York Press, 1989).
64. Yong-ho Ch'oe, "Private Academies and the State in Late Chosŏn Korea," in *Culture and the State in Late Chosŏn Korea*, ed. JaHyun Kim Haboush and Martina Deuchler (Cambridge, Mass.: Harvard University Asia Center, 1999), 15–45.
65. This refers to self-regulating organizations that also offered mutual assistance. See Sakai Tadao, "Yi Yulgok and the Community Compact," in *The Rise of Neo-Confucianism in Korea*, ed. Wm. Theodore de Bary and JaHyun Haboush (New York: Columbia University Press), 323–48; Martina Deuchler, "The Practice of Confucianism: Ritual and Order in Chosŏn Dynasty Korea," in *Rethinking Confucianism: Past and Present in China, Japan, Korea, and Vietnam*, ed. Benjamin Elman, John Duncan, and Herman Ooms (Los Angeles: Asia Pacific Monograph Series, University of California, Los Angeles, 2002), 292–334. For China, see Cynthia Joanne Brokaw, *The Ledgers of Merit and Demerit: So-*

2. THE EMERGENCE OF IMAGINED COMMUNITY   177

cial Change and Moral Order in Late Imperial China (Princeton: Princeton University Press, 1991).

66. It frequently happens when social status is encoded with the qualities of virtue, the coexistence of two possible arguments—that the elite had privileges because of their moral superiority or that moral superiority resulted in their noble status—had a potential for exacerbating rather than resolving the tension. For a discussion of the conflict between class and the qualities of nobility in eighteenth-century France before 1789, see Jay M. Smith, *Nobility Reimagined* (Ithaca: Cornell University Press, 2005), 26–179.

67. I am not suggesting that their new role was a transformation from transpolitical to national identity, which Gellner proposes as markers of the change from agro-literate polity to industrial society. In his generalization Gellner acknowledges that the Chinese bureaucracy was one of the rare instances in which the ruling strata were co-extensive with a state, and that it displayed a certain kind of nationalism. This certainly applied to the ruling elite of Chosŏn. Ernest Gellner, *Nations and Nationalism* (Ithaca: Cornell University Press, 1983), 13–17.

68. JaHyun Kim Haboush, "Open Letters: Patriotic Exhortations During the Imjin War," in *Epistolary Korea: Letters in The Communicative Space of the Chosŏn, 1392–1910*, ed. JaHyun Kim Haboush (New York: Columbia University Press, 2009), 131.

69. George L. Mosse discussed the nationalization of the masses to describe the politics that "draw the people into active participation in the national mystique through rites and festivals, myths and symbols which gave a concrete expression to the general will." Mosse, *The Nationalization of the Masses* (Ithaca: Cornell University Press, 1975), 2. I am using the term a little differently.

70. Greenfeld, *Nationalism*, 7.

71. Soon after the arrival of the Chinese troops, for example, the Righteous Army was assigned to transport food provisions. On February 11, 1593, it was only the Righteous Army of Kyŏnggi to which this duty was assigned (*SS* 34:12b [26/1/11#8]), but on February 23 the entire Righteous Army was assigned to it (*SS* 34:36b [26/1/23#5]).

72. SSS 28:4a [27/4#3].
73. The *Veritable Records of Sŏnjo* records a conference in which the king and high ministers discussed Kim, and it is clear that they regarded him as a threat and thought it judicious to get rid of him. SS 78:5a–6a [29/8/4#3].
74. The *Revised Veritable Records of Sŏnjo* records the impact of the news of Kim's death: "When the Japanese heard the news of [Kim's] death, they happily congratulated each other. The soldiers and the people of the southern region had relied on him and looked up to him. When he died under a false accusation, all who heard the news were chagrined and saddened. From this time scholars and the people of the region took this event as a warning, and those with military skills hid themselves and did not again mobilize the Righteous Army." SSS 30:6a–7a [29/8#1].

3. War of Words: The Changing Nature of Literary Chinese in the Japanese Occupation

1. There is, for example, an extant manuscript copy, which is believed to have been sent out by the government in 1593. This copy is owned by a private family in Kyŏngju city in Kyŏngsang Province, the area in which the poster must have been circulated. Kim Chongt'aek, "Sŏnjo taewang ŏn'gyo ko" [A consideration of King Sŏnjo's vernacular Korean edicts], *Kugŏ kyoyuk nonji* [Discourse on Korean education] (Taegu: Taegu kyoyuk taehak, 1975): 27–34.
2. Diplomatic relations between states were maintained through an elaborate system of ambassadorial missions. Depending on the nature of the relations and agreements, envoys were either exchanged or sent unilaterally. While the ambassadorial missions contained interpreters, all written communiqués were in literary Chinese, be they official or private.
3. In contrast to the period of Mongol domination, when there was a great deal of movement and travel in various directions by peoples in the region, personal travels abroad were rare during Chosŏn until late in the nineteenth century. Private individuals went to China, but they did so within the framework of ambassadorial missions. There

were several Korean missions a year to China, and those officials holding ambassadorial ranks in the mission were allowed to take a certain number of guests at their own expense. In this way a considerable number of literati men went to China, and some of them met and developed friendships with Chinese, and they exchanged letters mainly through people on ambassadorial entourages.

4. Benedict Anderson, *Imagined Communities: Reflections on the Origin and Spread of Nationalism* (New York: Verso, 1983), 14–15.

5. Sheldon Pollock discusses a mutually constitutive relationship of literature and community in the South Asian vernacular space of the late medieval period. See Pollock, "The Cosmopolitan Vernacular," *Journal of Asian Studies* 57, no. 1 (1998): 16–37.

6. JaHyun Kim Haboush, "Royal Edicts: Constructing an Ethnopolitical Community," in *Epistolary Korea: Letters in the Communicative Space of the Chosŏn, 1392–1910*, ed. JaHyun Kim Haboush (New York: Columbia University Press, 2009), 19.

7. Cespedes is viewed as having been influential in converting many Korean prisoners of war to Catholicism. Kim Yangsŏn estimates the number of converts at seven thousand. See Kim, "Imjin waeran chonggun sinbu Cespedes ŭi naehan hwaltong kwa kŭ yŏnghyang" [Activities and influences of the priest Cespedes in Korea during the Imjin War], *Sahak yŏn'gu* [Researches in Historical Studies] 18 (Sept. 1964): 705–39.

8. Virginia Mason Vaughan, "Preface: The Mental Maps of English Renaissance Drama," in *Playing the Globe: Genre and Geography in English Renaissance Drama*, ed. John Gilles and Virginia Mason Vaughan (London: Associated University Presses, 1998), 14.

9. SSS 25:3a–b [24/3#4]; Wm. Theodore de Bary and Donald Keene, eds., *Sources of Japanese Tradition*, 2nd ed. (New York: Columbia University Press, 2002) 1:466–67.

10. According to *Kokusho sōmokuroku* [General catalog of national books], Yoshino's memoir was written in 1593. However, the text that Haboush consulted seems to suggest that the memoir was written eighteen years after Hideyoshi's death, which would have made it 1616. See Yoshino Jingozaemon, *Yoshino Jingozaemon oboegaki* [Yo-

shino Jingozaemon's memoir], in *Zoku-gunsho ruijū* [Continued topical collection of all books] (Tokyo: Zoku Gunsho Ruijū Kanseikai, 1923–). [ED]

11. One *hiro* is about 1.8 meters (about 5.11 feet).
12. Yoshino, *Yoshino Jingozaemon oboegaki*, 379–80. This work, written in Japanese, is quoted in various other works. See Stephen Turnbull, *Samurai Invasion: Japan's Korean War, 1592–1598* (London: Cassell, 2002), 50–51. Turnbull mistakenly translates: "and there came to our ears the Chinese expression, 'Manō! Manō!'" He then says, "The contempt and ignorance which led Yoshino to think that the people of Korea spoke Chinese provides a clue." Turnbull is quoted in Samuel J. Hawley, *The Imjin War: Japan's Sixteenth-Century Invasion of Korea and Attempt to Conquer China* (Seoul: Royal Asiatic Society Seoul Branch, 2005), 138. Also in Sajima Akiko, "The Japan-Ming Negotiations," paper presented to the Imjin War conference at Oxford University, August 2001, 2–3.
13. Kitajima Manji, *Chōsen nichinichiki, Kōrai nikki: Hideyoshi no Chōsen shinryaku to sono rekishiteki kokuhatsu* [Daily record in Chosŏn, Korea diary: Hideyoshi's invasion of Chosŏn and its historical accusation] (Tokyo: Sohiete, 1982), 41–55; Jurgis Elisonas, "The Inseparable Trinity: Japan's Relations with China and Korea," in *The Cambridge History of Japan*, ed. John W. Hall (Cambridge: Cambridge University Press, 1991), 4:273.
14. The *Miscellaneous Record* reports on June 16 the burning of Yangsan (Nanjung chamnok, 1:333); on June 19 the burning of Yŏngsan and Ch'ŏngdo (1:334); on June 21 the burning of Ch'angnyŏng, Hyŏnp'ung (1:337); on the same day the burning of Hayang and the massacre of its residents (1:337–38); and on June 23 the burning of Indong, Sŏngju, and Ch'angwŏn (1:341–42). It says that Yangsang, Yŏngsan, Ch'ŏngdo, Ch'angnyŏng, Hyŏnp'ung, and Sŏngju were all reduced to ashes. *Nanjung chamnok*, 1:334, 337, 341.
15. This was at first attributed to logistical undesirability and then to his poor health. (See Hawley, *The Imjin War*, 123–24.)
16. Kitajima Manji explains that it was one of the duties of the accompanying Buddhist monks to write such proclamations and keep records. Kitajima, *Chōsen nichinichiki*, 44.

17. The proclamation is recorded in *Saisei nikki* (The diary of the western campaign), a journal kept by Tenkei, in *Zokuzoku gunsho ruijū* (Tokyo: Zoku gunsho ruijū kanseikai, 1969–1978), 3:677.
18. *Nanjung chamnok*, 1:342 (4/24/1592); 1:350 (5/3/1592).
19. Before the Japanese entered Seoul, the angry mob set fire to royal palace. *SSS* 26:9b [25/4#28].
20. Katō Kiyomasa ate Toyotomi Hideyoshi shuinjō [To Katō Kiyomasa. Toyotomi Hideyoshi's missive with red stamp], in *Katō monjo* [Documentation about Katō] quoted in Kitajima Manji, "The Imjin Waeran," paper presented to the Imjin War conference at Oxford University (August 2001), 9–10; Kitajima, *Chōsen nichinichiki*, 76–78.
21. Kimpaku Hidetsugu ate Toyotomi Hideyoshi oboegaki [To Kimpaku Hidetsugu. Toyotomi Hideyoshi's memoir], in *Seikan monjo* [Documentation on conquering Korea], in Kitajima, *Chōsen nichinichiki*, 67–71. For an English translation, see Yoshi Saburo Kuno, *Japanese Expansion on the Asiatic Continent: A Study in the History of Japan with Special Reference to Her international Relations with China, Korea, and Russia* (Berkeley: University of California Press, 1937), 1:314–18; Hawley, *The Imjin War*, 172–73.
22. Sō Yoshitoshi ate Toyotomi Hideyoshi shuinjō, in *Sōke Chōsenjin bunsho*, quoted in Kitajima, "The Imjin Waeran," 9–10. See also Kitajima, *Chōsen nichinichiki*, 90.
23. Tax was calculated in measures of grain. The total amount of tax from eight provinces was calculated at 81,916,186 koku. "Kōrai hatshū no kokunō oboe no koto" [What (the author) remembered about the collection of tax grains in eight provinces of Korea], *Tosa no kuni tokanshū* [Moth-eaten letters of Tosa Province] quoted in Kitajima, "The Imjin Waeran," 11.See also Kitajima, *Chōsen nichinichiki*, 90–91.
24. *Katō monjo*, in Kitajima, *Chōsen nichinichiki*, 91–92.
25. *Nanjung chamnok*, 2:502 (8/3/1592).
26. The Royal Ancestral Temple was not among the buildings that the angry mob burned, but the royal ancestral tablets were removed from the temple and taken with the royal court when it fled.
27. It is not known exactly when the tombs were destroyed. The *Revised Veritable Records of Sŏnjo* reports it as the twelfth month of the Imjin

year (1592) (SSS 26:44a [25/12#1]). The first time it appears in the *Veritable Records of Sŏnjo* is May 1593 (SS 37:17b [26/4/13#2]). The *Revised Veritable Records* seems to indicate that this was done in 1592 but that the Korean government did not hear of it until May the following year. The two tombs were both located in present-day Samsŏng-dong, south of Han River, in Seoul. At the time this was outside the walled city of Seoul.

28. Tenkei, *Saisei nikki*, 678.
29. These were dated with the Japanese imperial year and signed by several generals. The entry was followed by the author's comments: "The extremity of evil and atrocity could not surpass this, something that cannot be forgotten for ten thousand generations." *Nanjung chamnok*, 1:371 (5/20/1592).
30. Kankyōdō hyakushō ate Katō Kiyomasa bōbun [To people in Hamgyŏng Province, Katō Kiyomasa's poster], in *Taichōin monjo* [Taichōin documents], quoted in Kitajima, "The Imjin Waeran," 12. I am following the English translation provided at the conference, modified slightly. See also Kitajima, *Chōsen nichinichiki*, 99.
31. The total came to 244,360 *sŏk*. There were different categories of grain. "Chōsenkoku sozei chō" [Tax ledger of the Chosŏn state], quoted in Kitajima, "The Imjin Waeran," 13. See also Kitajima, *Chōsen nichinichiki*, 102. "Nabeshima Naoshige shuchi" [Nabeshima Naoshige's ruling over prefectures (in Hamgyŏng Province)], in Kitajima, *Chōsen nichinichiki*, 103–5.
32. Katō Kiyomasa to Ki (noshita) Hansuke, dated [Tenshō 20] 9/20/1592. See Hawley, *The Imjin War*, 268–69n10; Kitajima, *Chōsen nichinichiki*, 117–19; Elisonas, "The Inseparable Trinity," 275–76.
33. Jurgis Elisonas describes the situation as follows: true to their master's orders that they treat their conquered areas "according to Japanese rules" (*Nihon okime no gotoku*), "the generals of Hideyoshi's occupation forces in Korea taxed the peasants, confiscated their weapons, coerced them by taking hostages, and ruthlessly put down recalcitrants as though they were subjugating yet another Japanese province to his regime of unification through the methods of the Taikō kenchi." Elisonas, "The Inseparable Trinity," 275.

34. Tajiri Akitane, *Kōrai nikki*, entry of Bunroku 1 (1592) 7/18/1592, in Kitajima, *Chōsen nichinichiki*, 381.
35. *SS* 30:12b–13a [25/9/15#2].
36. Quoted in Kitajima, *Chōsen nichinichiki*, 106.
37. *Nanjung chamnok*, 1:460 (7/4/1592).
38. Ibid., 1:466–67 (7/9/1592).
39. Yi Chŏng'am, *Sŏjŏng illok* [The daily record of the western campaign] (Seoul: T'amgudang, 1979), 72–73.
40. Kitajima, *Chōsen nichinichiki*, 156–57.
41. This is the poster that said that Japan was no longer the Japan of the past. Yi mentions that because of the *idu*, the writing was coarse and difficult to comprehend. In the entry of the fifth of the sixth month, Yi records it in pure Chinese, presumably his own translation. Yi Chŏng'am, *Sŏjŏng illok*, 72–73.
42. Yi T'aegyŏng, *Yŏkchu chŏngmannok* [Annotated translation of the record of the campaign against barbarians] (Ŭisŏng: Ŭisŏng munhwawŏn, 1992), 98–99.
43. *Nanjung chamnok*, 1:371 (5/20/1592).
44. *Itsuku monjo*, quoted in Kitajima, *Chōsen nichinichiki*, 92–93.
45. Kenneth M. Swope, "The Three Great Campaigns of the Wanli Emperor, 1592–1600: Court, Military, and Society in Late Sixteenth-Century China" (Ph.D. diss., University of Michigan, 2001), 214–23.
46. Luis Frois, *Historia de Japam*, ed. Josef Wicki (Lisbon: Bilioteca Nacional de Lisbona, 1976–1982), 5:599, quoted in Elisonas, "The Inseparable Trinity," 280.
47. *SSS* 26:44b–45a [25/12#4].
48. Swope says that this figure is disputed. Swope, "The Three Great Campaigns," 247–48.
49. *Nanjung chamnok*, 2:623 (1/5/1593).
50. Swope, "The Three Great Campaigns," 250–54.
51. For a detailed discussion of the battle, see Hawley, *The Imjin War*, 324–27.
52. Tajiri Akitane, *Kōrai nikki*, entry of Bunroku 2 (1593) 1/23/1593, in Kitajima, *Chōsen nichinichiki*, 384. I modified Elisonas's translation ("The Inseparable Trinity," 280).

53. *Nanjung chamnok*, 2:633 (4/19/1593).
54. *SSS* 27:5a [26/1#4].
55. Swope, "The Three Great Campaigns," 257.
56. *SS* 43:2b [26/10/2#16].

4. Language Strategy:
The Emergence of a Vernacular National Space

1. Peter Lee and Wm. Theodore de Bary, eds., *Sources of Korean Tradition: From Early Times Through the Sixteenth Century* (New York: Columbia University Press, 1997), 1:57–59.
2. For a detailed treatment, see Kenneth M. Swope, "The Three Great Campaigns of the Wanli Emperor, 1592–1600: Court, Military, and Society in Late Sixteenth-Century China" (Ph.D. diss., University of Michigan, 2001), 89–156.
3. Kenneth M. Swope, "Bestowing the Double-Edged Sword: Wanli as a Supreme Military Commander," in *Culture, Courtiers, and Competition: The Ming Court (1368–1644)*, ed. David M. Robinson (Cambridge, Mass.: Harvard University Asia Center, 2008), 92–93. One *liang* was 1.327 ounces.
4. Zu reported to his superior that the defeat had been due to the nonparticipation of the Korean Army, charging that a portion of the army had surrendered to the Japanese. The Korean assessment was that Zu had been overly confident and, anxious to further his fame, reckless in his strategy. *SS* 28:18a [25/7/20#4]; 28:21b [25/7/24#3]; 28: 24a [25/7/26#4]; *Han'guksa*, 29: 75–77.
5. *SS* 28:26b [25/7/29#3].
6. Swope, "Bestowing the Double-Edged Sword," 93.
7. This is what China called itself. Although it became a proper noun, as in the case of Taiwan, it was used to connote a cultural center rather than a polity.
8. I translated the edict as it is recorded in the *Veritable Records of Sŏnjo* (*SS* 30:1b–2a [25/9/2#1]). Swope also includes his own translation in "Bestowing the Double-Edged Sword," 95–96.
9. *SS* 30:1b [25/9/2#1].
10. *SS* 30:2b [25/9/2#2].
11. *SS* 30:3b [25/9/4#7].

12. SSS 26:36a–37a [25/9#6].
13. SS 30:2b [25/9/2#2].
14. Swope, "Bestowing the Double-Edged Sword," 92–93.
15. Kija (Ch. Qizi) was, according to the *Book of Documents*, enfiefed as the feudal lord of Chosŏn by the founder of the Zhou dynasty, King Wu. When Kija moved to Korea, he is said to have devised a penal code that served as a civilizatory instrument. [MD]
16. SS 32:13b–14a [25/11/15#4].
17. SS 32:11b–13b [25/11/15#3].
18. SS 32:16a–17b [25/11/16#5].
19. SS 32:20a [25/11/18#2]; 32:23b [25/11/22#2].
20. East of the Taedong River actually meant the area south of the Taedong, beginning just south of P'yŏngyang.
21. *Han'guksa*, 29:89–90.
22. SS 33:21a–b [25/12/17#4].
23. SS 33:30a–b [25/12/25#2].
24. SS 33:30b–31a [25/12/26#2]; [25/12/27#2; #3].
25. Until the end of the war it was Koreans who were responsible for this task, and it was under the jurisdiction of the Korean king and his close officials. Gari Ledyard, "Confucianism and War: The Korean Security Crisis of 1598," *Journal of Korean Studies* 6 (1988): 103.
26. Li got the horse. SS 35:29a–30b [2/17/11] (in Sŏnjo's conversation with Yi Hangbok).
27. SS 34:23b–24a [26/1/13#6].
28. Before his departure he had an extensive discussion with the distraught Sŏnjo, who, as well as other officials present at the meeting, seems to have felt that the entire Korean court was under censure. Those present in the meeting probed for possible reasons for Li's censure. According to the attendant royal secretary, some people, among them Li's adjutant, took women, having either a female slave or a *kisaeng* accompany them on some public procession or another. But they felt that this was not the real reason. SS 34:24b–25a [26/1/14#3].
29. Swope, "Bestowing the Double-Edged Sword," 84.
30. O Hŭimun, *Swaemirok* [The records of trivial and insignificant matters] (Seoul: Kuksa p'yŏnch'an wiwŏnhoe, 1962), 265.

31. SS 34:46a–b [26/1/28#6].
32. Kenneth M. Swope, "Deceit, Disguise, and Dependence: China, Japan, and the Future of the Tributary System, 1592–1596," *International History Review* 24, no. 4 (2002): 771.
33. There is a detailed description of the battle, fought from February 6 to 8, in the *Veritable Records of Sŏnjo* (SS 34:13a–15a [26/1/11#13]). Also see Kenneth M. Swope, "Turning the Tide: The Strategic and Psychological Significance of the Liberation of Pyongyang in 1593," *War and Society* 21, no. 2 (2003): 1–22.
34. SS 34:15a [26/1/11#13].
35. Swope, "The Three Great Campaigns," 254–55.
36. SSS 27:4b [26/1#2].
37. Sŏnjo ordered that they should pursue the retreating enemy and wanted to behead a Korean general who let the Japanese escape, but Li Rusong asked that the general be pardoned. SS 34:38b–39a [26/1/24#9]; SSS 27:2a–4a [26/1#2].
38. Swope, "The Three Great Campaigns," 254.
39. Yoshi Saburo Kuno, *Japanese Expansion on the Asiatic Continent: A Study in the History of Japan with Special Reference to Her International Relations with China, Korea, and Russia* (Berkeley: University of California Press, 1937), 1:164.
40. Swope, "The Three Great Campaigns," 252–53.
41. At the discussion all objected except Prime Minister Yi Sanhae, who said that there were such precedents in ancient history. SS 26:1b [25/4/28#2].
42. SS 26:1b [25/4/17#4]; SSS 26:5a–5b [25/4#16]; *Nanjung chamnok*, 3:344–45.
43. SS 26:3a [25/4/30#1; #3]; Yu Sŏngnyong, who was in the entourage, described this in his *Chingbirok* [The book of corrections], trans. Nam Mansŏng (Seoul: Hyŏnamsa, 1970), 74–78, 288–99.
44. SS 26:8b [25/5/8#7].
45. Timothy Tackett, *When the King Took Flight* (Cambridge, Mass.: Harvard University Press, 2003), 9–25.
46. See chapter 1 for more details.
47. Yu Sŏngnyong, *Chingbirok*, 111–13, 305–6.

4. LANGUAGE STRATEGY   187

48. SS 27:3b [25/6/10#1].
49. SS 27:2a [25/6/2#5].
50. SS 27:4b [25/6/11#4].
51. It is notable that the content of this edict does not appear in the *Veritable Records of Sŏnjo*. It is assumed that once it was sent out, it was not recorded by historians. However, it is recorded in other books by those who received the edict. *Swaemirok*, 16–17. The same letter appears in the *Nanjung chamnok*, 1:453–54, but in a truncated form.
52. *Nanjung chamnok*, 2:515–17.
53. Ibid., 518–19.
54. Ibid., 540–42.
55. SS 29:1a [25/8/1#5]. Also *Han'guksa*, 29:72–73.
56. Discussions and reports as they appear in the *Sillok* show this view. SS 28:18a [25/7/20#4]; 28:21a [25/7/24#3]; 28:24a [25/7/26#4]; *Han'guksa*, 29:75–77.
57. The royal entourage was moving from Yŏngch'ŏn to Pakch'ŏn. SS 27:8b [27/6/14#4].
58. This was on the 22nd of the sixth month. SS 27:15a [25/6/22#2].
59. SS 27:6b–8a [25/6/13#7#8]; 27:8a [25/6/14#5].
60. "P'ilbu" refers to a common man of lowly station, but in this context a morally low person with no spirit.
61. SS 27:15b [25/6/24#1]; 27:16b [25/6/26#1] 27:17a–b [25/6/26#4#7].
62. SS 28:26b–28a [25/7/29#3]; 29:2a [25/8/2#1].
63. On the 19th of the eighth month, the king ordered that copies of the royal letter in Korean be forwarded to Song Ŏnsin, the governor of P'yŏngan Province, to be disseminated among the residents and that Yu Sŏngnyong carry them north to distribute to the people. SS 29:23a [25/8/19#1].
64. They include Kuno, *Japanese Expansion*, 1:159–73; Elisonas, "The Inseparable Trinity," 281–85; Swope, "Deceit, Disguise, and Dependence," 757–82; Hawley, *The Imjin War*, 299–428.
65. Swope, "Deceit, Disguise, and Dependence," 776–78; Elisonas, "The Inseparable Trinity," 284–85.
66. Mary E. Berry states that Hideyoshi did not object to dragged-out peace talks as he preferred ambiguity to an "unbecoming settlement,"

but when this was no longer possible he decided on the second invasion. Mary Elizabeth Berry, *Hideyoshi* (Cambridge, Mass.: Harvard University Press, 1982), 217, 232.

67. Ronald P. Toby, *State and Diplomacy in Early Modern Japan: Asia in the Development of the Tokugawa Bakufu* (Stanford: Stanford University Press, 1984), 77–83. Also see Kenneth R. Robinson, "Centering the King of Chosŏn: Aspects of Korean Maritime Diplomacy, 1392–1592," *Journal of Asian Studies* 59, no. 1 (2000): 109–22.
68. Ray Huang, "The Lung-ch'ing and Wan-li Reigns, 1567–1620," in *Cambridge History of China* (Cambridge: Cambridge University Press, 1988), 7:571.
69. Swope, "Deceit, Disguise, and Dependence," 772–73.
70. Swope, "Bestowing the Double-Edged Sword," 77.
71. Kuno, *Japanese Expansion*, 1:169–70. His wife and children were sold into slavery. Hawley, *The Imjin War*, 422–23.
72. Swope, "Deceit, Disguise, and Dependence," 780.
73. Sŏnjo's conferences with Li were in the third month of 1593 and with Song in the sixth month of 1593. *Han'guksa*, 29:96–7.
74. *SS* 41:36 [26/8/14#2]; 42:3a [26/9/1#12]; *Han'guksa*, 29:98–105.
75. *SS* 41:13a [26/8/6#8; #11]; 47:2a [27/1/2#2]; 60:2b [28/2/2#4]; 69:3b [28/11/3#2]. For example, in the tenth month of 1592, a Korean official who had been captured by the Japanese was released, returning with Katō Kiyomasa's letter to the effect that if Korea were to agree to territorial concessions, the Japanese would retreat from Korea and return the Korean princes whom they had captured. *SS* 31:16b [25/10/19#5].
76. For example, see the argument by Yun Tusu, the minister of the left. *SS* 47:2a [27/1/2#2]. Prime Minister Yu Sŏngnyong, on the other hand, continued to counsel the necessity of buying time. By the end of the sixteenth century the political elite was split in several factions. Yu Sŏngnyong was the leader of the Namin ("Southerners"), whereas Yu Tusu represented the Sŏin ("Westerners"). [MD]
77. This text is based on a manuscript copy, which is believed to have been sent out by the government on this occasion. The copy is owned by a private family in Kyŏngju city in Kyŏngsang Province,

in which the poster must have circulated. Kim Chongt'aek, "Sŏnjo taewang ŏn'gyo ko" [A consideration of King Sŏnjo's vernacular Korean edicts], *Kugŏ kyoyuk nonji* [Discourse on Korean education] 2 (1975): 27–34.
78. SS 42:20b [26/9/9#3].
79. It is interesting to note that this edict is not recorded in the *Veritable Records of Sŏnjo* but only in *Nanjung chamnok*, 4:231–33. The one at the beginning of the war is recorded only in the *Swaemirok*, although the *Veritable Records of Sŏnjo* records that the edict had been sent out.
80. JaHyun Kim Haboush, "Royal Edicts: Constructing an Ethnopolitical Community," in *Epistolary Korea: Letters in the Communicative Space of the Chosŏn, 1392–1910*, ed. JaHyun Kim Haboush (New York: Columbia University Press, 2009), 21, 24–26.

5. The Aftermath: Dream Journeys and the Culture of Commemoration

1. JaHyun Kim Haboush, "Constructing the Center: The Ritual Controversy and the Search for a New Identity in Seventeenth-Century Korea," in *Culture and the State in Late Chosŏn Korea*, ed. JaHyun Kim Haboush and Martina Deuchler (Cambridge, Mass.: Harvard University Asia Center, 1999), 46–90.
2. Inaba Iwakichi, *Kokaikun jidai no Man-Sen kankei* [Korea-Manchu relations during the reign of King Kwanghae] (Keijō: Osakayago shoten, 1933), 111–241.
3. Injo's court entered Namhan Fort on the fourteenth day of the twelfth month, 1636, and surrendered on the thirtieth of the first month, 1637. For a description of the forty-seven days and the ceremony of surrender, see Na Man'gap, *Pyŏngja namhan ilgi* [The records of the Namhan Fort in 1636] (Seoul: Sundang, 1977), 28–110; Kim Kwangsun, trans., *Sansŏng ilgi* [The diary of mountain fortress] (Seoul: Hyŏngsŏl ch'ulp'ansa, 1985).
4. Anthony D. Smith, *The Ethnic Origins of Nations* (Oxford: Blackwell, 1986), 6–46.
5. See Mary Elizabeth Berry, *Hideyoshi* (Cambridge, Mass.: Harvard University, 1982).

6. See Frederic E. Wakeman, *The Great Enterprise: The Manchu Reconstruction of Imperial Order in Seventeenth-Century China* (Berkeley: University of California Press, 1985).
7. Ch'a Munsŏp, *Chosŏn sidae kunsa kwan'gye yŏn'gu* [A study of military affairs during the Chosŏn period] (Seoul: Tan'guk University Press, 1996); Hŏ Sŏndo, *Chosŏn sidae hwayak pyŏnggisa yŏn'gu* [A study of firearms and weapons of the Chosŏn period] (Seoul: Ilchogak, 1994); Song Chŏnghyŏn, *Chosŏn sahoe wa Imjin ŭibyŏng yŏn'gu* [A study of the Chosŏn society and of the volunteer armies during the Imjin War] (Seoul: Haggyŏn munhwasa, 1998); Yi T'aejin, *Chosŏn hugi ŭi chŏngch'i wa kunyŏngje pyŏnch'ŏn* [Politics and the changes in the military garrisons structure in the late Chosŏn] (Seoul: Han'guk yŏn'guwŏn, 1985).
8. Han Myŏnggi, *Imjin waeran kwa Han-Jung kwan'gye* [The Imjin War and Sino-Korean relations] (Seoul: Yŏksa pip'yŏngsa, 1998); Sŏn Sŭngch'ŏl, *Chosŏn siadae Han-Il kwan'gyesa yŏn'gu* [A study of Korean-Japanese relations during the Chosŏn period] (Seoul: Chisŏng ŭi saem, 1994).
9. Chŏng Okcha, *Chosŏn hugi Chosŏn chunghwa sasang yŏn'gu* [A study of Korea-centered ideology in late Chosŏn] (Seoul: Ilchisa, 1998).
10. Im Ch'ŏlho, *Imjinnok yŏn'gu* [A study of *The Record of the Black Dragon Year*] (Seoul: Chŏng'ŭmsa, 1986); Im, *Sŏlhwa wa minjung ŭi yŏksa ŭisik* [Legends and people's historical consciousness] (Seoul: Chimmundang, 1989); Kim T'aejun et al., *Imjin waeran kwa Han'guk munhak* [The Imjin War and Korean literature] (Seoul: Minŭmsa, 1992); So Chaeyŏng, *Im-byŏng yangnan kwa munhak ŭisik* [The Imjin and Pyŏngja Wars and literary consciousness] (Seoul: Han'guk yŏn'guwŏn, 1980).
11. Ernest Renan, "What Is a Nation?," in *Nation and Narration*, ed. Homi K. Bhabha (London: Routledge, 1990), 19.
12. Kristin Ann Hass, *Carried to the Wall: American Memory and the Vietnam Veterans Memorial* (Berkeley: University of California Press, 1998), 34–86.
13. I was invited to participate in a ceremony to commemorate the Imjin War dead as recently as 1973.
14. *Imjinnok* [Record of the Black Dragon Year] can be described as a vivid example of this kind. See Im Ch'ŏlho, *Imjinnok yŏn'gu*, and also

Peter Lee, *The Record of the Black Dragon Year* (Seoul: Institute of Korean Culture, Korea University, 2000).
15. Mikhail Bakhtin, *The Dialogic Imagination: Four Essays*, ed. Michael Holquist, trans. Caryl Emerson and Michael Holquist (Austin: University of Texas Press. 1981), 428.
16. I use the edition of this narrative put out by the Association of Korean Language and Literature.
17. The edition at the National Library in Seoul (Kungnip chungang tosŏgwan) contains both *Kangdo mongyurok* and *P'isaeng mongyurok*, Ko 3636–38. Reprinted in Kim Kidong, ed., *P'ilsabon kojŏn sosŏl chŏnjip* [The complete anthology of classical Korean novels in manuscript] (Seoul: Asea munhwasa, 1980), 3:201–38.
18. Cho Tongil, *Han'guk munhak t'ongsa* [History of Korean literature] (Seoul: Chisik sanŏpsa, 1994), 2:483–93.
19. Yu Chongguk cites ten stories; see Yu Chongguk, *Mongyurok sosŏl yŏn'gu* [A study of dream journey novels] (Seoul: Asea munhwasa, 1987), 5–128. So Chaeyŏng mentions two new discoveries; see So Chaeyŏng, "Imjin waeran kwa sosŏl munhak" [The Imjin War and the novel], in *Imjin waeran kwa han'guk munhak* [Imjin War and Korean literature], ed. Kim T'aejun et al. (Seoul: Minŭmsa, 1992), 246–48.
20. The most conspicuous examples include Zhuangzi's famous butterfly dream in his eponymous philosophical treatise, continuing through innumerable stories in *zhiguai* and *chuanqi* genres to the great Ming play *Mudanting* [Peony Pavilion] and the famous Qing novel *Hongloumeng* [The Dream of the Red Chamber].
21. *Kuunmong* was circulated in both Korean and Chinese editions. Because no extant Korean edition predates the Chinese editions, scholars disagree over the language in which the novel was written. See Cho Tongil, *Han'guk munhak t'ongsa*, 3:118–25; Chŏng Kyubok, *Han'guk kojŏn munhak ŭi wŏnjŏn pip'anjŏk yŏn'gu* [A critical study of editions of Korean classics] (Seoul: Koryŏ taehakkyo minjok munhwa yŏn'guso, 1992). The same question is raised concerning *Hong Kiltong chŏn* [The tale of Hong Kiltong], long thought to be the earliest vernacular novel written in Korean. In fact, even the traditional attribution of authorship to Hŏ Kyun (1569–1618) is questioned. Some claim a much later composition. See Yi Yunsŏk, *Hong Kiltong chŏn yŏn'gu* [A

study of the tale of Hong Kiltong] (Taegu: Kyemyŏng University Press, 1997).

22. Judith Zeitlin, *Historian of the Strange: Pu Songling and the Chinese Classical Tale* (Stanford: Stanford University Press, 1993), 133–81.

23. JaHyun Kim Haboush, "Dreamland: Korean Dreamscapes as an Alternative Confucian Space," in *Das andere China* [The other China], ed. Helwig Schmidt-Glintzer (Wiesbaden: Harrassowitz, 1995), 659–70.

24. Of the four tales in this genre that predate the three discussed in this chapter, only one is narrated in this mode, namely, *Wŏnsaeng mongyurok* [Master Wŏn's dream journey]. This tale is a narrative in which the dreamer encounters seven famous tragic characters in Korean history: Tanjong (1441–1457, r. 1452–1455), the boy king who was deposed by his powerful uncle, King Sejo (1417–68, r. 1455–1468), and the six ministers, known as "six loyal ministers who died" (*sayuksin*), who were put to death when Sejo uncovered their secret plot to restore Tanjong. The authorship of *Master Wŏn's Dream Journey* has not been determined, but it is commonly attributed to either Wŏn Ho (fl. 1450), one of "six loyal ministers who lived" (*saengyuksin*), who, out of loyalty to Tanjong, lived their lives in retirement, or Yim Che (1549–1587), a well-known writer who lived a century after Wŏn Ho. See Yu Chongguk, *Mongyurok sosŏl yŏn'gu* [A study of dream journey novels] (Seoul: Asea munhwasa, 1987), 5.

25. Of twelve known dream journeys, five are about wars. After the mid-seventeenth century, dream journeys revert to the other mode of narration, in which the dream is employed as the dreamer's interior mental landscape.

26. Praesnjit Duara, "The Regime of Authenticity: Timelessness, Gender, and National History in Modern China," in *Constructing Nationhood in Modern East Asia*, ed. Kai-wing Chow, Kevin M. Doak, and Poshek Fu (Ann Arbor: University of Michigan Press, 2001), 367.

27. David Goodman, *Japanese Drama and Culture in the 1960s: The Return of Gods* (Armonk, N.Y.: M. E. Sharpe, 1988).

28. See Kim Sŏngnae, "Lamentations of the Dead: The Historical Imagery of Violence on Cheju Island, South Korea," *Journal of Ritual Studies* 3, no. 2 (1989): 251–85; Boudewijn Walraven, "Muga:

5. THE AFTERMATH 193

The Songs of Korean Shamanism" (Ph.D. diss., Leiden University, 1985), 1–11.

29. Tzvetan Todorov, *The Fantastic: A Structural Approach to a Literary Genre* (Ithaca: Cornell University Press, 1975), 25.
30. Ibid., 41.
31. Judith Zeitlin, *Historian of the Strange*, 7–8.
32. The dreamer in the *Master P'i's Dream Journey* dreams on the same night that he arrives, whereas the one in *Dream Journey to Kanghwa Island* dreams several days later. In the *Dream Journey to Talch'ŏn* there is a gap of several months between the time P'adamja arrives at the Talch'ŏn River and writes poems pitying the dead and when he dreams. Yun Kyesŏn, "Talch'ŏn mongyurok," in *Hanmun sosŏlsŏn* [Anthology of novels in literary Chinese], ed. Kugŏ kungmun hakhoe (Seoul: Taejegak, 1982), 140. Both So and Yu imply that P'adamja arrives and dreams on the same day. So Chaeyŏng, "Imjin waeran kwa sosŏl munhak," 245; Yu Chongguk, *Mongyurok sosŏl yŏn'gu*, 74. I examined several editions, and this is not the case.
33. Yun Kyesŏn, "Talch'ŏn mongyurok," 141.
34. *Kangdo mongyurok* [Dream journey to Kanghwa Island], National Library of Korea, Ko 3636–38, 1b.
35. Rosemary Jackson, *Fantasy: The Literature of Subversion* (New York: Methuen, 1981), 171–80.
36. Martina Deuchler, *The Confucian Transformation of Korea: A Study of Society and Ideology* (Cambridge, Mass.: Council on East Asian Studies, Harvard University, 1992), 179–202; Susan Naquin, "Funerals in North China: Uniformity and Variation," in *Death Ritual in Late Imperial and Modern China*, ed. James Watson and Evelyn Rawski (Berkeley: University of California Press, 1988), 37–70.
37. Yun Kyesŏn, "Talch'ŏn mongyurok," 141.
38. *Kangdo mongyurok*, 1b.
39. Yi Changhŭi, *Imjin waeransa yŏn'gu* [A study of the Imjin War] (Seoul: Asea munhwasa, 1999), 37–49.
40. Yun Kyesŏn, "Talch'ŏn mongyurok," 141.
41. Ibid., 142.
42. The miserable defeat of the Korean Army at the Talch'ŏn River and Sin Ip's role in it emerge as a familiar trope in postwar discourse on the

war with Japan. Hwang Chungyun's *Dream Journey to Talch'ŏn* focuses on this very issue. In it the defeat of the Korean Army is placed in a larger context of the social and military system of the Chosŏn government. Both Sin and his brother expound on the inadequacy of the military, which allowed the powerful to evade service while relying mainly on peasant soldiers with no training or expertise. Hwang's *mongyurok* has the same title as Yun's, except that *tal* is written with an extra "dog" radical. There is only one extant copy of Hwang's *mongyurok*, and the text is quite corrupt. It is reproduced in Hwang's collected works. See Hwang Chungyun, *Talch'ŏn mongyurok* [Dream journey to Talch'ŏn], in *Hwang Tongmyŏng sosŏlchip* [Collected novels of Hwang Tongmyŏng] (Taegu: Munhak kwa ŏn'ŏ yŏn'guhoe, 1984), 275–94. The character *tal* in Yun Kyesŏn's *Talch'ŏn mongyurok* is usually rendered without the dog radical, but the one in *Nanjung chamnok*, a multivolume history of the Imjin War written by a volunteer army leader, Cho Kyŏngnam (1570–1641), is with the radical. See Cho Kyŏngnam's *Nanjung chamnok*, in *Taedong yasŭng* [The unofficial narratives of the great East], 4 vols. (Seoul: Minjok munhwa ch'ujinhoe, 1972), 4:32a–43a.

43. One such painting of the party given by the Queen Mother of the West was auctioned at Sotheby's New York in 1993 (no. 34).

44. The perspective is that of the viewer, who faces north. The seating arrangement is typical of any formal gathering, which is reproduced in this dream. I am thankful to an anonymous reader for this clarification.

45. Yun Kyesŏn, "Talch'ŏn mongyurok," 156.

46. Ibid., 157.

47. Ibid., 159–60.

48. *SS* 41:17b [26/8/8#3].

49. *Chŭngbo munhŏn pigo* [Expanded encyclopedia of Korea] (Seoul: Kojŏn kanhaenghoe, 1959), 3:21a.

50. *Chosŏn wangjo ŭi chesa* [Sacrificial rites of the Chosŏn court] (Seoul: Munhwajae kwalliguk, 1967), 136–37.

51. Hass, *Carried to the Wall*, 43–55.

52. Thomas Laqueur, "Memory and the Naming in the Great War," in *Commemorations: The Politics of National Identity*, ed. John R. Gillis (Princeton: Princeton University Press, 1994), 152.

53. Hass, *Carried to the Wall*, 57; James Mayo, *War Memorials as Political Landscape: The American Experience and Beyond* (New York: Praeger, 1988), 94.
54. The depiction of Yi Kuksin as intensely evil has prompted some scholars to conclude that this work was written as a veiled attack on an individual. See Ch'a Yongju, *Mongyurokkye kujo ŭi punsŏk chŏk yŏn'gu* [An analysis of the structure of the dream journeys] (Seoul: Changhaksa, 1981), 164; Yu Chongguk, *Mongyurok sosŏl yŏn'gu*, 83–84. One article even traces a historical personage of the same name and suggests that he is possibly the object of the criticism. See So Taesŏk, "Mongyurok ŭi changrŭjŏk sŏnggyŏk kwa munhaksajŏk ŭiŭi" [Generic characteristics of dream journeys and their literary historical significance], in *Kyemyŏngdae Han'gukhak nonmunjip* 3 (1975): 531–32.
55. *Kangdo mongyurok*, 10a.
56. Ibid., 3b. The Chosŏn state conferred honors on persons of virtue in three categories: filial children, loyal subjects, and exemplary women. These honors were often accompanied by material remuneration. For details see Pak Chu, *Chosŏn sidae ŭi chŏngp'yo chŏngch'aek* [Policies on the conferral of honors during the Chosŏn period] (Seoul: Ilchogak, 1990).
57. *Kangdo mongyurok*, 4a. For a description of the Buddhist underworld, see Louis Frederic, *Buddhism: Flammarion Iconographie Guides* (Paris: Flammarion, 1995), 252–53.
58. *Kangdo mongyurok*, 10a.
59. Duara, "The Regime of Authenticity," 368–69.
60. "Pakssi chŏn" [The Tale of Madam Pak], in *Han'guk kojŏn munhak taegye* [Compendium of Korean classical literature], Chang Tŏksun and Ch'oe Chinwŏn (Seoul: Kyomunsa, 1984), 1:391.
61. Song Sanghyŏn, whose fierce although ultimately unsuccessful defense of Tongnae city earned Japanese admiration, for instance, received the posthumous title of Ch'ungnyŏl. *Hyojong sillok* 10:38a [4/3/4#6].
62. Jenny Sharpe, "The Unspeakable Limits of Rape: Colonial Violence and Counter-Insurgency," in *Colonial Discourse and Post-Colonial Theory*, ed. Patrick Williams and Laura Chrisman (New York: Columbia University Press, 1994), 226–35.

63. Peter H. Lee, *Anthology of Korean Literature* (Honolulu: University of Hawai'i Press, 1981), 110–11.
64. Mark Edward Lewis, *Writing and Authority in Early China* (Albany: State University of New York Press, 1999), 2–4.
65. Cho Tongil, *Han'guk munhak t'ongsa*, 3:9–129.
66. Ōtani Morishige, *Chosŏn hugi sosŏl tokcha yŏn'gu* [A study of readership of novels in late Chosŏn] (Seoul: Koryŏ taehakkyo minjok munhwa yŏn'guso, 1985), 17–74.
67. Martina Deuchler, "Despoilers of the Way-Insulters of the Sages: Controversies over the Classics in Seventeenth-Century Korea," in Haboush and Deuchler, *Culture and the State in Late Chosŏn Korea*, 91–133; Ch'oe Yong-Ho, "Private Academies and the State in Late Chosŏn Korea," in ibid., 15–45.
68. Kim Ilgŭn, *Ŏn'gan ŭi yŏn'gu* [A study of letters in Korean] (Seoul: Kŏn'guk University Press, 1986), 191–92, 202.
69. For Korea, see Haboush and Deuchler, *Culture and the State in Late Chosŏn Korea*, 1–13; for China, see Judith Berling, *The Syncretic Religion of Lin Chao-en* (New York: Columbia University Press, 1980); Donald S. Lopez, ed., *Religions of China in Practice* (Princeton: Princeton University Press, 1996).
70. Rosemary Jackson, *Fantasy: The Literature of Subversion* (New York: Methuen, 1981), 4.
71. See Robert Buswell, Jr., "Buddhism Under Confucian Domination: The Synthetic Vision of Sŏsan Hyujŏng," in Haboush and Deuchler, *Culture and the State in Late Chosŏn Korea*, 134–59; Boudewijn Walraven, "Popular Religion in a Confucianized Society," in ibid., 160–98.
72. Jean-Paul Sartre, "'Aminadab' of the Fantastic Considered as a Language," *Situations* I (1947): 56–72; Jackson, *Fantasy*, 86.
73. Yi Changhŭi, *Imjin waeransa yŏn'gu*, 65–66.
74. Gari Ledyard, "Confucianism and War: The Korean Security Crisis of 1598," *Journal of Korean Studies* 6 (1988): 81–119.
75. David McMullen, "Historical and Literary Theory in the Mid-Eighth Century," in *Perspectives on the Tang*, ed. Arthur F. Wright and David Twitchett (New Haven: Yale University Press, 1973), 307–44; Charles A. Peterson, "The Restoration Completed: Emperor Hsien-tsung and the Provinces," in ibid., 151–92.

76. SS 41:58a–b [26/8/30#2].
77. Sŏnjo left Seoul on the thirtieth day of the fourth month in 1592 and returned on the first of the tenth month in 1593. He stayed in what was called Chŏngnŭngdong haenggung. SS 43:1a [26/10/1#2; #3].
78. The eighteenth-century monarch Yŏngjo's use of Ming symbols and the eighteenth-century scholar Pak Chiwŏn's (1737–1805) story *Hŏsaeng chŏn* [The tale of Master Hŏ] illustrate Korea's predicament vis-à-vis Qing China. See JaHyun Kim Haboush, *The Confucian Kingship in Korea: Yŏngjo and the Politics of Sagacity* (New York: Columbia University Press, 2001), 40–45; Lee, *Anthology of Korean Literature*, 213–21.
79. Raymond Williams, *Marxism and Literature* (Oxford: Oxford University Press, 1977), 133–34.
80. Samuel Dukhae Kim, "The Korean Monk-Soldiers in the Imjin Wars: An Analysis of Buddhist Resistance to the Hideyoshi Invasion, 1592–1598" (Ph.D. diss., Columbia University, 1978).
81. Buswell, "Buddhism Under Confucian Domination," 134–59.
82. Pak Chonghwa, *Imjin waeran* [The Imjin War] (Seoul: Ŭryu munhwasa, 1972), 3:181–84.
83. SSS 28:4a [27/4#2]; SS 55:30b–31a [27/9/22#6]
84. Kim Tonghwa et al., "Hoguk taesŏng samyŏng taesa yŏn'gu" [A study of the great patriotic monk, Samyŏng], *Pulgyŏ hakpo* [Journal of Buddhism] 8 (1971): 13–205.
85. Abraham Lincoln, "Gettysburg Address," delivered at the Soldiers' National Cemetery dedication, November 19, 1863.
86. Wolfgang Iser, *Walter Pater: The Aesthetic Moment* (Cambridge: Cambridge University Press, 1987), 83.
87. Renan, "What Is a Nation?," 19.

Anderson, Benedict. *Imagined Communities: Reflections on the Origin and Spread of Nationalism*. New York: Verso, 1983.

Bakhtin, Mikhail. *The Dialogic Imagination: Four Essays*. Edited by Michael Holquist, translated by Caryl Emerson and Michael Holquist. Austin: University of Texas Press, 1981.

Bell, David A. *The Cult of Nation in France: Inventing Nationalism, 1680–1800*. Cambridge, Mass.: Harvard University Press, 2003.

Berling, Judith. *The Syncretic Religion of Lin Chao-en*. New York: Columbia University Press, 1980.

Berry, Mary Elizabeth. *Hideyoshi*. Cambridge, Mass.: Harvard University Press, 1982.

Boots, J. L. "Korean Weapons and Armor." *Transactions of the Korea Branch of the Royal Asiatic Society* 33, no. 2 (1934): 1–37.

Brokaw, Cynthia Joanne. *The Ledgers of Merit and Demerit: Social Change and Moral Order in Late Imperial China*. Princeton: Princeton University Press, 1991.

Buswell, Robert. "Buddhism Under Confucian Domination: The Synthetic Vision of Sŏsan Hyujŏng." In *Culture and the State in Late Chosŏn Korea*. Edited by JaHyun Kim Haboush and Martina Deuchler, 134–59. Cambridge, Mass.: Harvard University Asia Center, 1999.

Ch'a Munsŏp. *Chosŏn sidae kunsa kwan'gye yŏn'gu* [A study of military affairs during the Chosŏn period]. Seoul: Tan'guk University Press, 1996.

Ch'a Yongju. *Mongyurokkye kujo ŭi punsŏk chŏk yŏn'gu* [An analysis of the structure of the dream journeys]. Seoul: Changhaksa, 1981.

Chang Pyŏngok. *Ŭibyŏng hangjaengsa* [History of the volunteer armies' fighting]. Seoul: Hanwŏn, 1991.

Cho Kyŏngnam. *Nanjung chamnok* [The miscellaneous record of the war]. 4 vols. In *Kugyŏk Taedong yasŭng* [The translation of the unofficial narratives of the Great East]. Seoul: Minjok munhwa ch'ujinhoe, 1972.

Cho Tongil. *Han'guk munhak t'ongsa* [History of Korean literature]. 5 vols. Seoul: Chisik sanŏpsa, 1994.

Cho Wŏllae. *Imjin waeran kwa Honam chibang ŭi ŭibyŏng hangjaeng* [The Imjin War and the fighting of the volunteer armies in the Honam region]. Seoul: Asea Munhwasa, 2001.

Ch'oe Hyosik. *Imjin waeran'gi Yŏngnam ŭi ŭibyŏng yŏn'gu* [A study of volunteer armies in Yŏngnam during the Imjin War]. Seoul: Kukhak charyowŏn, 2003.

Ch'oe, Yong-ho. "Private Academies and the State in Late Chosŏn Korea." In *Culture and the State in Late Chosŏn Korea*. Edited by JaHyun Kim Haboush and Martina Deuchler, 15–45. Cambridge, Mass.: Harvard University Asia Center, 1999.

Ch'oe Yŏnghŭi. *Imjin waeranjung ŭi sahoe tongt'ae* [Social movements during the Imjin War]. Seoul: Han'guk yŏn'guwŏn, 1975.

Chŏng Kyubok. *Han'guk kojŏn munhak ŭi wŏnjŏn pip'yŏngjŏk yŏn'gu* [A critical study of editions of Korean classics]. Seoul: Koryŏ taehakkyo minjok munhwa yŏn'guso, 1992.

Chŏng Okcha. *Chosŏn hugi Chosŏn chunghwa sasang yŏn'gu* [A study of Korea-centered ideology in late Chosŏn]. Seoul: Ilchisa, 1998.

Chŏng T'ak, *Yakp'o/Yongsa ilgi* [The diary of Yakp'o during the war] (9/15/ Imjin year). Pusan: Pusan University, 1962.

Chosŏn wangjo sillok [Veritable records of the Chosŏn dynasty]. 48 vols. Reprint. Seoul: Kuksa p'yŏnch'an wiwŏnhoe, 1970.

Chosŏn wangjo sillok [Veritable records of the Chosŏn dynasty]. Translated and edited by Kuksa p'yŏnch'an wiwŏnhoe. http://sillok.history.go.kr (accessed February 5, 2015).

Chosŏn wangjo ŭi chesa [Sacrificial rites of the Chosŏn court]. Seoul: Munhwajae kwalliguk, 1967.

Chungbo munhŏn pigo [Expanded encyclopedia of Korea]. Vol. 3. Seoul: Kojŏn kanhaenghoe, 1959.

Colley, Linda. *Britons: Forging the Nation 1707–1837*. 3rd revised edition. New Haven: Yale University Press, 2009.

Connerton, Paul. *How Societies Remember*. New York: Cambridge University Press, 1989.
de Bary, Wm. Theodore, Donald Keene, et al. *Sources of Japanese Tradition*. Vol. 1: *From Earliest Times to 1600*. 2nd edition. New York: Columbia University Press, 2002.
de Bary, Wm. Theodore, and JaHyun Kim Haboush. *The Rise of Neo-Confucianism in Korea*. New York: Columbia University Press, 1985.
Deuchler, Martina. *The Confucian Transformation of Korea: A Study of Society and Ideology*. Cambridge, Mass.: Council on East Asian Studies, Harvard University, 1992.
——. "Despoilers of the Way-Insulters of the Sages: Controversies over the Classics in Seventeenth-Century Korea." In *Culture and the State in Late Chosŏn Korea*. Edited by JaHyun Kim Haboush and Martina Deuchler, 91–133. Cambridge, Mass.: Harvard University Asia Center, 1999.
——. "The Practice of Confucianism: Ritual and Order in Chosŏn Dynasty Korea." In *Rethinking Confucianism: Past and Present in China, Japan, Korea, and Vietnam*. Edited by Benjamin Elman, John Duncan, and Herman Ooms, 292–334. Los Angeles: Asia Pacific Monograph Series, University of California, Los Angeles, 2002.
Duara, Prasenjit. "The Regime of Authenticity: Timelessness, Gender, and National History in Modern China." In *Constructing Nationhood in Modern East Asia*. Edited by Kai-wing Chow, Kevin M. Doak, and Poshek Fu, 359–86. Ann Arbor: University of Michigan Press, 2001.
Elisonas, Jurgis. "The Inseparable Trinity: Japan's Relations with China and Korea." In *The Cambridge History of Japan*. Edited by John W. Hall, 4:235–300. Cambridge: Cambridge University Press, 1991.
Frank, Andre Gunder. *ReOrient: Global Economy in the Asian Age*. Berkeley: University of California Press, 1998.
Frederic, Louis. *Buddhism: Flammarion Iconographie Guides*. Paris: Flammarion, 1995.
Geary, Patrick J. *The Myth of Nations: The Medieval Origins of Europe*. Princeton: Princeton University Press, 2003.
Geertz, Clifford. *The Interpretation of Cultures: Selected Essays*. New York: Basic Books, 1973.

Gellner, Ernest. *Nations and Nationalism*. Ithaca: Cornell University Press, 1983.
Gilmont, Jean-François. "Protestant Reformation and Reading." In *A History of Reading in the West*. Edited by Guglielmo Cavallo and Roger Chartier, 213–37. Amherst: University of Massachusetts Press, 1999.
Goodman, David. *Japanese Drama and Culture in the 1960s: The Return of Gods*. Armonk: M. E. Sharpe, 1988.
Greenfeld, Liah. *Nationalism: Five Roads to Modernity*. London: Blackwell, 1992.
Grigely, Joseph. *Textualterity: Art, Theory, and Textual Criticism*. Ann Arbor: University of Michigan Press, 1995.
Haboush, JaHyun Kim. *The Confucian Kingship in Korea: Yŏngjo and the Politics of Sagacity*. New York: Columbia University Press, 2001.
——. "Constructing the Center: The Ritual Controversy and the Search for a New Identity in Seventeenth-Century Korea." In *Culture and the State in Late Chosŏn Korea*. Edited by JaHyun Kim Haboush and Martina Deuchler, 46–90. Cambridge, Mass.: Harvard University Asia Center, 1999.
——. "Creating a Society of Civil Culture: Early Chosŏn, 1392–1592." In *Art of the Korean Renaissance, 1400–1600*. Edited by Soyoung Lee, 3–14. New York: Metropolitan Museum of Art, 2009.
——. "Dead Bodies in the Postwar Discourse of Identity in Seventeenth-Century Korea: Subversion and Literary Production in the Private Sector." *Journal of Asian Studies* 62, no. 2 (2003): 415–42.
——. "Dreamland: Korean Dreamscapes as an Alternative Confucian Space." In *Das andere China* (The other China). Edited by Helwig Schmidt-Glintzer, 659–70. Wiesbaden: Harrassowitz, 1995.
——. "Open Letters: Patriotic Exhortations during the Imjin War." In *Epistolary Korea: Letters in the Communicative Space of the Chosŏn, 1392–1910*. Edited by JaHyun Kim Haboush, 121–40. New York: Columbia University Press, 2009.
——. "Royal Edicts: Constructing an Ethnopolitical Community." In *Epistolary Korea: Letters in the Communicative Space of the Chosŏn, 1392–1910*. Edited by JaHyun Kim Haboush, 17–28. New York: Columbia University Press, 2009.

Haboush, Jahyun Kim, and Martina Deuchler. "Introduction." In *Culture and the State in Late Chosŏn Korea*, 1–14. Cambridge: Harvard University Asia Center, 1999.

Haboush, JaHyun Kim, and Kenneth Robinson. *A Korean War Captive in Japan, 1597–1600: The Writings of Kang Hang*. New York: Columbia University Press, 2013.

Han Myŏnggi. *Imjin waeran kwa Han-Jung kwan'gye* [The Imjin War and Sino-Korean relations]. Seoul: Yŏksa pip'yŏngsa, 1998.

Han'guksa: Chosŏn chunggi ŭi woech'im kwa kŭ taeŭng [History of Korea: An outcry and its response of mid-Chosŏn]. Vol. 29. Seoul: Kuksa p'yŏnch'an wiwŏnhoe, 1995.

Hass, Kristin Ann. *Carried to the Wall: American Memory and the Vietnam Veterans Memorial*. Berkeley: University of California Press, 1998.

Hawley, Samuel Jay. *The Imjin War: Japan's Sixteenth-Century Invasion of Korea and Attempt to Conquer China*. Seoul: Royal Asiatic Society, Korea Branch; Berkeley: Institute of East Asian Studies, University of California, 2005.

Hŏ Sŏndo. *Chosŏn sidae hwayak pyŏnggisa yŏn'gu* [A study of firearms and weapons of the Chosŏn period]. Seoul: Ilchogak, 1994.

Hobsbawm, Eric J. *Nations and Nationalism Since 1780: Programme, Myth, Reality*. Cambridge: Cambridge University Press, 1990.

Hobsbawm, Eric J., and Terence Ranger. *The Invention of Tradition*. Cambridge: Cambridge University Press, 1983.

Huang, Ray. "The Lung-ch'ing and Wan-li Reigns, 1567–1620." In *Cambridge History of China*. Edited by Frederick W. Mote and Denis Twitchett, 7:511–84. Cambridge: Cambridge University Press, 1988.

Hwang Chungyun. "Talch'ŏn mongyurok" [Dream journey to Talch'ŏn]. In *Hwang Tongmyŏng sosŏlchip* [Collected novels of Hwang Tongmyŏng], 275–94. Taegu: Munhak kwa ŏn'ŏ yŏn'guhoe, 1984.

Im Ch'ŏlho. *Imjinnok yŏn'gu* [A study of *The Record of the Black Dragon Year*]. Seoul: Chŏng'ŭmsa, 1986.

——. *Sŏlhwa wa minjung ŭi yŏksa ŭisik* [Legends and people's historical consciousness]. Seoul: Chimmundang, 1989.

Inaba Iwakichi. *Kokaikun jidai no Man-Sen kankei* [Korea-Manchu relations during the reign of King Kwanghae]. Keijō: Osakayago shoten, 1933.

Iser, Wolfgang. *Walter Pater: The Aesthetic Moment*. Cambridge: Cambridge University Press, 1987.

Jackson, Rosemary. *Fantasy: The Literature of Subversion*. New York: Methuen, 1981.

Kangdo mongyurok [Dream journey to Kanghwa Island]. National Library of Korea. Ko 3636-8.

"Kangdo mongyurok." In *P'ilsabon kojŏn sosŏl chŏnjip* [The complete anthology of classical Korean novels in manuscript]. Edited by Kim Kidong, 3:201–22. Seoul: Asea munhwasa, 1980.

Kim Chongt'aek, "Sŏnjo taewang ŏn'gyo ko" [A consideration of King Sŏnjo's vernacular Korean edicts]. In *Kugŏ kyoyuk nonji* [Discourse on Korean education]. Taegu: Taegu kyoyuk taehak, 1975.

Kim Ilgŭn. *Ŏn'gan ŭi yŏn'gu* [A study of letters in Korean]. Seoul: Kŏn'guk University Press, 1986.

Kim Kidong, ed. *P'ilsabon kojŏn sosŏl chŏnjip* [The complete anthology of classical Korean novels in manuscript]. 30 vols. Seoul: Asea munhwasa, 1980.

Kim Kwangsun, trans. *Sansŏng ilgi* [The diary of mountain fortress]. Seoul: Hyŏngsŏl ch'ulp'ansa, 1985.

Kim, Samuel Dukhae. "The Korean Monk-Soldiers in the Imjin Wars: An Analysis of Buddhist Resistance to the Hideyoshi Invasion, 1592–1598." Ph.D. dissertation, Columbia University, 1978.

Kim Sŏng'il. *Kugyŏk Hakpong chŏnjip* [The translation of the complete anthology of Hakbong]. Seoul: Hakpong sŏnsaeng kinyŏm saŏphoe, 1976.

———. *Hakpong chŏnjip* [The complete anthology of Hakbong]. Seoul: Hakpong sŏnsaeng kinyŏm saŏphoe, 1976.

Kim, Sŏngnae. "Lamentations of the Dead: The Historical Imagery of Violence on Cheju Island, South Korea." *Journal of Ritual Studies* 3, no. 2 (1989): 251–85.

Kim Sŏngu. *Chosŏn chunggi kukka wa sajok* [The state and the elites in mid-Chosŏn dynasty]. Seoul: Yŏksa pip'yŏngsa, 2001.

Kim T'aejun et al. *Imjin waeran kwa Han'guk munhak* [The Imjin War and Korean literature]. Seoul: Minŭmsa, 1992.

Kim Tonghwa et al. "Hoguk taesŏng Samyŏng taesa yŏn'gu" [A study of the great patriotic Buddhist monk, Samyŏng]. *Pulkyo hakpo* [Journal of Buddhism] 8 (1971): 13–205.

Kim Tonguk. "P'anbon'go—Han'gŭl sosŏl panggakpon ŭi sŏngnip e taehayŏ" [The rise of woodblock-print vernacular novel]. In *Ch'unhyang chŏn yŏn'gu* [A study of The Tale of Ch'unhyang], 385–99. Seoul: Yonsei University, 1983.

Kim Yangsŏn, "Imjin waeran chonggun sinbu Cespedes ŭi naehan hwaltong kwa kŭ yŏnghyang" [Activities and influences of the priest Cespedes in Korea during the Imjin War]. *Sahak yŏn'gu* [Researches in Historical Studies] 18 (September 1964): 705–39.

Kitajima Manji. *Chōsen nichinichiki, Kōrai nikki: Hideyoshi no Chōsen shinryaku to sono rekishiteki kokuhatsu* [Daily record in Chosŏn, Korea diary: Hideyoshi's invasion of Chosŏn and its historical judgment]. Tokyo: Soshiete, 1982.

———. "The Imjin Waeran." Paper presented to the Imjin War conference at Oxford University. August, 2001.

———. "The Imjin Waeran: Contrasting the First and the Second Invasions of Korea." In *The East Asian War, 1592–1598: International Relations, Violence and Memory*. Edited by James B. Lewis, 73–92. London: Routledge, 2014.

Ko Kyŏngmyŏng. *Kugyŏk Chebong chŏnsŏ* [The translation of the anthology of Chebong]. 3 vols. Sŏngnam: Chŏngsin munhwa yŏn'guwŏn, 1980.

Kuno, Yoshi Saburo. *Japanese Expansion on the Asiatic Continent: A Study in the History of Japan with Special Reference to Her International Relations with China, Korea, and Russia*. 2 vols. Berkeley: University of California Press, 1937.

Kuwata Tadachika. *Toyotomi Hideyoshi kenkyū* [A study on Toyotomi Hideyoshi]. Tokyo: Kadokawa Shoten, 1975.

Kyŏngsŏng taehakkyo, hyangt'o munhwa yŏn'guso, ed. *Non'gae sajŏk yŏn'gu* [A study of Non'gae from historical perspective]. Pusan: Sinji sŏwŏn, 1996.

Laqueur, Thomas. "Memory and the Naming in the Great War." In *Commemorations: The Politics of National Identity*. Edited by John R. Gillis, 150–67. Princeton: Princeton University Press, 1994.

Ledyard, Gari. "Confucianism and War: The Korean Security Crisis of 1598." *Journal of Korean Studies* 6 (1988): 81–119.

Lee, Ki-Baek. *A New History of Korea*. Cambridge, Mass.: Harvard University Press, 1984.

Lee, Peter H. *Anthology of Korean Literature*. Honolulu: University of Hawai'i Press, 1981.

———. *The Record of the Black Dragon Year*. Seoul: Institute of Korean Culture, Korea University, 2000.

Lee, Peter H., and Wm. Theodore de Bary, eds. *Sources of Korean Tradition*. Vol. 1: *From Early Times Through the Sixteenth Century*. New York: Columbia University Press, 1997.

Lewis, Mark Edward. *Writing and Authority in Early China*. Albany: State University of New York Press, 1999.

Lincoln, Abraham. "Gettysburg Address," delivered at the Soldiers' National Cemetery dedication, November 19, 1863.

Lopez, Donald S., ed. *Religions of China in Practice*. Princeton: Princeton University Press, 1996.

Lukacs, Georg. *The Historical Novel*. Translated by Hannah Mitchell and Stanley Mitchell. Lincoln: University of Nebraska Press, 1983.

Marx, Anthony. *Faith in Nation: Exclusionary Origins of Nationalism*. New York: Oxford University Press, 2003.

Mayo, James. *War Memorials as Political Landscape: The American Experience and Beyond*. New York: Praeger, 1988.

McDermott, Joseph. "The Ascendance of the Imprint in China." In *Printing and Book Culture in Late Imperial China*. Edited by Cynthia J. Brokaw and Kai-wing Chow, 55–106. Berkeley: University of California Press, 2005.

McMullen, David. "Historical and Literary Theory in the Mid-Eighth Century." In *Perspectives on the Tang*. Edited by Arthur F. Wright and David Twitchett, 307–44. New Haven: Yale University Press, 1973.

Mosse, George L. *The Nationalization of the Masses*. Ithaca: Cornell University Press, 1975.

Na Man'gap. *Pyŏngja Namhan ilgi* [The records of the Namhan Fort in 1636]. Seoul: Sundang, 1977.

Naito Shumpo. *Bunroku Kencho eki ni okeru hiryojin no kenkyu* [A study of prisoners of war from 1592 to 1598]. Tokyo: Tokyo Daigaku shuppankai, 1976.

Naquin, Susan. "Funerals in North China: Uniformity and Variation." In *Death Ritual in Late Imperial and Modern China*. Edited by James Watson

and Evelyn Rawski, 37–70. Berkeley: University of California Press, 1988.
O Hŭimun. *Swaemirok* [The records of trivial and insignificant matters]. Seoul: Kuksa p'yŏnch'an wiwŏnhoe, 1962.
Ōtani Morishige. *Chosŏn hugi sosŏl tokcha yŏn'gu* [A study of readership of novels in late Chosŏn]. Seoul: Koryŏ taehakkyo minjok munhwa yŏn'guso, 1985.
Pak Chonghwa. *Imjin waeran* [The Imjin War]. 6 vols. Seoul: Ŭryu munhwasa, 1972.
Pak Chu. *Chosŏn sidae ŭi chŏngp'yo chŏngch'aek* [Policies on the conferral of honors during the Chosŏn period]. Seoul: Ilchogak, 1990.
"Pakssi chŏn" [The tale of Madam Pak]. In *Han'guk kojŏn munhak taegye* [Compendium of Korean classical literature]. Vol. 1. Edited by Chang Tŏksun and Ch'oe Chinwŏn. Seoul: Kyomunsa, 1984.
Palais, James B. *Confucian Statecraft and Korean Institutions: Yu Hyŏngwŏn and the Late Chosŏn Dynasty*. Seattle: University of Washington Press, 1996.
Peterson, Charles A. "The Restoration Completed: Emperor Hsientsung and the Provinces." In *Perspectives on the Tang*. Edited by Arthur F. Wright and David Twitchett, 151–92. New Haven: Yale University Press, 1973.
P'isaeng mongyurok [Dream journey of Master P'i]. National Library of Korea. Ko 3636-8.
"P'isaeng mongyurok." In *P'ilsabon kojŏn sosŏl chŏnjip* [The complete anthology of classical Korean novels in manuscript]. Edited by Kim Kidong, 3:223–38. Seoul: Asea munhwasa, 1980.
Pollock, Sheldon. "The Cosmopolitan Vernacular." *Journal of Asian Studies* 57, no. 1 (1998): 16–37.
———, ed. *Literary Cultures in History*. Berkeley: University of California Press, 2003.
Pomeranz, Kenneth. *The Great Divergence: China, Europe, and the Making of the Modern World Economy*. Revised edition. Princeton: Princeton University Press, 2001.
Renan, Ernest. "What Is a Nation?" In *Nation and Narration*. Edited by Homi K. Bhabha, 8–22. London: Routledge, 1990.
Ro, Young-chan. *The Korean Neo-Confucianism of Yi Yulgok*. Albany: State University of New York Press, 1989.

Robinson, Kenneth R. "Centering the King of Chosŏn: Aspects of Korean Maritime Diplomacy, 1392–1592." *Journal of Asian Studies* 59, no. 1 (2000): 109–25.

Rogers, Michael. "Medieval National Consciousness in Korea." In *China Among Equals*. Edited by Morris Rossabi, 151–72. Berkeley: University of California Press, 1983.

Sajima Akiko. "The Japan-Ming Negotiations." Paper presented to the Imjin War conference at Oxford University, August 2001.

———. "Hideyoshi's View of Chosŏn Korea and Japan-Ming Negotiations." In *The East Asian War, 1592–1598: International Relations, Violence, and Memory*. Edited by James B. Lewis, 93–107. London: Routledge, 2014.

Sakai Tadao. "Yi Yulgok and the Community Compact." In *The Rise of Neo-Confucianism in Korea*. Edited by Wm. Theodore de Bary and Ja-Hyun Kim Haboush, 323–48. New York: Columbia University Press, 1985.

Sartre, Jean-Paul. "'Aminadab' of the Fantastic Considered as a Language." *Situations* 1 (1947): 56–72.

Sharpe, Jenny. "The Unspeakable Limits of Rape: Colonial Violence and Counter-Insurgency." In *Colonial Discourse and Post-Colonial Theory*. Edited by Patrick Williams and Laura Chrisman, 221–43. New York: Columbia University Press, 1994.

Skillend, William. *Kodae sosŏl: A Survey of Korean Traditional Style Popular Novels*. London: School of Oriental and African Studies, University of London, 1968.

Smith, Anthony D. *The Ethnic Origins of Nations*. Oxford: Blackwell, 1986.

———. *Theories of Nationalism*. 2nd edition. Boulder: Holmes & Meier Publishers, 1983.

Smith, Jay M. *Nobility Reimagined*. Ithaca: Cornell University Press, 2005.

So Chaeyŏng. *Im-Byŏng yangnan kwa munhak ŭisik* [The Imjin and Pyŏngja Wars and literary consciousness]. Seoul: Han'guk yŏn'guwŏn, 1980.

———. "Imjin waeran kwa sosŏl munhak" [The Imjin War and the novel]. In *Imjin waeran kwa han'guk munhak* [Imjin War and Korean literature]. Edited by Kim T'aejun et al. Seoul: Minŭmsa, 1992.

So Taesŏk. "Mongyurok ŭi changrŭjŏk sŏnggyŏk kwa munhaksajŏk ŭiŭi" [Generic characteristics of dream journeys and their literary historical significance]. *Kyemyŏngdae Han'gukhak nonmunjip* 3 (1975): 531–52.

Sohn, Pow-Key. "Early Korean Printing," *Journal of the American Oriental Society* 79, no. 2 (1959): 96–103.

Sŏn Sŭngch'ŏl. *Chosŏn siadae Han-Il kwan'gyesa yŏn'gu* [A study of Korean-Japanese relations during the Chosŏn period]. Seoul: Chisŏng ŭi saem, 1994.

Song Chŏnghyŏn. *Chosŏn sahoe wa Imjin ŭibyŏng yŏn'gu* [A study of the Chosŏn society and of the volunteer armies during the Imjin War]. Seoul: Haggyŏn munhwasa, 1998.

Sŏnjo sillok [Veritable records of Sŏnjo]. 221 kwŏn. Vols. 21–25 of *Chosŏn wangjo sillok* [Veritable records of the kings of the Chosŏn dynasty]. Seoul: Kuksa p'yŏnch'an wiwŏnhoe, 1955–1963.

Sŏnjo sujŏng sillok [Revised Veritable records of Sŏnjo]. 42 kwŏn. Vol. 25 of *Chosŏn wangjo sillok* [Veritable records of the kings of the Chosŏn dynasty]. Seoul: Kuksa p'yŏnch'an wiwŏnhoe, 1971.

Sotheby's. *Korean Works of Art*. New York: Sotheby's, June 18, 1993.

Swope, Kenneth Michael. "Bestowing the Double-Edged Sword: Wanli as a Supreme Military Commander." In *Culture, Courtiers, and Competition: The Ming Court (1368–1644)*. Edited by David M. Robinson, 61–115. Cambridge, Mass.: Harvard University Asia Center, 2008.

———. "Deceit, Disguise, and Dependence: China, Japan, and the Future of the Tributary System, 1592–1596." *International History Review* 24, no. 4 (2002): 757–82.

———. "The Three Great Campaigns of the Wanli Emperor, 1592–1600: Court, Military, and Society in Late Sixteenth-Century China." Ph.D. dissertation, University of Michigan, 2001.

———. "Turning the Tide: The Strategic and Psychological Significance of the Liberation of Pyongyang in 1593." *War and Society* 21, no. 2 (2003): 1–22.

Tackett, Timothy. *When the King Took Flight*. Cambridge, Mass.: Harvard University Press, 2003.

Tenkei. *Saisei nikki* [The diary of the western campaign]. In *Zokuzoku gunsho ruijū*. 17 vols. Tokyo: Zoku gunsho ruijū kanseikai, 1969–1978.

Toby, Ronald P. *State and Diplomacy in Early Modern Japan: Asia in the Development of the Tokugawa Bakufu*. Stanford: Stanford University Press, 1984.

Todorov, Tzvetan. *The Fantastic: A Structural Approach to a Literary Genre*. Ithaca: Cornell University Press, 1975.

Tu, Wei-ming. "Yi T'oegye's Perception of Human Nature: A Preliminary Inquiry into the Four-Seven Debate in Korean Neo-Confucianism." In *The Rise of Neo-Confucianism in Korea*. Edited by Wm. Theodore de Bary and JaHyun Kim Haboush, 261–81. New York: Columbia University Press, 1985.

Turnbull, Stephen. *Samurai Invasion: Japan's Korean War, 1592–1598*. London: Cassell, 2002.

Vaughan, Virginia Mason. "Preface: The Mental Maps of English Renaissance Drama." In *Playing the Globe: Genre and Geography in English Renaissance Drama*. Edited by John Gilles and Virginia Mason Vaughan, 7–18. London: Associated University Presses, 1998.

Wakeman, Frederic E., Jr. *The Great Enterprise: The Manchu Reconstruction of Imperial Order in Seventeenth-Century China*. Berkeley: University of California Press, 1985.

Walraven, Boudewijn. "Muga: The Songs of Korean Shamanism." Ph.D. dissertation, Leiden University, 1985.

———. "Popular Religion in Confucianized Society." In *Culture and the State in Late Chosŏn Korea*. Edited by JaHyun Kim Haboush and Martina Deuchler, 160–98. Cambridge, Mass.: Harvard University Asia Center, 1999.

Waltham, Clae, ed. *Shu Ching; Book of History: A Modernized Edition of the Translations of James Legge*. Translated by James Legge. Chicago: Regenry, 1971.

Williams, Raymond. *Marxism and Literature*. Oxford: Oxford University Press, 1977.

Yi Ch'aeyŏn. *Imjin waeran p'oro silgi yŏn'gu* [A study of the records by prisoners of war of the Imjin War]. Seoul: Pagijŏng ch'ulp'ansa, 1995.

Yi Changhŭi. *Imjin waeransa yŏn'gu* [A study of the Imjin War]. Seoul: Asea munhwasa, 1999.

Yi Chŏng'am, *Sŏjŏng illok* [The daily record of the western campaign]. Seoul: T'amgudang, 1979.

Yi Hyŏngjong, ed. *Cho Chŏng sŏnsaeng munjip* [The literary collection of Cho Chŏng]. Seoul: Cho Chŏng sŏnsaeng munjip kanhaeng wiwŏnhoe, 1977.

Yi Kŭngik. *Kugyŏk Yŏllryŏsil kisul* [The translation of the narrative of *yŏllryŏsil*]. Edited by Kim Yungyŏng. 12 vols. Seoul: Minjok munhwa ch'ujinhoe, 1976.

Yi No. *Yongsa ilgi* [The diary of the dragon and snake war]. Pusan: Pusan University, Hanil munhwa yŏn'guso, 1960.

Yi Sangbaek. *Han'guksa, kŭnse chŏn'gi p'yŏn* [History of Korea: Early modern period]. Seoul: Ŭryu munhwasa, 1962.

Yi Sŏngnin. *Imjin ŭibyŏngjang, Cho Hŏn, yŏn'gu* [A study of a volunteer army leader, Cho Hŏn]. Seoul: Sin'gu munhwasa, 1993.

Yi Sungju, Kim Chŏnggyu, and Han Chunsŏ. *Pulmyŏl ŭi Yi Sunsin* [Immortal Yi Sunsin]. Seoul: Korean Broadcasting System, September 4, 2004–August 28, 2005.

Yi T'aegyŏng. *Yŏkchu chŏngmannok* [Annotated translation of the record of the campaign against barbarians]. Ŭisŏng: Ŭisŏng munhwawŏn, 1992.

Yi T'aejin. *Chosŏn hugi ŭi chŏngch'i wa kunyŏngje pyŏnchŏn* [Politics and the changes in military garrisons structure in the late Chosŏn]. Seoul: Han'guk yŏn'guwŏn, 1985.

Yi Yunsŏk. *Hong Kiltong chŏn yŏn'gu* [A study of the Tale of Hong Kiltong]. Taegu: Kyemyŏng University Press, 1997.

Yoshino Jingozaeon. *Yoshino Jingozaeon oboegaki* [Yoshino Jingozaeon's memoir]. Tokyo: Zoku gunsho tuijū kanseikai, 1931.

Yu Chongguk. *Mongyurok sosŏl yŏn'gu* [A study of dream journey novels]. Seoul: Asea munhwasa, 1987.

Yu Sŏngnyong. *Chingbirok* [The book of corrections]. Translated by Nam Mansŏng. Seoul: Hyŏnamsa, 1970.

Yun Kyesŏn. "Talch'ŏn mongyurok." In *Hanmun sosŏlsŏn* [A collection of novels in literary Chinese]. Edited by Kug'ŏ kungmun hakhoe. Seoul: Taejegak, 1982.

Zeitlin, Judith. *Historian of the Strange: Pu Songling and the Chinese Classical Tale*. Stanford: Stanford University Press, 1993.

Abelmann, Nancy, viii
ancestry and kinship, 39, 129, 141
Anderson, Benedict, 19, 24, 44, 74
Arabic, 74
arquebus, 29, 78. *See also* musket; weapons

Bakhtin, Mikhail, 125
Bao Gong dramas, xi
Bell, David A., 6–7
Berry, Mary E., 187n66
bows and arrows, 50, 60, 62, 85–86. *See also* weapons
Britain, 7, 139, 145
Britons: Forging the Nation 1707–1837 (Colley), 6–7
Buddhism: in dream journeys, 126, 129, 133, 136, 140–41, 151, 195n57; monks of in Japanese invasionary forces, 74, 79–80, 83–84, 88–89, 111, 163n17, 181n17; monks of in Righteous Army, 45, 58, 61, 133, 136, 151. *See also* religion

censorship, 147
Cespedes, Gregorio de, 76
Chakrabarty, Dipesh, 9
Ch'a Yongju, 195n54
China: aid to Korea against Japanese, 94–100; as historical nation, 5–6, 8, 14; Ming dynasty, x, 1–2, 15–16, 94–96, 111–12, 121–22, 150; peace negotiations with Japan, 91, 98–100, 103–5, 111–14; Qing dynasty, 2–3, 17, 150; Yuan dynasty, xi, 2–3, 77
Chinese Army, 71–72, 93–94, 100–105, 109, 113–14
Chinese classical language and script: and Confucian canon, 74; and discourse of nation, 18–19, 69, 74–75; and gender, 19; during Imjin War, 55–57, 79–80, 87; Korean government policy, 108, 110, 114–19; in postwar literary production, 147–48. *See also* language
Chinju battles, 60–63, 133
Chizhova, Ksenia, ix
Cho, Hwisang, ix
Cho Chŏng, 54
Ch'oe Kyŏnghŭi, 60–62
Ch'oe Yŏnghŭi, 59
Cho Hŏn, 45, 58, 134
choice, 44, 50, 69–71, 82
Cho Kyŏngnam, 163n15, 166n45, 168n62, 193–94n42
Chŏng Ch'ŏl, 110, 146

INDEX

chŏn'gi (*chuanqi*) (strange tales), 125, 128
Chŏng Inhong, 37, 54, 60–61
Chŏngnŭng, 82
Chŏng Pal, 29
Chŏng T'ak, 165n38
Chosŏn dynasty, 3–5, 65. *See also* Korean government
Christianity, 7, 76, 89, 179n7. *See also* religion
Chunghwa (Brilliant Center), 16
Ch'ungju city battle, 30, 130–32
circular letters (*t'ongmun*), 33–34, 55–57, 60. *See also* letters of exhortation (*kyŏksŏ*)
class structure, 165n39; class as driving force in Korean society, 12; local elites, 17–18, 25–26, 64–68; and Neo-Confucianism, 68; in premodern Europe, 6; and qualities of virtue, 177n66; and Righteous Army, 70–71; scholarly elites, x, 4, 66–67; social status in letters of exhortation, 46, 50; yangban, xii, 66
Colley, Linda, 6–7
colonialism: British, 145; Japanese, 12, 16, 72, 82–89; and Neo-Confucianism, x; scholarship on, 9, 11
comfort women (World War II), 81
commemoration: of anonymous war dead, 20, 127, 137–40; and discourse of identity and nation, viii, 4, 123–24; as immortality for the dead, 124, 136; and postwar literary production, 146–52; as social memory, 19–21
communal readings, 56
communicative rationality, 43
concubines, 81. *See also* service women
Confucianism: canon of, 8, 19, 74; in dream journeys, 136–37, 142–46, 148–49; and elites, 66–70; and Korean identity, 3–4, 12, 17–18, 67–70, 118, 121, 150; and letters of exhortation, 49–50; Mandate of Heaven, 63–65; moral autonomy in, 18; mortuary and funerary practices of, 124, 129, 139; Neo-Confucianism, x, 46, 65–68; patriarchy of, 142–46; and popular sovereignty, 64–65; and private armies, 34; and religion, 8, 19, 129, 141–42, 148–49; and remembrance, 19–21, 136–37
Confucian Kingship in Korea, The (Haboush), x–xi
Connerton, Paul, 19
Crump, James, xi
Cult of the Nation in France: Inventing Nationalism, 1680–1800 (Bell), 6–7

daily court gazette (*chobo*), 54
Daily Record of the Western Campaign (Yi Chŏng'am), 87
Daoism, 126, 132, 142. *See also* religion
dead bodies: and anonymity, 20, 127, 130–32, 137–42, 150–52; commemoration of, 20, 124–25, 127, 129, 137–39; in dream journeys, 121, 124–25, 127, 129–37, 139–46; ghosts, 127, 130–37, 140; unburiability of, 129–30, 142–46
democracy movement (1970s and 1980s), 12
Deuchler, Martina, viii, ix
Diary of the Campaign of Korea (*Kōrai nikki*) (Tajiri Akitane), 84
Diary of the Imjin War (*Imjin ilgi*) (Cho Chŏng), 54
Diary of the Western Campaign, The (Tenkei), 83
discourse of identity. *See* identity discourse
discourse of nation. *See* nation discourse

INDEX 215

dream journeys: Daoism in, 126; dead bodies and ghosts in, 121, 124–25, 127, 129–37, 139–46; and discourse of identity, 123; and imaginary memory, 152; patriarchy in, 129, 142–46, 149–50; subversive function of, 129–30

Dream Journey to Kanghwa Island (*Kangdo mongyurok*), 125, 129–30, 142–46, 150–52, 193n32

Dream Journey to Talch'ŏn (Hwang Chungyun), 135, 137, 193–94n42

Dream Journey to Talch'ŏn (*Talch'ŏn mongyurok*) (Yun Kyesŏn), 125, 128–35, 142, 144, 147, 150, 152, 193n32

Duara, Prasenjit, 127

East Asian studies, x
Ekei (Buddhist monk), 88–89
Elisonas, Jurgis, 182n33
Enlightenment, 7, 64
ethnicity, 3–4, 11–14, 42, 51, 82
ethnie, xii, 11, 39, 122
Eurocentrism, x, 9–10

Faith in Nation: Exclusionary Origins of Nationalism (Marx), 6–7
fantasy literature, 129, 148. *See also* dream journeys
feudalism, 6, 15
First Korean War, 1. *See also* Imjin War (1592–1598)
foreignness, 12, 29, 76–79
France, 7, 171n110, 177n66
Frank, Andre Gunder, 10
French Revolution, 6
Frois (Jesuit priest), 89

Geary, Patrick J., 8
Gellner, Ernest, 6, 8, 177n67
gender and gender roles: and Confucianism, 12, 142; and Imjin War and Manchu invasions, 82; and language, 19, 76, 87; and loyalty, 144–45; patriarchy, 129, 142–46, 149–50; patrimony, 6; rape, 81, 145; service women, 81–82, 85

Gettysburg Civil War cemetery (U.S.), 138
Goodman, David, 127
Great East Asian War, 1. *See also* Imjin War (1592–1598)
Great Wall, 2
Greenfeld, Liah, 6–7, 9, 71, 175n57
guerilla warfare, viii, 3, 24, 35–38, 60, 71, 89. *See also* Righteous Army (*ŭibyŏng*)

Habermas, Jürgen, 43
Haboush, JaHyun Kim: on East Asian studies, x; educational and intellectual background, x–xii; proposal for this study, vii; works by, x–xi, 153–57
Haboush, William J., vii–xii
Haengju ch'ima (Haengju skirt), 90
Haengju victory, 90
han'gŭl script, xi, 76. *See also* Korean vernacular language and script
hearts of the people concept, 45, 63. *See also* popular sovereignty
heteroglossia, 125
Hidetsugu (regent), 80
Hideyoshi. *See* Toyotomi Hideyoshi
historical nation concept, 5–6, 8, 14
Hobsbawm, E. J., 5, 14
Hŏ Kyun, 191n21
Hong Kiltong chŏn (The tale of Hong Kiltong), 191n21
Hong Taiji, 1, 17, 122
Huang, Ray, 112
Huguenots, 7
Hwang Chungyun, 135
Hwang Yun'gil, 27, 166n44
Hyegyŏng, Lady, xi

"Hymn of Constancy" (*Samiin kok*) (Chŏng Ch'ŏl), 146
Hyujŏng (Buddhist monk), 58, 151

identity discourse, 118, 121–24, 146–52
idu writing system, 87. *See also* Korean vernacular language and script
imagined community: and East Asian cultural imaginary, 74; and letters of exhortation, 47–48, 53; and volunteer army movement, 16, 26; and war commemoration, 21, 23, 72. *See also* nation discourse
Imhae (prince), 30, 33, 84
Imjin War (1592–1598): and discourse of nation, xii, 1, 11, 15, 23, 51, 71; guerilla warfare, viii, 3, 24, 35–38, 60, 71, 89; Japanese invasions and occupation, 1, 16–17, 27–38, 76–91, 105, 114, 180n14, 181n27; peace negotiations, 91, 98–99, 105, 111–14
Indian Mutiny against the British (1857), 145
Injo (king), 17, 122, 150
Inquisition (Spain), 7
Insŏn (queen), 147
internal seeds theory of industrialization and capitalism, 12–13
Iran, 5–6
Iser, Wolfgang, 152
Ishida Mitsunari, 81

Jackson, Rosemary, 129, 148
Japan: colonialism of, 12, 16, 72, 82–89; as historical nation, 5–6, 8, 14; invasions of Korea (1592, 1597), 1, 16–17, 27–38, 76–91, 105, 114, 180n14, 181n27; peace negotiations with China, 91, 98–99, 105, 111–14; pirates (*wakō* or *waegu*), 15, 97
Japanese language, 88–89, 91. *See also* language

Japanese plays and ghost characters, 127
Jewish expulsion from Spain (1492), 7

Kakitsu Treaty (1443), 15
Kangdo mongyurok (*Dream Journey to Kanghwa Island*), 125, 129–30, 142–46, 150–52, 193n32
Katō Kiyomasa, 33, 62, 79–81, 83–84, 90, 151
Keitetsu Genso, 27, 162–63nn9–10
Kim, Jisoo, ix
Kim Ch'ŏnil, 38, 62, 134
Kim Manjung, 126
Kim Myŏn, 37, 54, 60, 81–82
Kim Myŏngwŏn, 30, 103
Kim Simin, 61–62, 133
Kim Sisŭp, 126
Kim Sŏng'il, 27, 36, 40–44, 54, 174n32
Kim Su, 29, 35
Kim Tŏngnyŏng, 71–72, 178n74
Kim Yangsŏn, 179n7
Kim Yŏmul, 134
Kim Yŏn'gwang, 133–34
kinship and ancestry, 39, 129, 141
Kitajima Manji, 180n16
Kiyomasa. *See* Katō Kiyomasa
Ko, Dorothy, viii
Kobayakawa Takakage, 90
Ko Chonghu, 46–47, 62
Ko Inhu, 45
Ko Kyŏngmyŏng: death of, 46, 134; in *Dream Journey to Talch'ŏn*, 133–34; letters of exhortation, 38, 40–44, 56–58, 70, 167n53, 167n59; and volunteer army, 38, 58, 70, 133, 167n53, 167n59
Konishi Joan, 112
Konishi Yukinaga: Catholicism of, 76; and China-Japan peace negotiations, 91, 98–100, 105, 112; and Chinese-Korean defeat at P'yŏngyang, 94; in *Dream Journey to Talch'ŏn*, 130; and Japanese invasion,

29, 62, 79–80, 130; and Japanese retreat, 90–91
Korea Diary (*Chōsen nikki*), 84–86, 90
Korean government: and China-Japan peace negotiations, 113–14; and Chinese aid, 98–105, 121; Confucianization of society, 67–68; and Japanese invasion, 28–32, 34, 105–10; language policy, 108–11, 114–19; and Manchu invasions, 1, 122, 150; and volunteer army movement, 25–26, 34–38, 40, 65
Korean Royal Army, 3, 16, 29–33, 59
Korean vernacular language and script: and discourse of nation, 18–19, 73–74, 76; and gender, 19, 76; Japanese use during occupation, 87, 89; Korean government use of, 73–74, 108–11, 114–19; and letters of exhortation, 55–56; and postwar literary production, 147–48; writing systems, xi, 76, 87. *See also* language
Koryŏ, 14
Kuk Kyŏngin, 33
Kumo sinhwa (New tales of the golden turtle) (Kim Sisŭp), 126
Kŭmsan battles, 45, 58
Kuno, Yoshi, 16, 104
Kuroda Nagamasa, 76, 79, 87, 90
Kuunmong (A nine-cloud dream) (Kim Manjung), 126
Kwak Chaeu, 35–37, 60–62
Kwanghae (king), 30, 121
Kwŏn Yul, 54, 90
Kyŏn Yu, 174n32

land, 6, 39, 41, 48–49
language: diglossic linguistic space, 18–19, 76, 110, 147; in *Dream Journey to Talch'ŏn*, 131; and Japanese invasions and occupation, 77–80, 87–89; Korean government policy, 73–76, 91, 108–11, 114–19; of postwar literary production, 147–48; sacral languages, xii, 8, 19, 74. *See also specific languages*
Laqueur, Thomas, 139
Latin, 74
Ledyard, Gari, ix, xi
legitimacy of ruler, x, 7–9, 63–65, 118, 129
letters of exhortation (*kyŏksŏ*): class structure and social status in, 46, 50; and Confucianism, 46, 49–50; and defense of civilization, 49–51; dissemination of, 53–58; and ethnicity and discourse of nation, 39–48, 51; and free and personal choice, 70; language of, 55–56; loyalty and moral duty in, 42–46, 49–50; and volunteer army movement, 16, 25, 33–34, 38, 167n53
"letter written on horseback" (*masang kyŏngmun*) (Ko Kyŏngmyŏng), 42–43
Lewis, Mark Edward, 146–47
Li Guangtao, 28
Lincoln, Abraham, 152
Li Rusong, 71, 89–91, 101–4, 113
literacy, 8, 55, 173n16
loyalty: activist loyalty, 5, 18, 72; Confucianism and, 18, 46, 66, 68; and discourse of nation, 71; disloyalty (*pulch'ung*), 144–46, 149; gender and, 144–45; and Righteous Army, 42–47, 50, 59, 66, 108; and tributary relationship, 96, 98, 149

Manchus: conquest of China (1644), 1–3, 17, 121–22, 150; invasions of Korea (1627 and 1636–1637), xii, 1, 16–17, 72, 82, 142–43, 150–51
Mandate of Heaven, 63–65
Marlowe, Christopher, 77
Marx, Anthony, 6–7
Master P'i's Dream Journey (*P'isaeng mongyurok*), 125, 139–42, 148, 193n32

218　INDEX

memory, 19–21, 124, 131, 136, 139, 152. *See also* commemoration
Mencius, 46, 67
Ming dynasty, x, 1–2, 15–16, 94–96, 111–12, 121–22, 150
Miscellaneous Record of the War, The, 118, 147
modernity, 5–21
Mongols, xi, 2–3, 14, 77, 94, 142, 159n1
mongyurok (records of dream journeys), 125. *See also* dream journeys
moral autonomy, 18
moral duty, 39, 49–50, 68–70
Mosse, George L., 177n69
musket, 29, 60–61, 104. *See also* weapons

Nabeshima Naoshige, 83–84
Namhan Fort siege, 1, 122, 189n3
Namin faction in Korean government, 114
Nammyŏng (Cho Sik), 41
nationalism: and Imjin War, 11, 51, 71; and language, 74; and popular sovereignty, 175n57; of premodern Chinese bureaucracy, 177n67; scholarship on, 6–7, 11–13, 175n57, 177n67
Nationalism: Five Roads to Modernity (Greenfeld), 6–7
nation discourse: and Confucianism, 3–4, 12, 17–18, 67–70; East Asian, 8–21; and ethnicity, 11–14; European, 7–8; historical nation concept, 5–6, 8, 14; imagined community, 16, 21, 23, 26, 47–48, 53, 72, 74; and Japanese and Manchu invasions, 3–5; and language, 18–19, 73–74, 76; in letters of exhortation, 39–44, 46, 58; and modernity, 5–21; and otherness, 3, 7; and religion, 7–8, 171n110; scholarship on, 4–6, 9–21
Neo-Confucianism, x, 46, 65–68. *See also* Confucianism

Nobility Reimagined (Smith), 177n66
Non'gae (courtesan), 23, 62

"Oath of Revenge Sent to All the Towns of the Province [of Chŏlla]" (Ko Kyŏngmyŏng), 47
O Hŭimun, 33, 54
otherness, 3, 7, 78–79, 110, 118

Paek Kwang'ŏn, 174n33
Pakssi chŏn (The tale of Madam Pak), 145
patriarchy, 129, 142–46, 149–50. *See also* gender and gender roles
patrimony, 6. *See also* gender and gender roles
patriotism: and Buddhism, 136, 162; and Christianity, 171n110; and commemoration, 4–55, 72; and Confucianism, 68, 74; and discourse of nation, 4; in letters of exhortation, 42–43, 45; and popular sovereignty, 64; and volunteer army movement, 16–18
P'isaeng mongyurok (Master P'i's dream journey), 125, 139–42, 148, 193n32
Pollock, Sheldon, 75, 179n5
Pomeranz, Kenneth, 10
popular discontent, 30–31, 33, 106–7
popular sovereignty, 5, 8, 18, 44, 64–66, 71–72, 175n57
postal system, 53–54
practical learning (*sirhak*) school, 12–13
print technology and cultures, 57
Pulmyŏl ŭi Yi Sunsin, 24
Pusan massacre (1592), 16, 29, 78
Pyŏkchegwan battle, 104
P'yŏngyang: capture of by Japanese, 31, 95, 106–7; Chinese and Korean defeat at, 94, 109; Chinese and Korean recapture of, 89–90, 99–100, 102–4, 109
Pyŏn ŭnjing, 174n34

INDEX 219

Qing dynasty (China), 2–3, 17, 150. See also Manchus

rape, 81, 145. See also gender and gender roles
Record of the Campaign Against Barbarians (Yi T'aegyŏng), 87
Records of Trivial and Insignificant Matters (O Hŭimun), 33
reincarnation, 136, 143
religion: Christianity, 7, 76, 89, 179n7; and Confucianism, 8, 19, 129, 141–42, 148–49; Daoism, 126, 132, 142; and discourse of nation, 7–8, 171n110. See also Buddhism
Remaining Stories from the Three Kingdoms (Samguk yusa), 12
Renan, Ernest, 6
restoration (chunghŭng), 37, 51, 95, 110
revenge, 43, 46–47, 95
Revised Veritable Records of Sŏnjo, 160n17
Righteous Army (ŭibyŏng), 25; Buddhist monks in, 45, 58, 61, 133, 136, 151; and Chinese Army, 71–72; commemoration of heroes of, 23–25; organization and development of, viii, 3, 16, 24, 33–39, 58–63, 70–71, 89; Righteous Army of Vengeance (Poksu ŭibyŏngjang), 47. See also volunteer army movement
Robinson, Kenneth R., 112
Rogers, Michael, 14
Rousseau, Jean-Jacques, 65
royal edicts: circulation of, 55; edict of heartfelt pain, 117–18; edict of self-castigation (choegisŏ), 34, 36; language of, xii, 73–76, 91, 114–18

sacral languages, xii, 8, 19, 74. See also language
sacrifice (dying for the country), 24, 44–47, 69–70, 72, 135–39

Saisei nikki (The diary of the western campaign) (Tenkei), 181n17
Sangju battle, 30
scholarship: historical, x, xi–xii, 9–14, 122–23; literary, xi–xii, 123; modernists vs. primordialists, 7, 11, 13, 25; and nationalism, 6–7, 11–13, 175n57, 177n67
school of material force (ki), 67
school of principle (li), 67
Seishō Shōtai, 111
Sejo (king), 192n24
Seoul massacre, 88–91
service women, 81–82, 85. See also gender and gender roles
shamanic ritual, 128
Sharpe, Jenny, 145
Shen Weijing, 98–99, 105, 113
Shin Kilwŏn, 163n18
Shi Xing, 98, 105, 113
Shuihuzhuan (Water margin) novel, 147
Sim Tae, 55, 134
Sin Ch'aeho, 12
Sin Chap, 110
Sin Ip, 30, 130–32, 134–35
Sin Yŏl, 61
Smith, Anthony, 7, 11, 39, 122, 168n61
Smith, Jay M., 177n66
socialism, 12
Sō feudal house (Tsushima island), 15, 27
Sŏin faction in Korean government, 114
Sojunghwa (Small Brilliant Center), 15, 170n87
Song Chemin, 45–46
Sŏng Ch'ŏnhŭi, 58
Song Ŏnsin, 187n63
Song Sanghyŏn, 29, 133, 195n61
Song Yingchang, 90–91, 94, 98–100, 103, 105, 113–14
Sŏnjo (king), 30, 91, 96, 99, 101, 108–11, 113–14, 117–18
So Taesŏk, 195n54

Sō Yoshitoshi, 27, 29, 79–80
Spain, 7
spirits and ghosts, 124, 127, 130–37, 140
St. Bartholomew's Day Massacre (France), 7
structures of feeling, 26, 150
Sunhwa (prince), 30, 84
Swope, Kenneth, 60, 113

Tackett, Timothy, 106
Tajiri Akitane, 84, 90–91
Talch'ŏn mongyurok (*Dream journey to Talch'ŏn*) (Yun Kyesŏn), 125, 128–35, 142, 144, 147, 150, 152, 193n32
Talch'ŏn River battle (Ch'ungju city), 30, 130–32
Tamburlaine (Marlowe), 77
Tamerlane, 77
Tangun (mythical progenitor), 12
Tanjong (king), 192n24
taxes, 79, 81–89, 107, 117, 165
Tenkei (Buddhist monk), 80, 83, 163n17, 181n17
Toby, Ronald P., ix, 112
Todorov, Tzvetan, 128
T'oegye (Yi Hwang), 41, 67
Tokugawa Ieyasu, 2
Tokugawa Shogunate, 2, 122, 151
Tomb of the Unknown Soldier (U.S.), 140
Tongnae massacre, 16, 29
Toyotomi Hideyoshi, 1, 16, 27, 62, 79–87, 111–13
Trivial Matters, The (O Hŭimun), 103
Tsushima Island, 15, 27, 112
Turnbull, Stephen, 180n12
turtle ships (*kŏbuksŏn*), 23

Ukita Hideie, 90

Vaughan, Virginia Mason, 77
Veritable Records of Sŏnjo, 164n20

Vietnam Memorial (U.S.), 138
volunteer army movement: and discourse of nation, 16–18, 24–27; example of in later conflicts, 72; Korean state and, 25–26, 34–38, 40, 65; local elites and, 17–18, 25–27, 33, 37, 64, 66–68, 80, 167n53; origin of, 3, 16, 18, 51; popular sovereignty and, 18, 63, 71; studies of, 24–25. *See also* Righteous Army (*ŭibyŏng*)

Wang, Sixiang, ix
Wanli emperor, 94–96, 111–12
weapons: bows and arrows, 50, 60, 62, 85–86; firearms, 1, 29, 60–61, 78, 104
Weber, Max, 25, 40
"What Is a Nation" (Renan), 6
Williams, Raymond, 26
Wŏn Kyun, 24, 135
Wŏnsaeng mongyurok (Master Wŏn's dream journey), 192n24

Xie Fan, 94–97

yangban, xii, 66, 165n39. *See also* class structure
Yi Chŏng'am, 87
Yi Chun, 46
Yi Homin, 104
Yi Hŭidŭk, 84
Yi Hwang (T'oegye), 41, 67
Yi I (Yulgok), 32, 67
Yi Kwang, 38, 167n53, 167n59
Yim Kyeyŏng, 60–61
Yi No, 166n45, 168n62
Yi Royal Ancestral Temple (Chongmyo) and tombs, 82
Yi Sibaek, 145
Yi Sunsin, 23–24, 61, 89, 132, 135–36
Yi T'aegyŏng, 87
Yŏnggyu (Buddhist monk), 45, 133, 136

Yongin battle, 31, 38
Yongsa ilgi (The diary of the dragon and snake war) (Chŏng T'ak), 165n38
Yoshino (Japanese Army member), 78
Ypres (Menin Gate) Memorial (Belgium), 139
Yuan dynasty, xi, 2–3, 77. *See also* Mongols
Yu Chongguk, 195n54
Yujŏng (Buddhist monk), 58, 151
Yukinaga. *See* Konishi Yukinaga

Yu Kungnyang, 134
Yun Ansŏng, 167n53
Yun Kŭnsu, 98–99
Yun Kyesŏn, 125, 147
Yun Tusu, 102, 110, 174n29, 188n76
Yu Sŏngnyong, 102, 106–7, 166n44, 187n63, 188n76

Zeitlin, Judith, 126, 128
Zetaku (Buddhist monk), 83–84
Zu Chengxun, 94, 103, 109

GPSR Authorized Representative: Easy Access System Europe, Mustamäe tee
50, 10621 Tallinn, Estonia, gpsr.requests@easproject.com

www.ingramcontent.com/pod-product-compliance
Lightning Source LLC
Chambersburg PA
CBHW021943290426
44108CB00012B/949